THE RISE OF THE STEWARTS

By the same Author

THE FOUNDATIONS OF SCOTLAND

ROBERT BRUCE KING OF SCOTS

THE SCOTLAND OF QUEEN MARY
AND THE RELIGIOUS WARS

THE PASSING OF THE STEWARTS

SCOTLAND AND MODERN TIME

SCOTTISH PAGEANT - FOUR VOLUMES

THE RISE OF
THE
STEWARTS

BY

AGNES MURE MACKENZIE
C.B.E., LL.D., M.A., D.Litt.

OLIVER & BOYD LTD.
EDINBURGH : TWEEDDALE COURT
LONDON : 39A WELBECK STREET, W.1.

First edition published by
Alexander Maclehose & Co., London
1935

Reprinted by
Oliver & Boyd, Edinburgh
1957

PRINTED IN GREAT BRITAIN BY
BRADFORD AND DICKENS
LONDON, W.C.1

AD IUVENES
QUI VISIONES VISAS
FORTES SEQUUNTUR

" This realme of Scotland is our inheritance as a por-
cione of the warld allowit to our natione and antecessouris,
quhame we succeid.   Than quhair may thair be bettir weir
than to meanteine this our naturall inheritaunce ? "

The Regent Albany in 1522.   (*Bishop Lesley.*)

FOREWORD

THE time covered by this book is that from the death
of Robert I in 1329 to that of James IV in 1513—the
reigns of David II and of the first six kings of the
House of Stewart. In substance, therefore, it is
largely a study of the achievement of that house. Its
predecessor, *Robert Bruce, King of Scots,* dealt with the
breaking of Scotland into chaos, its foreign occupation,
its recovery, unification, and victory. Here again,
but with a larger, slower, movement, we have the major
lines of the same process : the disastrous débâcle under
David II, the painful resolute clearance of the country,
the aftermath of long war, the brilliant recovery, that
was shattered suddenly by the stroke of Flodden.
The book's real subject, therefore, is a study in
government, not in abstract terms, but in the furiously
concrete ones in which its problems, for nearly two
hundred years, presented themselves to the men who
governed Scotland. The period is one but little
known, save by various highly coloured incidents, too
often distorted by being detached from their context :
yet its understanding is deeply necessary to the comprehension not only of our later history, but of that
of the seventeenth century in England, which had
powerful repercussions upon our own.

I have tried in special to show the whole range of the problem of government, regarding not only Scottish domestic matters, not only relations with Scotland's immediate neighbour, but attempting to give at any rate an outline of our country's part in the comity of Europe, and of those European affairs that affected our own. Certain estimates may, perhaps, be unfamiliar. I approached my material with an open mind, resolving to consider the facts as I found them, although in terms, to be sure, of a scale of values which differs from that of at least the dominant school of the nineteenth century. Moreover, on reading the standard historians, I have applied to various of their judgments the control of going myself to their raw material, and of supplementing certain of their omissions, a process which on more than one occasion has rather markedly altered the orthodox picture.

Two minor points in the treatment may be mentioned. I have quoted more freely than is customary from the contemporary documents, not because these possess an accuracy denied to modern political correspondence, or because Bower or Hardyng is less biassed than the average modern newspaper of repute, but because these papers give the mind of the time : for one of the most vital, and neglected, elements in the art of history is to determine what the men meant who made it, and their lies reveal that as fully as their ledgers. Besides this, I have laid at times some stress on points of family genealogy. This is not from a merely Highland liking for it, but because it is often most illuminating to know that X is a close relation of Y, while complicated questions of succession, that are ultimately questions of descent, have more than once had widely reaching results, as in Harlaw or the murder of James I.

I am indebted to those writers and editors whose names appear in the bibliography; to the Marquis of Lothian for permission to reproduce the noble Holbein portrait of James IV; to Brigadier-General R. A. Carruthers, C.B., C.M.G., for kindly reading the chapter upon Flodden; to Mr Stephen Bone for the fine cover; to Mr Ahier for the map; to Miss Betty Aylmer for the drawings of contemporary costume that help the reader to visualise what he reads.

St. John's Wood, *August*, 1935.

CONTENTS

xi

CHRONOLOGY

THE dates throughout this book are in modern reckoning, counting 1st January as the beginning of the year. The purpose of this list is not to give a summary of events in Scotland, but to fit these into the framework of contemporary Europe.

1328. Treaty of Northampton. Perpetual peace with England.
1329. Death of Robert I. Accession of David II.
1330. *Edward III assumes government.*
1332. Baliol expedition. Dupplin. Treaty of Roxburgh.
1333. English war reopens. Fall of Berwick. Halidon Hill.
1334. Baliol cedes the South. David sent to France. Robert Stewart strikes first blow for recovery.
1335. Kilblene.
1336. Edward's march to Inverness. *Flanders expels her Count.*
1337. *Flanders tempts Edward III.* Scotland rallies under Robert Stewart. Black Agnes in Dunbar. *? Death of Giotto.*
1339. *Edward vainly attacks Picardy.* Recovery of Perth.
1340. *Sluys.*
1341. *Breton war.* Return of David.
1342. Truce of Maestricht (triangular).
1345. *Anglo-French war reopens.*
1346. *Edward invades France. Crecy.* Invasion of England. Neville's Cross. David prisoner. Robert Stewart Regent.
1347. *Fall of Calais.* Truce of Calais (triangular).
1348. *Black Death in France and England.*
1350. Black Death. *Death of Philip VI. Accession of John II.*
1352. Pope Innocent attempts general peace.
1354. *Turks cross into Europe.*
1355. *Edward invades France.* Invasion of England. Berwick retaken. Nesbit Muir.
1356. Baliol resigns claim, Berwick lost again. Burnt Candlemas. Much of South cleared. *Poitiers.*
1357. David ransomed.
1358. *Jacquerie. Étienne Marcel.*
1359. *Edward in France again.*
1360. *Peace of Brétigny.* French break alliance.
1361. *Burgundy receives a French Duke. Turks in Adrianople.*
1363. Band against David. He remarries. Secret Treaty of Westminster.
1364. Estates refuse Treaty. *Death of John II. Accession of Charles V. Cocherel.*

1414. *Council of Constance.*
1415. *Henry V in France. Agincourt. Hus burnt.*
1416. Foul Raid. English invasion. Scots Church supports Conciliar Movement.
1417. *Henry in France again. Burgundy in Paris. End of Schism.*
1419. *Henry takes Normandy. Burgundy murdered.* Scots troops sent to France.
1420. Death of Albany. Murdoch Stewart Governor. *Treaty of Troyes.*
1421. Buchan in France. Baugé.
1422. *Death of Henry V. Accession of Henry VI. Death of Charles VI. Accession of Charles VII.*
1423. Crevant. James I makes treaty with England.
1424. James I returns. Verneuil. Arrest of Albany's son. *Gloucester quarrels with Burgundy.*
1425. Breaking of Albanies. Parliament of Inverness.
1427. Contention with Pope. Agreement with Norway.
1428. *Siege of Orleans.*
1429. *Relief of Orleans.* England proposes peace. Alexander of the Isles revolts.
1430. England proposes peace. *Charles crowned. St Joan captured.* Alexander subdued.
1431. *Henry crowned in Paris. St Joan burnt. Council of Basel.* Scots Church supports it. Revolt in Highlands.
1435. *Treaty of Arras.*
1436. *Charles in Paris.* Marriage of Princess Margaret. English war renewed.
1437. Murder of James I. Accession of James II.
1438. Queen against Crichton.
1439. Livingstone against Crichton. Civil disturbance. Queen remarries. Livingstone Guardian.
1440. Execution of Douglas.
1443. Renewal of civil war.
1448. English invasion. Invasion of England. Renewal of French alliance.
1449. *Anglo-French war reopens. Recovery of Normandy.* King's marriage. He begins to rule.
1450. *Formigny. Fall of Suffolk. Jack Cade.* Fall of the Livingstones.
1451. *Recovery of Guyenne.* Glasgow University.
1452. Douglas stabbed. *Birth of Leonardo.*
1453. *Châtillon. End of Hundred Years War. Madness of Henry.* James Douglas intriguing with England. *Turks take Constantinople. End of Eastern Empire.*

1454. *First known printed documents. Peace of Lodi.*

1455. Douglas war again. Arkinholm. York's letter. *Wars of the Roses. I St Albans.*

1456. James supports Henry.

1458. *Turks conquer Serbia.*

1460. *Northampton.* James again supports Henry. James killed. Accession of James III. Roxburgh finally recovered. *Wakefield. Death of York. Turks conquer Morea.* ? Birth of Dunbar.

1461. *Mortimer's Cross. II St Albans. Edward IV on English throne. Death of Charles VII. Accession of Louis XI. Turks conquer Trebizond.*

1462. Treaty between Edward and John of the Isles. *Turks conquer Wallachia.*

1463. *Wars of Roses reopen.* Border fighting. French and Scots make truce with England. Death of Queen Marie. *Hexham.*

1465. Death of Bishop Kennedy.

1466. Boyd coup d'état.

1467. ? *Birth of Erasmus.*

1468. Treaty with Scandinavia.

1469. King's marriage. He assumes active rule. Fall of Boyds. *Clarence and Warwick.*

1470. *Henry restored.*

1471. *Barnet and Tewkesbury. Henry murdered. Equator crossed.*

1472. Orkney and Shetland annexed. Archbishopric of St Andrews. *Louis at war with Burgundy.*

1474. Treaty of marriage with England. Forty-five years truce. *Accession of Isabella of Castile.*

1475. *Treaty of Pecquigny. Birth of Michael Angelo.*

1476. Surrender of John of the Isles.

1477. *Nancy. Death of Charles of Normandy. House of Austria in the Low Countries. Maximilian marries Mary of Burgundy.*

1479. James quarrels with his brothers. *Accession of Ferdinand of Aragon.*

1480. War again. *Turks in Italy.*

1481. Wood's victory off S.E. coast. Papal truce.

1482. *Treaty of Arras.* Albany in England. Invasion of Scotland. Lauder Bridge. Berwick finally lost. James and Albany reconciled. *Naples, Milan, and Florence against Venice.*

1483. Fresh breach with Albany. *Death of Louis XI. Accession of Charles VIII. Death of Edward IV. Accession of Edward V and Richard III. Birth of Luther.*

1484. Invasion by Albany. His final defeat.

1485. *Bosworth. Death of Richard III. Accession of Henry VII.*
1487. *Diaz rounds Cape. Maximilian King of the Romans.*
1488. Civil war. Sauchieburn. Death of James III. Accession of James IV. *Accession of Anne of Brittany.*
1489. Isle of May.
1491. Henry tries to kidnap James. Renewal of French alliance. Fresh war in Highlands. *Marriage of Anne and Charles.*
1492. Archbishopric of Glasgow. *Columbus in the Bahamas. Moors driven out of Spain. Henry VII invades France. Treaty of Étaples.*
1493. England offers perpetual peace. James in the Isles. *Maximilian unites the Hapsburg dominions.*
1494. James in the Isles. Founding of Aberdeen University. *Charles invades Italy.*
1495. *League of Venice.* Pacification of Highlands. Perkin Warbeck. *Treaty of Vercelli.*
1496. James supports Warbeck.
1497. Truce of Ayton.
1498. James in Isles. Reverses Highland policy. *Death of Charles VIII. Accession of Louis XII. ? Birth of Rabelais.*
1499. Henry renews marriage proposals. *Louis in Italy.*
1501. James consents to English marriage. Rising in Isles.
1502. Perpetual peace with England. *France and Spain at war in Italy.*
1503. James's marriage. *Death of Alexander VI. Election of Pius II, then Julius II. Birth of Sir Thomas Wyatt.*
1504. *French lose Naples.*
1505. James and Gueldres.
1507. Henry arrests Arran. First Scots printing.
1508. France and England attempt to draw James into war. *League of Cambrai.*
1509. *Death of Henry VII. Accession of Henry VIII. Birth of Calvin.*
1510. *Peace between Pope and Venice.*
1511. *Holy League against France.* James tries to reconcile France and the Pope.
1512. James working for peace. Treaty of Edinburgh. *Ravenna. English invade France. Spanish invade Navarre.* Victories at sea.
1513. *Death of Julius. Election of Leo X.* West's mission. *League of Mechlin. Novara. Guinegate.* Flodden. Death of James IV. Accession of James V.
1514. *France makes truces. Death of Louis XII. Accession of Francis I.*
1515. Franco-Scots truce with England.

I

1329–1424

And in those times there was no peace to him that went out nor to him that came in, but great vexations were upon the inhabitants of the lands. And they were broken in pieces, nation against nation and city against city : for God did vex them with all adversity.

II Chronicles, xv. 5-7.

CHAPTER I

INTRODUCTORY

Antecessorum gesta laudabilia . . . ad memoriam reducentes, non solum praesentibus ea quae praeterita sunt placabilia recitando proficimus : immo etiam virtutis viatoribus per providorum exempla praeteritorum, tanquam per lucernam veritatis viculum ostendimus.

Liber Pluscardensis.

BRUCE'S death let loose the Four Horsemen upon Scotland. The middle and later years of the fourteenth century are among the darkest in all our history. That any country could live through that time, and emerge still a country, still under her own flag, with the seeds of true national life still alive in her soil, bears witness to the spirit of those men who at Arbroath in 1320 declared that so long as only a hundred of them remained they would never surrender what they had undertaken. There was a time when it nearly came down to the hundred : greed and disunion and treachery did their worst, pestilence, famine, and economic chaos, under the shattering blows of new foreign aggression. Yet we came through. The grandsons of men who had fought, with little hope, through that black generation saw Scotland still in danger, to be sure—for when has Scotland ever been out of danger ?—but on her feet again and a power in Europe.

The change from the Scotland of the mid fourteenth century to that of the later part of the fifteenth is very

3

largely the work of three of her kings, men of the house
that succeeded that of Bruce. They had to change a
wrecked country, with little left living but fierce
nationalism, into a nation, not a mere nationality ; to
grip the powerful forces of disorder, the strong individual greeds, and fuse them together, force the wild
sectional loyalties and hatreds to serve not a man or a
district but an undying government and a country, as
preliminary to establishing that country united, civilised, prosperous, and safe from internal and foreign
tyrannies alike. Put merely thus, the problem is
formidable : and there were further complicating
factors. One was the presence, on the very edge of the
wealthiest provinces, within striking distance of most
of the greater towns, of a rich, powerful, and active
enemy, with somewhere from five to eight times
Scottish man-power, and an unappeasable greed to
extend her possessions. The other was the constant
luck of the house, the repeated minorities that not only
threatened to undo their work but made them a
sequence of young sovereigns, only two of whom—
significantly, the greatest—lived to reach their forties,
and they only barely : the longest lived of ' the Jameses '
was scarce forty-two, while the others died at twenty-
nine, thirty-seven, forty, and thirty-one . . . and of the
eight sovereigns of the First House of Stewart, three
died in their beds, and two among those of heart-break.

To understand the work of the Stewarts in Scotland,
it is needful to know something of their house in the
centuries before it was called to reign, and to know

what the problems were they had to face when Robert II, an old man already wearied, first found himself, as the great Bruce's grandson, *sedens in sede regno super montem de Scone.* The first of these points may be handled very briefly.

We are sometimes told the first Stewart kings were upstarts, and that they were foreigners. Neither statement is true. Their house, though not royal, was a very great one, and had served Scotland for six generations, from their founder, the High Steward of David I, to the father of Robert II, the defender of Berwick, and Robert himself in youth and the prime of his manhood. Their origin goes beyond that, to Celtic France, the Armorica that gave Caesar such work to win it, and to the beginning of the Middle Ages.

The Wandering of Nations, that is the main note of the seven centuries we call, and not unjustly, the Dark Ages, comes to an end with the last establishment of Scandinavian states, the conquest of Southern Italy by the Normans, and their conquest of England twenty-six years later. If any one date can be said to mark the beginning of the great epoch of the Middle Ages, it is the united effort of Western Europe to hold back the advancing culture of Asia in the First Crusade of 1096. The generation covered by these dates is a significant one for the whole of Europe considered as a whole, and not less for the individual nations. In the Empire it saw the great Franconian house of Henry the Fowler, the clash of Henry IV and Pope Gregory VII, that ended in the snow outside Canossa. Italy witnessed the rise, or fall, of the Popes to a position as great temporal princes. In France the stage was set for the great struggle between the centralising power of the Crown and the disintegrating forces of feudalism that is the framework of French mediaeval history, and supplies so many parallels with our own. Lost Spain turned her face to Europe when Alfonso and the Cid rode into Toledo. England was violently wrenched from her insular culture, her insular dynasty, and linked to France. For our own country, the North Sea was narrowed. When Duncan I, the king who joined the four Caledonian kingdoms, was killed at Bothgowan in the year 1040, Scotland's outlook was still to Ireland and Scandinavia. When his son Malcolm III fell in 1093, she had turned her face to central Christendom, to the Continent, and was taking her place as a division of Europe.

It is to this turbulent, formative generation, that we can trace the beginning of the Stewarts, although the dignity whence they took their name was not to be theirs for two generations yet. The first of the house of whom there is any record appears in the late eleventh century, in the stormy Celtic duchy of Brittany, that Alan Wrybeard the century before had made an all but independent state. This was one Alan, a vassal and possibly a kinsman of the Count of Dol, that fighting small city of the Breton Marches, whose ' Mount ' looks to St Michel over sea and quicksand. He went a crusader under Geoffrey of Boulogne, the first of the

French Kings of Jerusalem, of a house linked by marriage to that of the Kings of Scots. Now, Alan had a younger brother, Fléald or Flahault, who like many French younger sons of his generation went to look for an establishment in life in the swirl of the new Franco-Scandinavian kingdom the Tanner's Grandson was pounding out of England. It seems that he throve. At the end of the century he appears with a lordship on the March of Wales, a countryside whose lords led no easy life. He called his son Alan after his elder brother : this Alan succeeded to his lands in the March, and King William's son Henry made him Sheriff of Shropshire. The son of this Sheriff Alan, grandson therefore of the Flahault who came from Dol, was the first Scots Stewart, and the founder of the house whose royalty came to an end in 1807, with a priest's tomb in an Italian church, after a history tragic among kings beyond any dynasty that has worn a crown.

What brought them to Scotland was this. King Henry of England, son of the Conqueror, married a Scots princess : and since Scotland was rent by the succession wars between Donald Ban her uncle and her brothers, she brought with her, or had sent her, the youngest of these last, the sixth and seventh, two small boys, the Princes Alexander and David. At her husband's Norman court they were brought up, and grew to the age of knighthood, marrying in England. By fatality strange enough, but lucky for Scotland, these last sons of Malcolm III both reigned in turn, for nearly half a century between them. David was Prince of

South Scotland for seventeen years, and King of Scots for close on thirty more. Called north to this unexpected inheritance, he brought with him certain young Norman gentlemen, his friends at his brother-in-law's court. He reigned well, knew men and affairs, and chose his friends well : their Norman talent for administration, that made their race political heirs of Rome, made them good servants for a prince and king faced with a hundred fiercely difficult problems : and since Scotland and England were on terms of friendship, cemented by a close dynastic union,[1] it was not likely to strike a man of his time that the fact that many of these new Norman vassals were also vassals of the King of England might conceivably pose a fiercer problem yet . . . as indeed it did not till a hundred and thirty-seven years after David died, as an old man and a venerated monarch.

Now, one of these ' Norman ' friends of the young prince was a son of Sheriff Alan the son of Flahault, a Norman by culture and by blood a Breton. Sheriff Alan had three sons, as a matter of fact. Jourdain, the eldest, had the Breton heritage of his father's uncle, Alan of Dol. William, the second, had the English lands, and founded the house of the Fitzalan Earls of Arundel. Walter, the third son, as third sons do in the stories, sought his fortune, and in the third kingdom in three generations. He went to Scotland, to David's

[1] The Empress Maude and the Queen of her rival Stephen were both nieces of David's, and Henry II, the first Plantagenet king, his great-nephew : it was from David that Henry received his knighthood.

principality of the South. David thought well of him, gave him Kyle and Renfrew, and had him about his person as his High Steward, that is, the chief officer of the Royal Household. He outlived his great master by nineteen years, seeing in that time the reign of the young Malcolm IV and the breaking of the Princes of Galloway, and beating back from his own lands of Renfrew the invasion of Somerled (1164) that ended in the death of that dangerous man, the Norse-Celtic King of the Isles, who was backing the rival dynasty of Lulach. He outlived Malcolm, saw William I make alliance with Louis VII, the king's capture at Alnwick, the kingdom's at Falaise. He did not live to see the latter recovered, far less Fortune's revenge in the Treaty of Worms, when the Emperor played on Henry's son and England the same trick that Henry had played on William and Scotland. He died in 1177, and was buried in Paisley Abbey that he had founded, leaving his lands and office to Alan, his son by Eschyna de Mole, whose brother had founded the short-lived greatness of the Durwards.

The broken tradition of dynastic friendship was healed twelve years later by the Treaty of Canterbury, the wisest act of Richard Cœur de Lion, that rescinded completely the Treaty of Falaise, and opened the Hundred Years Peace between Scotland and England. Alan the Steward went with King William's brother to serve with Richard in the luckless Second Crusade, and was so fortunate as to return. He supported his sovereign through the latter's quarrels with Richard's brother John, that all but plunged their countries into

war. He died in 1204, succeeded by his son, another
Walter, the first to take his official title as surname.
William's young and able heir, Alexander II, made
Walter Justiciar as well as Steward, and gave him the
headship of the embassy that was charged to bring
home Queen Marie, that ' lady of unbelievable beauty,'
from France. He died in 1241, having seen the main
work of that important reign, and being present when
in the year 1238 Robert Bruce, Lord of Annandale,
son of the King's cousin, was nominated as next heir to
the throne, on the death of the King's first wife, Joan
of England, without children. His name appears on
the roster of lords present between those of Bruce and
the father of Bruce's rival, John Baliol, husband of
Devorgilla of Galloway: and the next is John Comyn,
Lord of Badenoch.

Walter married a daughter of the Earl of Angus, and
had three sons. John died on the Crusade under St
Louis, in the unhappy business at Damietta, and the
heirship fell to his brother Alexander. The third son,
Walter, married the co-heiress of Menteith, and since
her sister, who had married into the great house of the
Comyns, died childless, succeeded to the undivided
earldom, and founded the first cadet branch of the
Stewarts.[1] Their sister Margaret married Neil Earl of

---

[1] In the mid fourteenth century, Walter's great-grand-daughter
Mary, heiress of the line, married Sir John Graham, whose execution
by the English in 1347 left as heiress again his daughter Margaret.
She brought the earldom to her husband Robert Stewart, Duke of
Albany, son of Robert II, and Regent after the virtual deposition of
his own elder brother, Robert III.

THE EARLY STEWARTS AND THE ANCESTRY OF THE
SECOND HOUSE

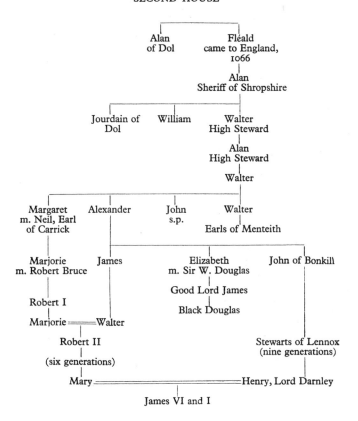

Carrick and her daughter was the mother of the great Bruce.

The main line, of course, is that of Alexander. He was one of the Guardians or Regents for the young King whose birth had ousted Bruce of Annandale from his heirship. He helped to save Scotland from the jarring factions of Alexander III's minority, Bruce and Durward the Justiciar on the one side, and Comyn and Queen Marie on the other, with the latter's second husband, John de Brienne. He married a daughter of MacRorie of Bute, of the seed of Somerled, who brought him lands adjacent to his own, that enabled him to command the Firth of Clyde : and he took a leading part in the victory of Largs, that broke the menace of Norway for good and all, and gave the Far North and the Isles to Scotland.

Alexander had two sons, James and John, and a daughter Elizabeth, who all served Scotland. She married the hard-fighting Sir William Douglas, who as Governor of Berwick bore the first brunt of the Three Hundred Years' War, and died soon after in an English prison : and their son was Bruce's Douglas, Good Lord James. James Stewart, the elder son of Alexander, fell heir to the Stewardship in 1283, at the age of forty. He married a sister of the Earl of Ulster, and in 1286, a few months after the King's unhappy death, he and his brother and his brother-in-law appear at Turnberry with the group of nobles who wished to put by the claim of the three-year-old Queen in favour of that Bruce of Annandale who had once been named heir by

Alexander II. The attempt to give Scotland a stronger head than a child Princess of Norway soon failed, and the little Queen Margaret was recognised. James, who was one of the six Guardians or Regents, refused to share in the negotiations for a union of the two British crowns by her marriage ; and in the succession contest after her death he resumed his support of the claims of the House of Bruce, backing the old man as against Baliol. When Baliol was driven to war against Edward I he sank the feud, holding Roxburgh against Edward's first invasion : but his anti-Baliol sympathies made him take a somewhat half-hearted share, for that time, in the struggle, and when Baliol's cause seemed ruined, after Dunbar, he surrendered on terms. None the less, he was for Scotland, if not for her puppet king : indeed, he is the first of the great nobles who after the breaking of the Hundred Years' Peace shows sign of what may be called national feeling. In the next year, when a popular resistance began to take shape in sporadic risings over most of Scotland, it was he who joined with the Bishops of Glasgow and Moray in co-ordinating these small local risings into a national one. He was one of the chief men among those Southern leaders whose bickerings nearly wrecked the beginning resistance, and surrendered with them at Irvine in 1297. Then, finding the apparent collapse not final, he took arms again with Wallace, and fought at the victory of Stirling Bridge. He saw Wallace's brilliant first success, his disastrous failure at Falkirk the next year, where John Stewart, his own younger brother,[1] was killed, the dragging of the war under the Comyns, its apparently final collapse and the seeming obliteration of Scotland in 1304-5. The next year brought the hazardous coronation of Bruce's grandson, Robert Bruce Earl of Carrick. James, then over sixty, joined Bruce immediately after, saw the apparent ruin of the adventure, its resumption in 1307, and the successes of that year and the next. When he died in 1309, Scotland had been won back to the line of the Tay, and King Robert had held his first Parliament at St Andrews, where James Stewart is named among those who were present.

Walter, his heir, a brilliant, short-lived soldier, was born late in his father's life, in 1292, the year that ended with Baliol's coronation. Presumably he served as a lad with his father : he was first cousin alike of the great Douglas, of the wife of Douglas's colleague, Thomas Randolph, and of Bruce's imprisoned Queen, Elizabeth of Ulster, but he would be only a child in the Comyn wars, and at Bruce's coronation not *hors de page*.

[1] John Stewart married Margaret, heiress of Bonkill, and his family were *Alexander* (or *John*) the progenitor of the Stewarts Earls of Angus, whose heiress carried that dignity to a Douglas ; *Alan*, of the Stewarts of Darnley, Earls of Lennox, and of the French house of Stuart d'Aubigny ; *Walter*, of the Stewarts of Garlies, Earls of Galloway ; *James*, of the Highland branches, the Stewarts of Lorne, Earls of Athol, Buchan, and Traquair, and the Stewarts of Appin and Grandtully ; and *Isobel*, wife of Bruce's great general, Thomas Randolph, Earl of Moray, and mother of Black Agnes, Countess of March, and her two brave brothers. The descendants of Alan, second son of John, came to the throne by the marriage of Henry Lord Darnley to the heiress of the senior line, Queen Mary, and their descendants are the Stewarts of the United Kingdom, the Second House.

We know that as a squire of twenty-two he led the men of his great family lands to the muster of Bannockburn, was his cousin Douglas's lieutenant in command of the centre during the main action, and was knighted in the field before the battle. His service there was rewarded the next year, by his betrothal to the King's only child, the Princess Marjorie, newly released from eight years of an English prison. The Parliament of Ayr, just before their marriage, postponed the Princess's rights, with her own consent, to those of her uncle Edward Bruce and his heirs, Marjorie and her children to come after, with the wise veteran Randolph to be Regent. In less than a year, Princess Marjorie was killed, leaving a new-born son, called Robert after his mighty grandfather. Edward Bruce's death at Dundalk in 1318 brought this baby back into the direct succession as the only legitimate descendant of the King, whose three younger brothers had all of them died, childless, on English scaffolds : the Parliament of that year could do no other than to recognise the little Robert Stewart as heir.

His young father fought gallantly in the few years left him. His quality as a soldier is proved by the fact that when Berwick, the last of Scotland to be recovered, was taken, the young man of twenty-six was made the Governor of that dangerous post. He justified King Robert's confidence by his splendid defence of it in the next year, when he turned the tide of the attempted storm by his sally through the burning Mary-port. For some years his little son remained heir-presumptive :

it was not until 1324 that the birth of a Prince of Scotland excluded him. Two years later, Walter Stewart, then only thirty-four, died of a fever. His death was to be a grievous loss to Scotland, for young as he was his fame ranks next after that of King Robert's three great Captains, Randolph and Douglas and Sir Edward Bruce. None of them, nor their master, lived to be old, though only two of the four were to die in battle, and they on foreign fields.

When in 1329, only a year after his final victory, King Robert went to the rest that he had earned, he left Scotland to a King of five years old, newly married to a child princess of England : and the boy's heir was his nephew, Robert Stewart, now thirteen, who was to succeed him as the first Stewart sovereign, but not till after nearly forty years of the most wretched reign in our history.

CHAPTER II

DAVID II : 1329–71

' Tristia felicibus succedunt.'
Fordun and Bower, *Gesta Annalia*.

THE reign of Robert Bruce's unworthy son opened in glory. Scotland, mourning her great king, had good cause for pride. 1286 had left her without a head. The jarring feuds of the next nineteen years had left her, in spite of struggles, of the long resistance of Wallace and the Comyns, without a body. In 1305 she was a country no more, had fallen into the heavy Plantagenet gripe, and was to be henceforth no more than a province of England. She was to be as extinct as the Kingdom of Arles, as Poland seemed to be in 1913, as the Eastern Empire. Within a year of that, Bishop Wishart and Lady Buchan crowned Bruce at Scone. The broken country gathered her strength and rose. It took eight years to drive out the enemy, and fourteen more to make them acknowledge defeat. At Northampton, in May 1328, the English king and Parliament yielded at last, in the fullest possible terms, all Scotland had fought for. There was to be peace. . . . But between the Hundred Years' Peace that this war had broken were the years from 1290 to 1328 : and the young King of England, who was seventeen, with the makings of a great soldier, was chafing against the shameful tutelage of his mother and her lover Mortimer, and seeking for glory in the terms in which he conceived it. He came of the fated house of Plantagenet, who had never forgotten the loss of their vast French lands, and were to spend themselves, through their whole course, in the lust for the foreign thrones of France and Scotland, that they won, the former twice and the second thrice, but could never hold, till they went down at last in a worry of wild beasts about their own, and left it to an adventurer's grandson from Wales.

King Robert I died with the new peace unbroken, leaving his kingdom and his little son to the firm guardianship of the Earl of Moray, Thomas Randolph, the soldier who had led the left wing at Bannockburn and taken Edinburgh Castle by a wild audacity of escalade, the diplomat who had outplayed the Pope in the chess of international politics. For a couple of years all was well. Randolph guided affairs with wisdom and a heavy-handed justice, and Scotland was recovering already, for all through the last fourteen years of the war most of the actual fighting had been in England. To the responsible men of 1330 it must have seemed that the country now had her chance to recover the prosperity of the previous century, that old men could remember, the fruit of the steady progress under the last Alexanders. It was not to be.

At the end of 1331, Randolph crowned and knighted his young charge, aged seven. Across the Border young David's brother-in-law was coming to manhood : he asserted himself, sent his mother to the prison in which she died, and her lover to the block, and assumed the headship of his own government. The rest of David's reign is the story of one long bitter struggle with Edward, first in war, then in diplomacy, with the recurring threat of war to back it. The issue of the struggle was success, but hardly victory : what there is of that is on the other side, though it did not avail for anything in the end, except to harm both. The whole period is both complex and unhappy, without the epic thrill of Bruce's War : one is scarcely surprised that most historians shirk it. None the less, to understand the course of events is essential to comprehension of later relations in the triangle of Scotland, France, and England : and this time, the middle fourteenth century, left a deep and permanent mark on our national life.

Almost before the little King was crowned, and within a year of Edward's beginning to rule, the clouds were already gathering south of the Border. The diehards of the old Comyn-Baliol faction, who had opposed to the last the rule of a Bruce, had lost their Scots lands. They included a son of the forfeited (Umfraville) Earl of Angus, and the forfeited Earl of Athol,[1] who besides the loss of his lands had considerable grounds for a feud with the Bruces, as his mother was a daughter of Red John Comyn, and his aunt had been the wife of Edward Bruce, who had quarrelled with her and left her. Certain great English nobles, before the war, had held lands in Scotland, which the war had lost them. It

---

[1] David, 11th Earl. The earldom at this time was held by a junior branch of the House of Fife.

appears that at the time of the Treaty of Northampton some private arrangement (it is not, as is commonly said, a term of the treaty) had been made for the return of their properties to Henry Percy, Thomas Lord Wake, and the Henry de Beaumont whose cavalry Randolph's spearmen had smashed at St Ninians.[1] Randolph gave Percy his lands, but hesitated over the others. It is possible that he may have wished for some reciprocal arrangement : none of the Scots who had lost English lands, save Douglas, had had anything restored. It is certain also that political considerations might well give him pause. Beaumont and Wake had violently opposed the Peace : Beaumont, heir to the Comyn feud with the Bruces, claimed Buchan, the key to all North-east Scotland, and very vulnerable from the sea, while Wake claimed Liddesdale, the gate of the West March. Clearly, he disliked the idea of handing over important strategic points to men not only foreign but frankly hostile. He temporised : the young Edward III backed the demands of his nobles, and tension grew between the two Governments. The *Exheredati*—the Disinherited—drew together. What lit the bonfire was that the outed faction had an heir of their own available for the Crown. The nominal aim at least of the Comyn war, between 1297 and 1304, had been the restoration of John Baliol : William Wallace's commission as Guardian represents him as acting on Baliol's behalf.

---

[1] He had married the niece and heiress of Bruce's inveterate enemy, John Comyn, Earl of Buchan, and was the last gaoler of the latter's brave Countess.

Now, King John Empty Jacket was dead long since in France, but he had left a son to inherit his claims. Edward II, by way of a threat against King Robert, had celebrated one of his truces with Scotland by inviting this young man to England, and making much of him. He was still available as a figure-head.

They determined—the leader seems to have been Beaumont—on what is now called a *putsch*, an armed raid to overthrow the Government, and place them at the head of Scots affairs. In August of 1332 they landed at Kinghorn, after some resistance by the Earl of Fife. Randolph, moving to oppose them, died suddenly. Barbour, Wyntoun, and Bower all say he died of poison : modern historians commonly say ' of the stone.' The earliest authority for the last is Hector Boece, who lived about 1500, and was a gentleman, as Spottiswoode puts it, of some ' felicity of ingenie.' The extreme convenience of the demise is suspicious, and an English friar who was about the court appears to have bolted : but an innocent man in the circumstances might well have done that, and like other famous cases of ' poisoning ' Randolph's death may have been due to internal disease.[1] He died, at any rate, at a moment when he was desperately needed. The King was nine, and James Douglas in his grave in the Kirk of St Bride.

The Estates, meeting at Perth, had to choose a new Regent in a hurry. They chose the King's cousin, the

[1] Appendicitis has been suggested : but if, as is recorded, Randolph, then very ill, got up and dressed himself richly to receive an English envoy, concealing his pain, it sounds scarcely probable.

Earl of Mar, son of Christina Bruce : and Mar's birth
seems to have been his sole qualification.   He marched
to oppose the invaders.   He had seen service in the wars
after Bannockburn, but he was no general, and in a night
action, near Perth, at Dupplin Moor, he was badly and
disgracefully defeated.   It is true that there was
treachery : the enemy were guided across a ford and
enabled to approach the Scottish camp before Mar
could get his men in order of battle : but there was also
gross carelessness over pickets, and according to later
Scottish evidence, Mar's men were largely drunk.
There were instances of a redeeming devotion.   Randolph's son and heir, with Menteith, Robert Bruce
(King Robert's natural son) and Alexander Fraser
attempted a rally, but they were not supported, and lost
their lives.   Mar was killed also.   The Scots were
jammed on the river and massacred.   John Craib, the
Aberdeen-Flemish sea-captain who had served Walter
Stewart so well in the siege of Berwick, attacked the
invaders' ships, and took the chief, the *Beaumondscogge*,
but the small success was an insufficient check.   Perth
lay open : they marched on it and repaired the
' slighted ' fortifications, and on the 24th September,
Edward Baliol was crowned King of Scots at Scone, by
his prisoner the Earl of Fife, the very brother of the
gallant lady who in the same place had crowned Robert
Bruce.

Edward of England had so far behaved correctly,
officially disowning the affair, and adhering, up to this
point, to the detailed treaty he and his parliament had

subscribed a little more than three years before, that
had been ratified by his sister's marriage. Now, however, the temptation was too strong. Scotland, devoted
to the Bruces, could settle the business if she were left
alone, though the situation was necessarily complicated
by the absence of a recognised head to the government.
Baliol, if he were to have any effective success, would
certainly need help of some kind from without, and
might be ready to pay his father's price . . . and Edward
may have recalled his first campaign, that had ended
with his bursting into tears at its inglorious collapse. A
war would be sport : (*il*) *desiroit lez armys et honors* :
and the Treaty of Northampton had been most unpopular in the South of England.

He called a council, and the Englishman Gray's
account of it is of interest. It was clearly impossible
frankly to back a pretender against a friendly sovereign,
his brother-in-law. The Treaty of Northampton, however, had specifically safe-guarded the Franco-Scots
Alliance. The alliance was definitely a purely defensive
one, and Edward and his parliament had passed it.
Now, however, he proceeded to make a grievance of it,
and declared that Randolph's formal confirmation of
the alliance, at the beginning of his Regency, was a
hostile move against England. He pointed out further
that the Treaty had compelled him to surrender his
' rights ' to Scotland, but that now the situation had
changed and a new war was possible : *fust avys au dit
roi qe pur nouel mocioun nouel guer.* He was now free to
take the most profitable course—*fraunk a faire soun*

profite—which clearly was to back Baliol and make him yield what David's supporters certainly would not.

With the joyful concurrence of his Council, therefore, he proceeded to ignore the recent Treaty, and deal with Baliol as King of Scots. Within two months of the anti-king's coronation, Baliol had signed the Treaty of Roxburgh, that yielded all that the Treaty of Northampton had professed to secure—the results of the twenty-two years of Bruce's War. Baliol would hold his crown as vassal of England : he calmly proposed to marry the little Queen Joan (who was eleven) declaring that her marriage was but a betrothal. *Pur les grauntz Honeurs et Profitz que nous avons sentis et trouez en la souffrance nostre dit Seigneur le Roi [Dengelterre] et la graunt et bone Aide de ses dites bones gentz de son Roiaulme et poair,* he gives Edward III 2000 *livrees* of ground on the Marches, and in full gift, the town, castle, and county of Berwick, and agrees to come in person, with all his power, at his own expense, whenever Edward or his heirs should require : as a penalty clause, if Baliol or his successors fail to appear in the field when summoned by Edward (who already, probably, had his eye on France, where Philip was quarrelling with Robert d'Artois) they must pay the impossible sum of £200,000 sterling, failing which, Scotland shall ' revert ' to Edward.

The latter, having thus put himself right with the active but resourceful Plantagenet conscience, proceeded to mobilise. So far, the affair had been no more than a local insurrection, complicated by the inopportune de-

mise of first one and then another head of the Government and Commander-in-Chief. The third phase of
the Three Hundred Years' War begins now : its earliest
part, the nine years from this re-opening to David's
assumption of the Government in 1341, is one of the
most confused and entangled periods in our history.
There is no centralised action, no organising principle
except resistance, and that was uncoordinated. There
were brave men in plenty, but the few who might have
been capable of leading a national movement were lost
almost as they appeared. The real national leaders,
through these nine years, were the ghosts of Robert
Bruce and his great captains.

The barely re-established national machinery did not
break quite at once. The Estates chose a new Regent,
and more wisely, the stepfather of the dead Mar, King
Robert's brother-in-law, Andrew Moray of Bothwell,[1]
vir validus et magni regiminis—strong, self-controlled,
just, devout, and merciful, a man of high character and
an excellent soldier. Other leaders rose who had the
old blood in them—John Randolph, now Earl of Moray
in succession to his brother and his father ; and the
brother and the natural son of the great Douglas, Sir
Archibald, who had served with him in the brilliant
Weardale campaign, and Sir William of Liddesdale,
called the Flower of Knighthood. Troops were raised,
and before the year was out, Douglas and Randolph had

---

[1] He was son to the young Andrew de Moray who was prominent
in the rising of 1297, became Wallace's colleague in command of the
army, and fell mortally wounded at Stirling Bridge.

fallen on ' the Winter King ' at Annan, and forced him
to bolt in his shirt on an unsaddled horse, with one boot
on and the other left behind him.

This aggression upon Edward's protégé gave him
colourable excuse for an invasion, the more as the
promised Berwick had not chosen to give itself up.
He moved north, and before he could cross the Border,
Scotland had lost two of her three best leaders, in minor
skirmishes : the new Regent, Bothwell, had been taken
at Roxburgh, in a gallant attempt to rescue his own
squire, and Douglas of Liddesdale was also prisoner.
The Estates, compelled to choose a successor to Bothwell, appointed a very much less useful man, Archibald
Douglas, a man brave to rashness, but with none of the
qualities of a commander, while the mere fact of having
to make a new election wasted time at a moment when
time was valuable.

It was now summer, and Edward's army could move.
He struck for Berwick, attacking by land and sea. The
townsmen, under Seton their Governor and the Earl of
March, who commanded the castle, put up a gallant
resistance, sinking or firing great part of the English
fleet. Philip VI implemented the Treaty of Corbeil by
sending over a French relieving squadron, but it was
destroyed off Dundee before it could act, and the loss of
Bothwell apparently delayed the Scottish army. Berwick, hard driven, had to negotiate, and Seton at length
agreed to surrender the town if it were not relieved by
a given time, hostages guaranteeing the arrangement.
Within that time (the evidence is English) the new

Regent brought his army within sight of the town, and threw into it a reinforcement of men and provisions. He then marched past Edward, perhaps intending the sort of strategic diversion that had been so successful in 1319. Edward claimed that this did not constitute a relief. Seton, however, declared that he had been re-lieved, and refused to open the gates. His young son was among the hostages : the elder had been killed in his father's sight, at the burning of the ships. Edward produced him now, and threatened to hang him unless the town surrendered. His parents—Lady Seton was in Berwick—were foremost in refusing to make the bar-gain, and watched from the wall as the boy was duly hanged.

Save as example, their devotion was wasted. Edward turned on Douglas : he was at this time not quite twenty-one, but already and instinctively a soldier to compare with his grandfather. On the 19th of July, 1333, he brought the Scots to action at Halidon Hill, a couple of miles from Berwick. He faced Douglas across a ravine, with a bog in the bottom, and he was well supplied with archery. Douglas's force was mainly hobelers, the light mounted infantry his brother had handled so magnificently. He had no archers, and with incredible folly he threw his men at the strong English position, across bog and uphill under a murderous fire, to which, of course, they had no means of replying. They fell in swathes, and a cavalry charge downhill completed a massacre. Douglas was killed, and many other nobles : the army was shattered. Edward put his prisoners to death, and entered Berwick. The victory left him master of all Scotland below the Forth, and (as we may see from the songs of Lawrence Minot) the English thought Bannockburn revenged and undone. It was five years from the Treaty of Northampton.

In fact, they were justified in the belief. Edward Baliol was nominally King again, not merely repeating his submission now, but completely ceding Galloway and Lothian, which were ' planted,' after the example of Ireland, with English merchants, clergy, and tenants. The speedy over-running of the South is due not only to the destruction of the army and its leaders, but to the fact that the castles had been destroyed in the previous war, and most of them were not yet rebuilt, so that there were few *lieux-forts* to serve as nuclei for a resistance. There was a hideous time for the loyalists : they were dispossessed of lands and gear, flogged and imprisoned. The Flemish ports were full of penniless refugees, ' beating the streets,' as a jeering English song of the time describes it. Throughout the whole country, according to Andrew Wyntoun, only the children at play called Bruce's son King, and in the whole length and breadth of Lowland Scotland, only five castles, one of them a mere peel, were holding out for the lawful King of Scots.

It was the third apparently final conquest in the space of thirty-six years. The men who surrendered to it may be forgiven : if ever resistance seemed completely hopeless, a mere waste of strength and of suffering, it was then. But there were men—women too—in those desperate years who chose rather to die in a lost fight than live remembering that they had surrendered. There is no great organised movement : there could not be. (Wallace was rousing a country almost uninjured, still prosperous from long peace.) Only groups here and there resisted where they stood, refused to go down, died fighting or came through somehow, made a breathing space, fired the weaker by their example. The record flickers with small local heroisms—Malcolm Fleming guarding the child King and Queen in Dumbarton, till in spring a French ship managed to get them away, and they were safely installed in Château Gaillard ; old John Thomson in Lochdoun ; Thomas Lauder in Urquhart ; Vipont, breaking the English dam at Lochleven Castle, and sweeping his foes away with the loch water they had engineered to overwhelm himself.

In a year, four Regents had died, been killed, or been captured. To succeed Douglas, two men were chosen now to act together. One was John Randolph, son of the great soldier, Earl of Moray since his brother's death at Dupplin, and jointly responsible with the dead Douglas for the driving of Edward Baliol from Annan. The other was his kinsman, the young heir-presumptive to Scotland, Robert Stewart. The latter's appointment seems to be mainly a gesture, as he was not yet eighteen : he was a tall handsome lad, gay and warm-hearted and with charming manners, *valde hilaris et amabilis.* Young as he was, he distinguished himself by the first active counter-stroke for recovery. Randolph apparently went to France for help, while his co-Regent took refuge with Malcolm Fleming in Dumbarton, in striking distance of the Stewart country, which was now held by Athol as Baliol's lieutenant. Thence he crossed to Bute, which was also in Athol's hands, and the men of the island rose for their young lord. A body of them, marching unarmed to join him, encountered Athol's deputy, Alan Lisle, and defended themselves by so hot a fire of stones that his force was routed. Bute was recovered, and the gallant ' Brendanes ' were freed as reward from multure dues thereafter. Robert, with his cousin Campbell of Lochow, then landed on the mainland, raised the Stewart men, and in no long time had cleared Renfrew, Cunningham, and Carrick, while Randolph, who by now had returned from France, drove Athol north into Lochaber, where he surrendered and took King David's side—no addition to it, as he soon stirred up trouble between the Regents.

Similar small independent campaigns were going on elsewhere. In the South-east Alexander Ramsay of Dalhousie was carrying on a fierce guerilla war from a base in the caves of Roslin, and men flocked to him as they had done to Wallace. Douglas of Liddesdale and Moray of Bothwell had been ransomed, and both were at work on the strategic lines of *King Robert's Testament*.[1]

---

[1] A rhyme current at this time, which professes to give the essence of that great soldier's practice. Modernised, so far as rhyme permits, it goes :

> On foot should be all Scottish weir,
> By hill and moss themselves to rear.

They tell a story of Bothwell at this time that illus-
trates the nature of the man. His small force had word
of a much greater English one marching against them.
Bothwell was at mass, and no one dared interrupt till
the mass was over. Then they told him, and he
answered calmly, 'No hurry,' and gave deliberate
orders for a retreat. As they mounted he found that a
strap of his armour was broken, sent his squire for a
special coffer out of his baggage, extracted a piece of
leather, and at the completest leisure cut a new thong,
and fashioned it precisely to his liking. Wyntoun, who
tells the story, remarks with a chuckle that some of the
knights who looked on at the repairs thought they never
saw a strap take so long to make, but Bothwell finished
at last, imperturbably, and brought his men off in a
masterly retreat.

Athol, having brought about an open quarrel between
Randolph and young Robert Stewart, changed sides
again in 1335, and laid siege to Kildrummie, which was
held by Bothwell's wife, Christina Bruce. Bothwell and
Liddesdale, having joined forces, marched to raise the

> Let woods for walls be bow and spear
> That enemies do them no deir. (harm)
> In safe places go keep all store,
> And burn the plainland them before.
> Then shall they pass away in haste,
> When they shall find the land lie waste.
> With wiles and wakings of the night,
> And muckle noises made on height,
> Them shall ye turn with great affray,
> As they were chased with sword away.
> This is the counsel and intent
> Of Good King Robert's Testament.

siege, and on St Andrew's Day defeated and slew him at Kilblene in Braemar : Beaumont, his father-in-law, had been with him, and revenged him by putting his prisoners to death, some with torture. His elimination from politics was a gain to Scotland, for he had been a restless, unstable creature, stirring trouble wherever he went.

In spite of these various little local successes, the country was still in grave danger. Even the successes themselves, as with Beaumont after Kilblene, invited reprisals : there is a dreadful vindictiveness in this war. In 1336 Edward could still march as far as Inverness, burning the towns of Elgin and Aberdeen, and sacking the country, to the very churches. He rebuilt, using forced labour, some of the greater castles—Leuchars, St Andrews, Edinburgh, Stirling, and Roxburgh—and garrisoned them. While he thus pinned down the East, his young brother, John of Cornwall, harried the West, burning churches over the heads of refugees, a proceeding to which Edward, to his credit, took objection : they quarrelled over it when they met at Perth, and a Scots historian says that Edward stabbed him. He certainly did die at Perth just then.

Before Edinburgh Castle had been rebuilt, Edward's ally, the Duke of Namur, landed in Lothian : Liddesdale and Bothwell, still working in concert, fell on him and drove him into Edinburgh, where he made a stand on the Rock, killing his horses to make a sort of laager of the bodies. He was starved out, and surrendered with the honours of war ; his captors set him free without ransom, and his men likewise. Bothwell, escorting him courteously over the Border, was captured once more, a very serious loss.[1]

The most famous exploit of the war, perhaps, is the defence of Dunbar by Randolph's sister, Agnes, Countess of March, through the first half of 1337. There are vivid stories of her upon the walls, singing gay insulting rhymes to the besiegers, and leading her maids with dusters under fire to mock the results of Salisbury's mangonels. She kept him off through five months of siege and blockade, and was almost starved out, for the English held the sea with Genoese galleys, till Ramsay of Dalhousie ran the blockade under cover of night from the Bass, and Black Agnes had the pleasure the next morning of sending Salisbury, short of provisions himself, a politely annoying gift of white bread and wine, whereat he gave up and withdrew from the sea-beaten walls.

Bothwell was ransomed again, but killed soon after, and the war went on grimly, with a new horror of famine. Men ate raw acorns, and far worse than that : there are hideous tales of cannibals here and there, and no law ran any more. Robert Stewart, on Bothwell's death, was again made Regent. He was consistently a patriot, and he had courage and intelligence and, in his youth and middle life, energy as well : but to force order upon such a chaos was impossible for a lad of

---

[1] The *Liber Pluscardensis* has an odd story of this episode. A Flemish knight of Namur's challenged one Richard Shaw to run a course. They met, the Fleming was killed, and on the body being streiked for burial, turned out to be no knight, but a lady of Flanders.

c

twenty-two. In any case, the most immediate need, before any reconstruction could be attempted, was to clear Scotland of the enemy. He set about that, with the aid of a curious figure, one Bulloch, a priest who had become a soldier of fortune, and after serving as Baliol's Chancellor, changed sides in 1338, bringing Cupar with him : he was a specimen of the *condottiere* who is one of the typical figures of the age, an efficient soldier and a cool-headed creature who could take calm account of the panic at an eclipse.[1]

Help came from France too. Philip VI sent over an expeditionary force under Garancières, and in August of 1339, Robert succeeded in taking Perth with them. Stirling fell soon after. The land north of Forth was gradually cleared in the course of the following year, and in April of 1341 the young Regent, aided by Bulloch and Liddesdale and a sea-captain of the name of Currie, recovered Edinburgh Castle, playing a trick like Binnock's at Linlithgow in 1313.

Robert Stewart's push south marks the turning of the tide. To describe the dreadful 'thirties in more detail is hardly needed. Scotland held on grimly for seven bitter years, and at last the invading pressure began to slacken, for Edward's greed found a larger temptation elsewhere. In the early part of 1341, Robert Stewart was able to bring the young King home, and the son of Bruce was once again in his kingdom.

---

[1] His later career is also typical of his kind. He became King David's Chamberlain, lost favour and his post, and died starved to death in a dungeon at Lochindorb.

Events, in the last few years, had been happening abroad that were to shake Europe for a century, all but wreck France, and bring down the Plantagenets in a gory scramble : and until the Union of the Crowns, or indeed until the mid-eighteenth century, our own history was deeply influenced by them. Everyone has heard of the Hundred Years' War, but its causes and course, as given by English historians, are commonly, let us say, so simplified that it is difficult to understand them, and certainly to grasp the part of Scotland : yet since the war, both during its course and after, profoundly affected Scottish politics, it is necessary to know what it was about, even although the picture is less romantic than that familiar to us in the schoolroom.

Flanders, the mart of Europe and Edward's ally, had been at odds with its French Count, Louis de Nevers. In 1336, his exasperated subjects turned him out : and he was a kinsman of the King of France. He fled to the French court. Van Artevelde, the leader of the rising, feared Philip, who was overlord of Flanders, and sought for help. Now, Flanders was the main market for the wool that was the principal export of England, as much the basis of the nation's wealth as coal and iron were under Victoria. Artevelde put on the economic screw, and backed by Philip's kinsman Robert d'Artois, who had fled to England to avoid the block for forgery and poison, he added a shrewd diplomatic stroke. His Flemings might shrink from a rising against their suzerain the King of France : but they would rise for a rival King of France, who would keep out their hated

Count, and help their cloth-trade. He covered his prosaic woollen weapon by throwing a royal mantle over the sacks, and suggesting that Edward might claim a second throne. Now, Edward's mother had been a Daughter of France, and but for the Salic Law, which cut out succession in the female line, he was senior to Philip VI, her first cousin, whose father had been her father's younger brother. The Flemings conveniently ignored the fact, as English historians still not uncommonly do, that on the principles by which he claimed, Edward, though senior to Philip VI, was junior not only to their own ex-Count's son, but to the King of Navarre and the heir of Burgundy, who were sons of his cousins of two *elder* lines.[1]   Edward, incidentally, had accepted the settlement of the French Crown on Philip, and done homage to him for his duchy of Guyenne.   From a variety of motives, however, he decided in 1337, nine years after, to denounce his fealty, ignore his superfluous cousins, and proclaim himself the rightful King of France.

In England, it was a decidedly popular move.   The

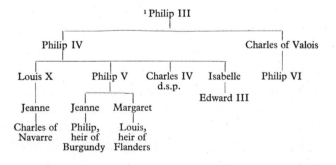

[1] Philip III

Philip IV — Charles of Valois

Louis X   Philip V   Charles IV   Isabelle   Philip VI
                       d.s.p.
                                    Edward III

Jeanne   Jeanne   Margaret

Charles of   Philip,   Louis,
Navarre   heir of   heir of
          Burgundy   Flanders

wealthy merchants had their very existence bound to
the Flemish markets, and could not afford to be on ill
terms with Flanders. The riches of the nobles also
depended largely upon wool, and both they and the
commons were weary of the Scots war, which in spite of
its brilliant opening at Halidon Hill, was yielding little
glory after all. Scotland had nothing left in the way of
loot, and France was fat with it, while there was an old
tradition of dislike, going as far back as the conquest by
Normandy and strengthened by the loss of four provinces from the great Plantagenet inheritance. None the
less, Edward could not act at once. A great and wealthy
country like France was a different problem from
small, war-shattered Scotland, and he had to lay a
political foundation, which occupied him through the
later 'thirties. No doubt the Scots government knew of
his intentions, and the prospect of his imminent dis-
traction, and a consequent easing of the heavy pressure
if they could only hold out a little longer, would encourage resistance, and help Stewart's drive south in
1338-9 ; while desire to keep Edward still occupied in
Scotland might sharpen Philip's sense of his treaty
obligations towards his ally, and have something to do
with the sending of Garancières.

Edward formed alliances with the Emperor, who made
him his Vicar for the provinces on the left bank of the
Rhine, and with various princes of the Netherlands,
and the matter looked ill for France, who could now be
attacked on north-east and south-west at once. His
first military move was an expedition to Picardy in

1339. It failed completely, but in the following year
the French fleet paid for its admiral's lack of skill, and
was heavily beaten off Sluys. Edward made little more
progress for some time, but the turning of his attention
to the South made matters very much easier for Scotland, and this and the fact that North France was now
in danger decided the Regent to bring home the young
King.

It was one of those actions that have everything for
them in reason, and founder in practice on a man's
character. David was seventeen, verging on manhood.
He was lawfully the King, Robert Bruce's son. His
very presence in his shattered kingdom was like a glint
of the flags of Bannockburn. But he had nothing of
his father in him except a decent share of physical
courage, a handsome presence, and some charm of
manner. He had left Scotland at the age of ten, knew
little of it, and was disinclined to give up a life of ease at
the brilliant French court for a task that might have
daunted a stronger man, that of holding Scotland clear
of the enemy, and building her ruins into a nation
again.

He landed at Inverbervie in the spring of 1341, and
his twenty-five-year-old nephew resigned the government into his hands. David had grace enough to confirm the latter in the earldom of Athol, conferred upon
him by the Regent Bothwell, and sense enough to make
Randolph, Liddesdale, and Ramsay of Dalhousie
Wardens of the Marches, while for a time he was much
about Kildrummie, in the bracing company of his aunt

Christina, mother of the Regent Mar and widow of the Regent Bothwell, a resolute and energetic woman.

Matters, at first, went reasonably well. Hostilities had slackened a good deal, for though Edward had ceased for the time to attack France directly, he was occupied by the Breton Succession War, *la Guerre des deux Jeanne*. The heir of the male line, Jean de Montfort, claimed against Jeanne de Penthièvre, who was the daughter of his elder brother. She was married to that hard-fighting saint, Charles de Blois, who was Philip's nephew, and Philip took their part, which brought Edward in on the side of Jean de Montfort, whose claim precisely reversed the principles on which he himself was claiming the Crown of France. North France was soon in a very ugly mess, with Charles of Navarre, known succinctly as Charles the Bad, pouring oil on the flames. The distracted Philip appealed to his Scots allies for a diversion, and Randolph and the young King raided the Border. At the end of 1341, however, when Edward had crossed to Brittany with an army, the Pope intervened, and negotiated a truce for the next three years, proclaimed at Maestricht on the 18th January, 1342, between Philip and David on the one hand, and Edward and his allies on the other.

The truce lasted for two years of its official three, when it was broken by Philip's treacherous revenge on Clisson. The lull, for Scotland, is more apparent than real. The economic and social effects of a war for existence, the third and most dangerous in a half-century, were made worse by the weakness of a government whose head was a petulant and impulsive boy, careless of his responsibilities as King, and incapable of bridling his jarring nobles : even already an ill-judged appointment had set two of his best leaders, Dalhousie and Liddesdale, at odds with each other, and was to lead to the ghastly murder of both. There was no law. There was little enough of food. The greater cities were either looted or razed, and trade was ruined. Murrain swept through what was left of the country's cattle, and disease through the starved insecurity of her people.[1]

In 1345, war broke out again, between Philip and the Montfort faction in Brittany. Edward promptly intervened, and Scotland was soon, and disastrously, involved. Edward prepared to attack France on three sides. He was held up at first by the death of his wife's brother, William of Holland and Hainault, the passing of these lands to the Imperial House, and the defection of the Emperor, who was involved in the Tyrol Succession Question : it was not till the next year that he could move in force, but then he did so with shattering effect. On the 27th of August, 1346, he won his most famous victory, completely breaking Philip's army at Crécy : he then proceeded to give siege to Calais, the key of Northern France. Philip sent a desperate appeal to his ally for a diversion, and David crossed the Tweed and marched on Durham.

---

[1] It has been reckoned that temporal lands in 1366 had gone down to half their value under Alexander III, and church lands to something like two-thirds.

The move, in fact, was of great service to France : the army of the North of England was held from joining Edward before Calais, for Queen Philippa turned it to meet the invader. (According to Froissart, she rode with it, and addressed it before the action as its commander.) For Scotland, however, there was grave disaster. The twenty-two-year-old David was no general, and none of the more experienced men in his service could curb his weak impetuous obstinacy. He played for another Bannockburn, and got it in reverse, or very nearly, for the ultimate effects were less far-reaching. He did present England with another Crécy, an apparently overwhelming victory. Near Durham, at Neville's Cross, in mid-October, the two forces met. David chose his ground ill, tangled among enclosures, where the English archers had an easy mark. Sir John Graham pled for cavalry to break them, but could not get it, and the Scots centre and right wing were mown down without being able to retaliate. David himself, twice wounded, was taken prisoner : he had fought gallantly enough, for he did not lack personal courage. The Earls of Fife, Menteith, and Wigtown, and the veteran Liddesdale were also taken, while Randolph, Strathearn, and three of the great Officers of State, the Chancellor, Chamberlain, and Marischal, were killed. Robert Stewart, who with the husband of Black Agnes had commanded the left wing, saved what could be saved, rallying his division and bringing at least part of them off in good order—a ' desertion ' which his young uncle never forgave.

David was ridden through London on a tall black charger, and deposited in the Tower. He stayed a prisoner for eleven years, and Robert Stewart was again made Regent, with the title of *Locum Tenens* or Lieutenant.

Thanks to the courage of the burghers of Calais, the results of the defeat were not so serious as might have been expected. Some weeks before the battle, in early September, Edward had closed his siege lines about that city. It held on grimly until well past the middle of the succeeding year, and though it fell at last, its capture had cost Edward's army so heavily that, the King of Scots being now his prisoner, he made truce with both France and Scotland in late September, *ès champs près de Calais.*

Robert Stewart, meanwhile, in addition to his heavy responsibilities as head of the Government, was involved in a domestic trouble also, of serious importance to the dynasty, and consequently to Scotland. The young King was imprisoned, and he was childless. This mattered the less, dynastically speaking, as the popular and energetic Robert was his next heir, and Robert was married and had several children. But just about the time of the King's capture, the validity of his marriage was called in question, while the only other living descendants of Bruce were the King's two sisters, one of whom, the Countess Dowager of Sutherland, was a childless widow, while the other had made a more. or less surreptitious marriage to a squire of no standing, and had only a very young daughter. If anything should happen to Robert Stewart—and in the last few years the mortality among Regents had been high—the only possible male heir was his son, failing whom, any accident to David would certainly mean a worse succession problem than even the famous one of 1290.

The whole matter is sufficiently obscure. We do not know how the marriage, of ten years' standing, came to be challenged. It has been further obscured because Protestant historians of the sixteenth century, such as George Buchanan, whose interest it was to blacken the House of Stewart, gravely misrepresented the facts that are known, and added several inventions of their own, which were uncritically copied by later writers. Distinguishing carefully between fact and inference, and using all due caution in the latter, we may say they are these. At the age of twenty, in 1336, the year of Edward's march to Inverness, and one of the most terrible of the war, Robert had married Elizabeth, daughter of Sir Adam Mure of Rowallan in Ayrshire, one of his own vassals. We may guess that the marriage, as it well might be at such a time, was a rather hurried affair, with less ceremony and less legal paraphernalia than that of a great lord would normally involve, but no one seems to have questioned it. Both Robert and everyone else appear to have considered it perfectly valid ; he was certainly unfaithful to his wife, but it was as his wife that he regarded her. Both he and she, however, were ignorant of certain facts that by canon law would render it invalid unless they had a special dispensation : and ten years later these facts were brought to light, conceivably by interested parties.

The point is this : certain degrees of kinship, as brother and sister, formed a quite insurmountable bar to marriage.   Others, from first cousins to grandchildren of cousins, were also a bar, but one which could be cancelled by authority, pronouncing on the individual case.   This latter provision, wise enough in its original theory, came to be regarded as a mere source of income, and led to some most hampering abuses, for kinship was considered to be established not merely by blood or even by marriage, but by relations furth of marriage, and even by sponsorship.   The effect on the noble class of a very small country was complicated, to put it very mildly.   Now, it appears that Robert and his wife were discovered to be kin in the fourth degree : if the kinship (which does not happen to be traceable) were in the female line, they might quite well have been really ignorant of it.   The other impediment, that Elizabeth was distantly related to Robert's former mistress, Isobel Butler, was even more likely to be overlooked, for each of them might well be ignorant of Isobel's relation to the other.   They applied to the Pope for a retrospective dispensation, legitimising their children.   The dynastic importance was clearly recognised, for both David and Philip of France backed the application.   It was duly granted, in December of 1347 : the legitimation was accepted by the Estates, and John, their eldest son, succeeded in due course to his father : but though conflict at the moment was avoided, it was to come, and seriously, later, and was in fact to be one of the forces that led to the murder of Robert Stewart's grandson, perhaps the ablest of all the Stewart Kings.

The Truce of Calais had suspended hostilities for a while, and in the next year, 1348, both France and England had other things to think of than a war. The appalling visitation called the Black Death, which seems to have been borne by the trade routes from China, swept north over Europe, killing off, it is said, a third of the population, and they as a rule among the young and strong, rousing a wild and widespread hysteria, and dealing to the Church in special a blow from which it took long to recover, for the best of the clergy were by the very nature of their work in the front of danger. It was a strange, mad time, morale disintegrating under the recklessness of panic terror. The plague did not come to Scotland till 1350 : then, sweeping her on the heels of war and famine, it left her bled white. It almost ended the war. The three countries most con-cerned in that were so weakened that the new Pope, Innocent VI, elected in 1352 and a man of some vigour, almost succeeded in making a general peace, and might have done so but for Charles of Navarre.

The awful invasion of the pestilence stilled political and military movements alike, and in spite of the failure of Pope Innocent, it was some time before Scotland was again involved in the war. She employed the time in negotiating for the return of the gentleman whom the English persisted in calling *Monsieur David de Bruis qui*

se dit roy Descoce. Discussion dragged on and on : it
was not till July of 1354 that a treaty was at last signed
at Newcastle. Edward failed to achieve any recognition
of his claim to the superiority, but the Scots agreed to
pay a ransom of 90,000 merks, in nine yearly instalments . . . which amounted to nearly twice as much as
what was left of the Crown revenues.

The treaty, however, was never carried out. Charles
of Navarre was making trouble again for the luckless
John II, who succeeded his father Philip in 1350. In
1355 Edward saw his opportunity for another attempt
on France, and used his bridgehead of Calais (whose
citizens had been evacuated by force and replaced with
English) to base an invasion. John appealed to his
father's ally for a diversion, sending over troops again
under Garancières, and a subsidy of 40,000 *moutons d'or.*
The diversion was carried out, and with much better
fortune than the last. A mixed force under Garancières and Thomas Stewart, Earl of Angus, took Berwick from the sea, by escalade, while William Ramsay
of Dalhousie and the Earl of March made a raid into
England, trailed their coats there, lured an English
force back over the Border to where William Douglas [1]
was lying in wait for them, and defeated them heavily on
Nesbit Muir, taking many prisoners. The successes,
however, were more profitable to France than they were
to Scotland. Edward had to withdraw from France,
leaving his son to ravage the Languedoc, and deal with

[1] Son of the Regent Archibald. He became first Earl of Douglas a
little later. See the Douglas genealogy at the end of this book.

Scotland in a winter campaign, which though it achieved little else, did a great deal of damage. On his way he got rid for good of one King of Scots, though unfortunately for his desires, not the one who mattered. On the 21st January, 1356, Edward Baliol, for a pension of £2,000 a year, was induced to make public and formal resignation of his shadowy royalty. Sir Walter Manny, the famous Flemish knight who is deservedly one of Froissart's chief heroes, recaptured Berwick, and Edward swept through Lothian. The Scots repeated Bruce's strategy of 1322, evacuating population and provisions. Edward's fleet was destroyed by a gale, and he was starved out, but not before he had wrought so much devastation to a countryside beginning to recover that the raid was recalled as ' the Burnt Candlemas.'

It was his last attempt to win Scotland by force. Robert Stewart still held the country north of Forth, and Douglas speedily cleared much of the South, Stewart's young heir, John of Kyle (who was later Earl of Carrick and Robert III) beginning his career under him by reducing Annandale. It was possible to return John's loan of Garancières by sending a Scots force to France, where it was involved in September in the apparently crushing disaster of Poitiers, in which several prominent Scots were taken prisoners : young Douglas was dragged to safety by his own men, but his cousin Archibald, later Third Earl and ' the Grim,' the natural son of ' Good Lord James,' was captured. King John joined King David as prisoner in London,

leaving the Dauphin, an unlikeable but much more intelligent person, to cope with the general mess of
affairs in France, which included, within the next year
and a half, not only the chronic treacheries of Navarre,
but the Jacquerie and the affair of Étienne Marcel.

Edward's main preoccupation now was France, where
he seemed to be approaching complete success. Scotland was still unsubdued in his rear, however, after
fourteen years of endeavour towards its conquest, and
the Scots fleet was sufficiently strong at sea for English
merchants to have to sail in convoys. The raid of the
spring had apparently taught him a lesson : he decided
to give up any further attempt at a conquest by force
of arms, and to work for the future by diplomacy. It is
more than likely that the decision was confirmed by his
observation of David's character and by the fact that the
latter, whose wife had joined him soon after Neville's
Cross, was, at the age of thirty-two, still childless. He
determined, at all events, to let David go, and resume
a kingship he still refused to acknowledge, superseding
the nationalistic Robert Stewart. His price was now
raised to 100,000 merks, but he threw in, besides the
person of David, a ten years' truce and an agreement for
freedom of trade between the countries—a clause whose
advantage just then was clearly with the Scots—adding
the provision that no subject of either country should be
received to the other's allegiance.

The ransom was bitterly heavy for a wrecked country,
but the truce and the trade agreement both were welcome, and Scotland desired to have her King again :

his nominal reign had lasted twenty-eight years now, but his actual rule a little more than five, with his aunt and other counsellors to guide it : for nineteen years he had been out of Scotland. He returned in October 1357. His subjects received him with joy, and set about paying for him. The Estates voted the King, at a low price, the whole output of wool (one of the major exports) and made inquisition into property, with a view to raising the balance of the sum, while David proceeded to encourage their efforts by a flagrant personal extravagance and by cancelling the various gifts and remissions that had been made by his nephew and deputy.

Before very long, the country awoke to the fact of a fresh danger, whose centre was the recovered King himself. David had found his gilded captivity, about a gay and extravagant court, more pleasant than the backbreaking task of lifting a ruined country out of chaos. Moreover, he strongly disliked his heir-presumptive : the invidious contrast between their respective achievements was not endearing, and it is possible that Robert, apart from unwillingness to give up the power he had wielded now for so many years, saw his uncle mismanaging what he himself had laboured to preserve, and expressed himself too frankly. At all events, there was bad feeling between the two, and it gave Edward opportunity.

His policy now was to conciliate Scottish feeling in general, while binding Scotland by a heavy debt, and to work on King David, with the assistance of the Queen

D

his sister, and possibly of David's English mistress, in order now to induce him to consent not to formal submission, for which he no longer could hope, but to an alteration of the succession. His secret diplomacy makes it very plain that the change in his public attitude to Scotland was merely a change of means and not of end.

David went back to England every year—Queen Joan had not returned with him to Scotland, and never did, though she lived for five years longer—and had opportunity to feel the contrast. Scotland was finding infinite difficulty in paying the instalments of the ransom, and had soon lost liking for her recovered King, while England was on a summit of success. Edward had, it is true, failed to accomplish the proposed Treaty of London, which would have given him more than half France and the mouths of all the rivers. The Dauphin refused it, renewed the Scots alliance, and sent 50,000 marcs toward's David's ransom. But the Peace of Brétigny, late in the next year, made Edward master of nearly half the country, put her in debt to him for three million crowns, and forced her to give up the Scots alliance, King John being dispensed by the Pope from all engagements *entre nous nostre royaume et noz subgiez dune part et nostre treschier cousin le roy d'Escosse son royaume et ses subgiez dautre part.*

The breach of engagement, of course, was a stroke for Edward. It not only isolated Scotland, but caused a good deal of feeling there against France. Edward

worked hard to improve Anglo-Scottish relations generally. Scots merchants, students, and pilgrims were now
made ostentatiously welcome in England, while David
was lavishly entertained and made much of . . . still
unrecognised, however, as King of Scots. One cannot
blame David, in the circumstances, for wishing to settle
the war without more fighting : unfortunately, Edward
saw to it that the only way in which that was possible
was one his subjects considered worse than a war.
(There was a certain amount of Scots trade with Ireland.) And David attempted to go behind their backs.

It was some time, however, before he reached that
point. He went to and fro every year between the two
kingdoms, seeing the contrast between his luxurious
English holidays and the dismal hard work of reorganis-
ing Scotland. The country, in fact, was recovering a
little : trade must have been mending, for in a single
month English safe-conducts were issued to sixty-five
merchants. But the terrible floods in recovering
Lothian, the fresh wave of plague in 1361-2, were no
help : and the social conditions are revealed by the fact
that to avenge some slight upon the Queen, David's
English mistress, Katharine Mortimer, was murdered
on the open highway at the orders of Thomas Stewart,
Earl of Angus, and David could do nothing to punish
him. The burden of the ransom, with its corollary of
debased coinage, rising prices, and the perpetual threat
of recurring war, was nightmare. The country was
splitting into parties, the King heading one that wished
to give up the struggle, and unite, on terms at any rate,

with England, while opposite him his nephew, still his
heir, led that for independence and the alliance with
France ; and in between it seems there were moderate
men who were deceived by Edward's change of front,
and worked honestly for peace where there was no
peace.

In 1363, the two factions nearly came to civil war.
The national party had clearly got some wind of the
King's intentions, for the leaders proceeded now to
form a band, whose avowed purpose was to compel the
King either to abdicate or publicly to acknowledge his
nephew's heirship. Robert himself, it would seem, was
not a party, the active leaders being March, Douglas,
and the two eldest of Robert's surviving sons, John of
Kyle, later Robert III, and Robert, later the Regent
Albany, who was now by his recent marriage Earl of
Menteith. David, significantly, looked for support to
the enemies of his own house, the Baliol *émigrés* across
the Border, with young Athol, Percy, and the *exheredati* . . . and a good deal of money seems to have
come in from a source it is not difficult to guess. There
was every prospect of an armed rebellion—Douglas in
fact seized Dirleton, a royal castle—but neither party
dared go to extremes, David for fear of immediate deposition and possible death, the others for the risk of an
English invasion. In May they met at Inchmurdach,
in the palace of the Bishop of St Andrews, and made
peace. Robert renewed his allegiance to King David,
and David formally named him his heir, and gave his
eldest son the earldom of Carrick, closely associated

with the royal house.[1] Having thus, perforce, recognised his heir-presumptive, he proceeded to attempt to
cut him out, by the quite unexceptionable method of
producing in his stead an heir-apparent. The childless
Queen Joan had died the year before, so he married
again; and to the general scandal, chose as his Queen
his mistress Margaret Drummond, Lady Logie, who
was not even of a noble family, though it is incorrect to
call her low-born.

Having dealt this neat réplique to his hated heir, he
and his bride went out of the way of trouble on a pious
(and expensive) pilgrimage to the shrines of Walsing-
ham and Canterbury. The journey included the usual
visit to Edward. Whatever that monarch thought of
his sister's successor, he treated her with much civility.
His opportunity had come at last. David had fairly
quarrelled with his heir, and was in debt to the point
of pawning his jewels. The new Queen Margaret,
whose influence on the King had just received spectacular demonstration, also hated Robert Stewart with
much fervour. Edward now proceeded to recognise
David's kingship, which up to this point he had refused
to do, to remit the unpaid portion of the ransom, and
make all possible concessions to Scots feeling—on
condition that David would cut out his nephew, and
appoint as heir instead his nephew by marriage, that
is, Edward's son.

[1] The great Robert I had inherited it from his mother, and it had
later been held by his brother Edward, by David himself, and after
the latter's accession, by Edward Bruce's son. It is held at present
by the heir to the throne.

David, perhaps urged on by his Queen, consented, and since Edward was eager to bind him as soon as might be, they went into the business in elaborate detail. Both knew that the first suggestion of the arrangement would rouse an immediate and violent storm in Scotland. (When a suitor who finds attempts at rape are useless comes into the market with a wedding-ring, one can hardly be astonished if the lady receives his proposals more coldly than Pamela did.) Apparently, by way of conciliation, they brought out and studied the old Treaty of Birgham, which Edward's grandfather and the Scots Estates had subscribed in 1290, just before the war, as the terms of a peaceful and welcome Union of Crowns by the marriage of the child Queen of Scots to the Prince of Wales. The terms of the secret Treaty of Westminster repeat it so closely it cannot be accident. There was now no question of an incorporating union : the new heir was not to be the Prince of Wales, but his next brother, Lionel, Duke of Clarence, and Scotland was to remain a separate kingdom, *sanz Union ne Annexion*. King Lionel was to be crowned at Scone by Scots prelates. The independence of the Scots Church was confirmed. Scots Parliaments were to be held in Scotland. No Scot was to go out of the kingdom for process of law. The ecclesiastical and civil offices were to be held by Scots, and the grants of Robert I and David II were to stand. There was to be free trade between the two kingdoms, and provision was made for bribes for the various barons. The terms are if anything more favourable to Scotland than those of

Birgham, which was largely the work of accredited
Scottish envoys, and willingly subscribed by the Scots
estates and approved by the Scottish people. But
Lionel was not receiving the Crown Matrimonial as
bridegroom of a Queen of Scots : and blood enough
had been shed in seventy-three years to dissolve the
ink from that hopeful and friendly parchment, fire
enough lit in Scots towns to melt its seals. Edward and
David, however, must have considered that no one
would mind what did not trouble themselves : the treaty
was secretly ratified by both, on the 26th November,
1363, for which purpose, since only a king could validly
sign it, David was recognised at last to be King of
Scots.

David went home at once. It is tempting to consider
what were his thoughts, and his hopes, on that winter
journey. On the 13th of January he met the Estates
at Scone. Without, apparently, admitting that he
had already bound himself, he suggested the transference of the succession, and there was an immediate
conflagration. They would by no means yield, nor
give the smallest assent to the proposals : *nullo modo
voluerunt concedere nec eis aliqualiter assentire.* The
phrase is from the sober official record, but the rhythm
has a suggestion of set teeth. Wynton draws the picture : he was a boy at the time, but probably had his
account from eye-witnesses.

> Til that said al his legis nay,
> Na thai consent walde be na way
> That ony Inglis mannys son
> Into that honour sulde be done . . .

Sen of age and of vertu thar
The lauchful ayris apperande are . . .

' The Kynge was rycht wa and angry ' : but though
the Scots Parliament had in 1290 been very willing for
federal union with England, under no bribes or safe-
guards, or threats either, would they so much as consider the question now.   It marks the achievement of
the two great Edwards, in three-quarters of a century
of hard effort.

The Parliament, probably, expected war, but more
moderate counsels were prevailing on both sides.   England had had enough, and so, with complete certainty,
had Scotland so long as she was left alone.   A fresh truce
was made, which had the effect of removing some in-
flammable material, since many nobles went off to
foreign wars, from Spain (where, fighting for Henry of
Trastamare, they met their old foes, now allies of
Pedro the Cruel) to the crusade of the Teutonic Knights
against the heathen of Lithuania.   The *politiques*,
though. they would not yield to a union with England,
were ready enough to consider a friendly gesture :
Prince Lionel,[1] to make up for his disappointment, was
granted by the Estates considerable lands in Man and
Galloway, while certain of the *exheredati* were restored,
and Edward was promised a contingent of troops for an
Irish expedition.   The general relations of the two
countries had leisure to improve, for the failure of the
English adventure in Spain and the growing reorganisa-

---

[1] The record only mentions Edward's *filius junior*, but the prince so
described is presumably Lionel.

tion of shattered France (where Charles le Sage had succeeded in 1364, and Guesclin was cleaning up the Free Companies) kept England fairly quiet through the later 'sixties.

The easing of pressure had a double effect. On the one hand, there was an opportunity for reconstruction, and a real attempt at it. The Parliaments of the later 'sixties show much reformative legislation, on the process of justice, the amending of the debased coinage, the equalising of taxation, and rather notably, a number of checks on the absolute power of the Crown, that throw a considerable, and unfavourable, light on the King's conduct and that of his entourage.[1] It is clear that the Estates were looking forward with hope, for in 1367 they considered the cases of tenants who had been evicted from the Border districts still in English hands, and arranged for a record to be made of their rights, against the time when they could recover them. Two important features of the later politico-legal system have their origins also at this time, the Committee for Causes, which was to grow into the Court of Session, and the Committee of the Articles, both of them coming into existence almost by chance, as

[1] Actions at law, once begun, could not be stopped. Royal remission of damages for injury was null unless the injured party were satisfied. No Crown officer could execute a warrant under the royal seal unless its tenor were in accord with law. No ' purveying ' or forced provisioning was to be made for the King's Household, beyond the recognised feudal dues of the Crown, and his horses were not to graze on farmers' lands. Most significant of these measures for control, the King was not to gift Crown property without the consent of his Council : i.e., we have the germ of a vote for the appropriation as well as for the granting of supply.

temporary arrangements for the convenience of parliamentary business.

If the suspension of foreign war gave scope for civil reorganisation, it did so also for civil bickering, and the trouble between the factions rose again. The heir-presumptive and the new Queen had never been on friendly terms : someone seems to have tried to effect a reconciliation, for towards the end of the 'sixties—the date is uncertain—his own heir, John of Carrick, married her niece, Annabel Drummond of Stobhall, who had her aunt's beauty and a better reputation. The family alliance failed to make peace, however. The Queen and Robert Stewart quarrelled again : she induced her husband to imprison him, and his two eldest sons, the leaders in the band of 1363, and nearly precipitated a civil war ; for John of the Isles, who was Robert's son-in-law, made a band with Archibald Campbell and John of Lorne, the husband of David's niece, and threatened armed intervention. Before the disturbance could come to a head, however, the Queen appears to have over-reached herself. She had apparently given up hopes of a child who would cut out the hated Robert : now she claimed, falsely, to be pregnant, perhaps with some intention (the claim seems otherwise rather pointless, at least) of a ' Warming-pan plot.' Whether this really was the case or not, in 1369 David undoubtedly quarrelled with his wife, and contrived to obtain from his not too reluctant bishops a declaration that their marriage was null. The lady fled to the Papal court and appealed, but although she succeeded in getting the judgment reversed, she died in Avignon before she could return. Her disgrace had reinstated Robert Stewart, and he was released and reconciled with the King.

Affairs abroad still made for the peace of Scotland. Her old ally had been recovering, and superbly. Charles V, in nine years, had done wonders in the way of reconstruction within his kingdom, and abroad had buttressed himself by marrying his brother, already Duke of Burgundy, to the heiress of Flanders. He had backed the winning candidate in Spain, and had the Castilian fleet at his disposal. England's star was in eclipse. Her failures in Spain and Scotland had been expensive, the Black Prince had lost his personal popularity in Guyenne, and Guesclin, a genius at soldiering and a leader of the quality of Bruce, had worked out a new way of war, perhaps modelled on Bruce's, which it certainly resembled in principle. In 1369 the Gascons, who had received none of their promised pay in the Spanish war, and were now being heavily taxed to pay its costs, appealed to Charles, who summoned the Black Prince to do them justice. Prince Edward promptly defied him, and Charles declared the truce was at an end. King Edward at once invaded France in force, landing at Calais, and found himself completely baffled by Guesclin. Foreseeing another French war, and a long one, he made a hasty attempt to make sure of his rear by renewing the truce with Scotland, offering to lower the instalments of David's ransom to the more manageable sum of 4,000 merks.

The Scots were not too well pleased with their old ally for throwing them over at the Peace of Brétigny, and a truce was made to last for fourteen years.

David lived after that for not much more than a year. On the 22nd of February, 1371, he died in Edinburgh, aged forty-seven, leaving Scotland in ruins, but still independent, still under her own flag, by no doing of his, and the throne passed to his nephew Robert Stewart.

HERE
ENDS
CHAPTER
II

CHAPTER III

ROBERT II : 1371–90

'But Jehoiada waxed old, and was full of days.'
II Chronicles, xxiv. 15.

ROBERT II had barely succeeded to the throne when his kingship was challenged, by the Earl of Douglas, nephew of Good Lord James,[1] who claimed himself to be lawful King of Scots, and threatened to back the claim by force of arms, a foreshadowing of much that was to come. He was checked by the prompt action of Sir Robert Erskine, and conciliated by being created Justiciar and Warden of the East March, and by the marriage of his son and heir James to the new King's fourth daughter Isobel : and King Robert was crowned peaceably at Scone on the 26th of March, 1371, three-quarters of a century, to the day, since the first act of the Three Hundred Years' War, and sixty-five years, less one day, since the crowning of his heroic grandfather. At the coronation, the 1318 Act of Settlement was read, and the continuance of the line was provided for, John, Earl of Carrick, Robert's eldest son, being named High Steward and Prince of Scotland : and the nomination was ratified by the Estates, who did homage to him as well as to King Robert. Queen Euphemia, Robert's second wife, whom he had married during his uncle's imprisonment, was crowned separately, later in

---

[1] See appendix to this chapter (p. 78).

the year : she was a daughter of the Earl of Ross, and widow of Robert's old comrade-in-arms, John Randolph, Earl of Moray.

The new dynasty was in no very enviable position. Of three heavy wars in three-quarters of a century, none of which Scotland had herself initiated, the first had ended in complete disaster, the second, two years later, had begun with it, had ended indeed in political and military triumph, but had continued the process of economic exhaustion, and the third and longest, opening four years later, had again begun with apparentiy final ruin, and had dragged through twenty-four years to success at last, but to a success that was not victory in the sense that the Treaty of Northampton had been victory : and while there had been no serious fighting now for fifteen years, and the late truce had twelve years yet to run, there was no guarantee war might not break out again.   Scotland was Scotland yet, and the enemy, for the time, unlikely to make another attack in force : but Berwick, Roxburgh, much of Annandale, were still in English hands,[1] and half King David's ransom was

---

[1] ' The English government, after Scotland was lost, retained the official staff which Edward I had designed for the administration of the country.   It was huddled together within Berwick as a centre, and was in readiness to expand over such districts of South Scotland as England acquired from time to time—was ready to spread over the whole country when the proper time should come. . . . The active field for this body, however, was contracted by degrees, and at last it was confined to the town and liberties of Berwick, which were thus honoured by the possession of a Lord Chancellor, a Lord Chamberlain, and other high offices, while the district had its own Domesday Book and other records adapted to a society on the model of the Kingdom of England.'

J. HILL BURTON, *History of Scotland.*

still unpaid. The country was stripped stark, drained in people and goods by war and pestilence, and fresh serious famine marked the inauguration of the new reign: corn had to be imported from England and Ireland.

There was a further handicap—disunion. Robert I had, largely by sheer personality, fused Scotland together ; and united Scotland had shown her power to resist very heavy odds. But no subsequent leader had been able to achieve this unity, and the great houses, under David's weak rule, were so many mutually hostile principalities. More serious, just now, than even the internecine feuds of the nobles, was the problem of the Western Isles, and those parts of the Highlands that were attached to them. For generations the Isles had been a virtually independent sovereignty, owing a loose and easy allegiance not to near Scotland but to distant Norway. It was very little more than a hundred years since they had become, officially, part of Scotland, and in the Baliol-Comyn war, Alexander, the son of the Lord of the Isles who had seen the transfer, had allied with England as an independent prince. Alexander's defeat and forfeiture, and the personal friendship of Bruce with his brother and successor Angus Og, had made the relation with Scotland close for a while : Bruce was popular in the West Highlands, and all through his wars they and the Isles contributed some of the finest material for his army, his own chosen followers. But the bond was personal, to the King, not the Crown : to the Island chiefs it was rather an alliance than a submission—an alliance that could be transferred to another quarter. John of the Isles, the son of Bruce's friend, was, it is true, Robert II's son-in-law : but until near the end of the next century, the Isles bore very much the same relation to Scotland as Brittany to mediaeval France, and like it were a continual source of danger.

For a further complication still, the royal house was now on a new footing, It was, to be sure, and had been for over two hundred years, a great and powerful one, with vast lands, and since the new King had thirteen legitimate children, who had all grown up to marriageable age, it was, from one point of view at any rate, secured and buttressed by many alliances. His heir, the Earl of Carrick, as has been said, had married the niece of Queen Margaret, who came, like her royalised aunt, of the smaller gentry. But Walter, the next son, before his early death, had married Isobel, Countess of Fife in her own right. Robert, the ablest of the sons, the future Regent Albany, had married (as her fourth husband) Margaret Graham (see note on page 10), Countess of Menteith in her own right ; and afterwards Muriel Keith, daughter of the Marischal. Alexander was to marry—he had not yet done so—Euphemia, Countess of Ross in her own right, while of the daughters of the King's first marriage, Margaret was married to the Lord of the Isles; Elizabeth to the Constable, Thomas Hay; Jean to John Keith, the heir of the Marischal [1] ; and Marjorie and Isobel, a few months

[1] She afterwards married Sir John Lyon, and became the ancestress of the Earls of Strathmore, and of the present Duchess of York.

after their father's coronation, to John, brother of the
Earl of March (to whom was given the earldom of
Moray, vacant since Randolph's death at Neville's
Cross), and James, heir of Douglas. The four children
of the King's second marriage were still young : of
these, David was to be given the earldom of Strathearn,
which had lapsed, as a male fief, on the death of Malise,
the 8th earl, without a son ;[1] and Walter married the
heiress of Brechin, and later, though not till his
brother's regency, was to receive his father's old earldom of Athol. Katharine later married the first Earl of
Crawford ; and Egidia, ' the very beautiful,' who might,
they said, have been the Queen of France, chose rather
to marry for love, the brave and attractive Sir William
Douglas of Nithsdale, a natural son of Archibald the
Grim. Besides all these, there was a tribe of others by
the left hand ; John, made Sheriff of Bute, and ancestor
of its present marquises, Thomas, Archdeacon of
St Andrews, and another John, ' the Red Stewart ' of
Dundonald, all three full brothers, sons of Lady Moran;
then three more, by Marion Cardney ; and at least two
more, all dependent for their position on that of their
father.

The earldoms of Athol, Carrick, Fife, Menteith,
Ross, and Strathearn were in, or soon to be in, the royal
house : the Earls of March, Moray, Douglas, Crawford,
the Lord of the Isles, the hereditary Constable and Marischal, were all closely linked with it. But the phalanx
of apparent support had—even was—a weakness. The

---

[1] More will be heard later of this succession.

E

House of Stewart was *primus inter pares* : but the emphasis might easily slip from the *primus* and fall rather heavily upon the *pares*. The House of Alpin had been royal, at their end, for very nearly seven hundred years, counting from Fergus the first King of Scots : one member of the house might dispute another's right to the crown, and frequently did, but none denied the right of the house itself. The failure of the old line left the throne to men who were no more than the great-great-great-grandson and the great-great-great-great-grandson respectively of a King of Scots—a diluted royalty. Of these, the first was a puppet, soon rejected : the second had been the Saviour of Scotland, and his Parliament could say, fourteen years from his crowning, ' by reason of his desert as of his rights . . . our common and just consent has made him our King.' The late King was his son, and the new King his grandson : but David had lowered the prestige of the name of Bruce, especially among the nobles who knew him personally : and by the time of Robert's accession those who had known the great King were old men. The traditional prestige was still strong, however, in the other classes, where it endured as a very lively legend. Moreover, Robert was heir by clear descent, son of the eldest daughter of Robert Bruce, and of the brave young Steward, still remembered : he himself had for years at a time been at the head of Scottish government, played a gallant part in the national resistance, and had an unblemished record of patriotism, and an attractive personality. His only serious recorded vice was one

that rarely does anything but endear a man to the masses
—inability to resist a pretty face.

This weakness may have helped, with worthier
causes, to produce a man unequal to ruling the Scotland
of the thirteen-seventies. He was only fifty-five, but
already failing—a noble, dignified figure of a man, in
spite of the ophthalmia that, perhaps as result of his
imprisonment, had marred his good looks and made his
eyes ' as red as scarlet cloth ' : he was upright, intelligent, generous, tender-hearted, and courteous to all
men, but his youthful energy had gone with his beauty.
It is possible that historians, blaming the supineness
of his rule as king, have not allowed enough for what
must have been fairly serious eye-trouble. To lead in
war, to grip a quarrelling council and impress his
authority upon it, a man needs before anything else a
quick and lively perception of what is toward. If he
cannot see faces, and perhaps as well has the dullness of
hearing common in elderly life, and there are no arti-
ficial means of aid, the thing is impossible. To add to
these difficulties, the new Prince of Scotland had not
the parts that would let him aid his father : he was a
gentle, kindly half-invalid, lamed in his early life by
a kicking horse, unfit for war. His next younger
brother was dead : the next was intelligent indeed, and
reasonably able, a scholar but no soldier, with, one
would say, a touch of King Claudius in him ; and the
others a violent brute and two mere boys. The general
problem of ruling Scotland, in fact, hard enough at the
accession of the Stewarts, was greatly made worse by

the personality of the first two kings of the house, though neither was wilfully disloyal to the country's interests, nor, for the matter of that, was either a fool. That last point deepens the tragedy of their failure, for both were wise enough to comprehend the evils they had not strength to stand against.

Robert's primary policy was sound enough : to ensure that his kingdom should have a chance to recover. His foreign policy was aimed at this end—to continue the truce with England, whose run of French disasters was keeping her quiet, and renew the alliance with recovering France. This latter was effected at once on his accession, when Archibald Douglas, the Bishop of Glasgow, and the Dean of Aberdeen were sent to negotiate a treaty of defensive alliance against England, sealed by Charles V at Vincennes in June and Robert at Edinburgh in October. It provides that no subject of either country shall take service with England, that neither shall make a separate peace with England, and that if there is any dispute over succession to the Scottish Crown, the King of France is to support the candidate approved by the Estates—a clause which serves to show that the alliance was not with the dynasty but with the Scots nation. It is known that besides the public treaty, Charles put forward certain private proposals as well, for more active measures against the common enemy : if Robert would induce the Pope to annul the truce with England, he would send over troops, and a subsidy to assist an invasion. There is no sign, however, that Robert agreed.

Indeed, he was working for peace within and without. He sought, as a primary charge, to pay off the arrears of David's ransom : Edward's teeth were drawn, but the old Leopard was still truculent, and refused to acknowledge Robert, in his receipt, as King of Scots. Robert, being very visibly King of Scots, took no notice, though his envoys, as was only their duty, protested, and received very scant politeness. So long as Edward observed the truce, however, which at the moment he was thankful to do, he could use whatever form of words might please him.[1] The King was more concerned to restore order to the extravagance of the royal household, the disordered legal system, the wasted country. For the first years of his reign, in fact, he showed a good deal of his youthful energy, and the Estates apparently did their best to support him.

The question of the succession was giving rise, it would seem, to anxiety. The King was growing old, the Prince was in frail health, and though nearly forty, had as yet no son. In 1373, the Estates considered the position and passed a new Succession Act, assigning the inheritance of the Crown through the King's sons in order unless they in turn had sons. This brought Robert of Menteith, the future Albany, very close to the throne, and he held that close position for five years yet, till the birth of John's son David, the future Duke of Rothesay, cut him out. It is more than possible

---

[1] He evidently thought better of the discourtesy, for by the next year Robert has become *ly tresnoble et puissant prince, Robert nostre chier cousin Descoce.*

that these five years affected his later attitude to his nephews.

Edward III was heavily occupied overseas. In 1372 his fleet was wiped out off La Rochelle. He sent John of Gaunt to Calais next year with 30,000 men, to sweep across France. By the time they reached Auvergne, they had no horses. Not more than 6,000 of them reached Bordeaux, and the very knights had to beg there from door to door. In 1375 he had to make truce, and two years later came grimly to his end, abandoned by all his servants except one priest. The Black Prince his heir had died in the previous year, leaving only a child, whose guardians were his by no means scrupulous uncles. Charles V broke the truce, and sent five armies against Guyenne : in three years nothing was left of the Plantagenet conquests but Bayonne and Bordeaux in the South, and Brest, Cherbourg, and Calais in the North.

Robert, with the enemy thus engaged abroad, was most anxious to keep clear of foreign war. His treaty obligations forbade a peace, but both he and the English strongly desired to avoid hostilities, and though Charles tried again to induce him to move, he would not. Unfortunately, he was unable to control his nobles, who claimed the privilege of private war, not only with each other, but abroad. In the year of King Edward's death, there was serious trouble. Roxburgh was still English. A gentleman of the Earl of March went to its annual fair, and was killed in a riot. March claimed redress, and when it was refused, took up the feud, captured Roxburgh, and sacked it. In spite of the efforts of both governments, unauthorised hostilities broke out on the Border. Percy led what is called the Warden's Raid on Duns : the countrymen surrounded his sleeping camp, and using the tactics of *King Robert's Testament* (' wiles and waking of the night, And muckle noises ') fell on his horse-lines with shouting and blowing of horns, and started a stampede of the terrified beasts. The camp was thrown into confusion, much damage was done, and many of Percy's men-at-arms ' had to walk home with their lances on their shoulders,' while a number of Merse farmers, their wives assisting, were able to refill their stables gratis. Berwick also was retaken, and fell again, and to Border war was added war at sea, Mercer, the son of a rich Scots merchant in France, heading a squadron of Scots, French, and Spanish ships, and doing a great deal of damage to English trade, until he was taken and killed by a rival squadron, fitted out, since the English government would do nothing, by a London merchant of the name of Philpot.

The Governments on both sides tried to quieten matters, which had not been improved by another burst of plague. In 1380 a commission headed by the Prince and Douglas met John of Gaunt, the uncle of young King Richard, and negotiated another truce to last three years, the balance of David's ransom—by this time 25,000 merks, a quarter of it—to be suspended until the end of the time. This truce is merely a sort of ratification of the old one of 1369, running concurrently with the end of that. The next year saw violent domestic disturbance in England, in the Peasants' Revolt. It is significant of the improved relations between the Courts that John of Gaunt fled into Scotland for refuge, was nobly entertained at Holyrood, and sent home in due course with an escort of eight hundred Scots men-at-arms.

Both governments wished to make the truce the basis of a permanent peace, a *pees finale*. Robert wanted it : Richard and his chief councillor Suffolk wanted it : and France was not averse. In 1384, in fact, a general truce was negotiated between France, Spain, and Scotland on the one part, and England and her allies on the other. Before all the High Contracting Parties had signed it, the truce died still-born. The English war-party, headed by the King's uncle, Humphrey of Gloucester, were intriguing against Suffolk, whom they were very soon to send to the block. The Scottish nobles were straining at the leash, the Douglases foremost. Charles had sent over a subsidy of 40,000 *livres tournois, aut fait de la guerre commune,*[1] escorted by a force of some thirty knights, and these latter expected their hosts to show them sport.

They did. Douglas died just as the old truce expired. Immediately his son James (the King's son-in-law) and Archibald the Grim, who was James's cousin, were in arms, with their French guests for company.

---

[1] It was distributed among various nobles, in sums varying from 7,500 to Douglas, 5,500 to Carrick, through 700 to the Cardinal-Bishop of Glasgow, down to 40.

Lochmaben and all Annandale were recovered, Teviot-dale also, save for Jedburgh and the retaken Roxburgh. The French knights seem to have enjoyed themselves, and their account induced the young Charles VI (who had succeeded his father in 1380) to send over a larger force in the next year, in the hope that an invasion by the Scots would synchronise with his projected reprisal-attack on England.

In the spring John of Gaunt headed an English raid from the sea, by the Firth of Forth. He sacked Inch-colm Priory and Queensferry, but mindful of his late kindly treatment at Holyrood, allowed the burgesses of Edinburgh to ransom their persons and apparently their goods, and evacuate the town before he burnt it. His expedition suffered more than it inflicted. It was a mortally cold March, there was little food available, and he had to withdraw in worse case than he came.

Charles VI carried out his intention of sending troops, and the arrangement worked as badly as might be. The first French auxiliaries were a mere handful, easily housed as private guests of the nobles. Now he sent over a force of a couple of thousand, under the Admiral, Jean de Vienne, Comte de Valentinois. They brought fourteen hundred suits of armour, which was useful, but they themselves were of more trouble than service. They were offended, to begin with, because King Robert, who probably disapproved of the arrangement, was in the Highlands (where there was also disturbance) and did not come to receive them. They expected the same entertainment as their predecessors, and the wrecked country simply could not give it : and when they tried to shift for themselves there was trouble : the easy-going Continental methods of paying with the lance-butt did not go down in Scotland. The Scots farmers stood on their rights and the Statute of 1318, and the Estates backed them : Vienne had to pay his bills, and did not like it.[1] Nor was there amusement to counter the inconvenience. The French had expected a sporting raid on England : Clisson, according to Froissart, who was in Scotland that year, had said he would rather fight the English in England than half as many of them in France. Douglas, however, to whom they were attached, was fighting a war and not a tournament : he was perfectly capable of *de biaus faictes darmes*, but for business purposes he preferred to make use of his uncle's tactics, avoid a pitched action, and leave the great English armies to march and starve and founder their heavy horses.

One approached, under Richard himself and John of Gaunt. Vienne eagerly tried to make Douglas fall on them. Douglas proceeded to take him out reconnoitring, showed him from the hill the English army passing in column of march, and requested him to contemplate the military situation. Vienne was soldier enough to take the point, but both he and his knights

---

[1] The regulations for the mixed Franco-Scottish force are extant, and rather interesting. Both nationalities are to wear the St Andrew's Cross on breast and back, but on a black ground. There are complicated arrangements for discipline, and it is notable that the articles include regulations for the protection of enemy non-combatants. A soldier guilty of firing a church, of rape, or of killing a woman or child, might lose his hand.

were annoyed and resentful about it. The auxiliaries, in fact, caused more trouble than they were worth : the mixed force tried, and failed, to take Carlisle, while Richard's force burnt Melrose, Dryburgh, and New-battle Abbeys, and what was left, or rebuilt, of Edinburgh, including St Giles's.

It was full war again. Richard had decided to cut his losses in France, and compromise with his war-party by giving them their heads over Scotland—a sound enough decision in the circumstances. The old King Robert, under this fresh strain of the war he had been striving to prevent, broke up completely in health and perhaps in mind, and abandoned even an attempt at control. The Prince, who shared his father's policy of peace, was little more vigorous, and the government, for all practical purposes, slipped into the hands of Robert of Menteith.

In 1388, he and Douglas, his brother-in-law, planned new invasion. Menteith crossed the Sark and ravaged Cumberland. Douglas took the East March, chased Harry Percy, whom the Scots called Hotspur, into Newcastle, and captured his pennon. Douglas was not in force to besiege the strong town. He came before the walls and displayed the pennon, informing Percy that if he wanted it back he could come and seek it before his pavilion door, and marched north. Hotspur was no man to let a challenge pass. He followed them.

> They lichted high on Otterburn,
> Upon the bent sae broun.
> They lichted high on Otterburn,
> And threw their pallions doun,

and there in the night he fell upon their camp. It was very near disaster for the Scots. Hotspur's forced march brought him up unexpectedly, but he blundered on the horse-lines in the dark, and gave the main camp time to stand to arms for the fight Froissart calls the fiercest of that generation. *Il étoit toute nuit. Si ne véoient que de l'air et de la lune.* Under the August moon Percy sought his pennon, and there was a wild mêlée among the tents. Douglas, half-armoured, went down with three mortal wounds in the front of the fray : his chaplain bestrode him and laid about with a snatched battle-axe. Montgomery, they say, his nephew, came to the rescue before he was quite dead, and Douglas bade him conceal his death and fight on :

'Rayse up again my banner which lyeth on the ground . . . but sirs, show neither to friend nor foe what case ye see me in for if myne enemyes knew it they wolde rejoyes, and our friends be discomfited.'

Montgomery obeyed, and the battle raged till Percy surrendered at last as the dead man's prisoner, and the English were killed or taken or in flight. The battle cost England nearly every gentleman of fighting age in Northumberland and the County Palatine. It was otherwise of small military importance, but it added immensely to the Douglas legend, and the Douglas ὕβρις, and that was to cost both them and the Stewarts dear, and Scotland also.

In the next year King Robert, who was now seventy-three, withdrew from even nominal charge of affairs, and virtually abdicated. IIis heir was, significantly, passed over, and Robert of Menteith, now fifty, appointed as Governor. He, in the same year, had added to both his power and his possessions, for he had induced his widowed sister-in-law, the Countess of Fife, to bequeathe him her earldom, since she had no children. She died now, and he heired it. His first act as Governor was to depose his next brother, Alexander, Earl of Buchan, called not without reason the Wolf of Badenoch, from the Justiciarship of North of Forth—a proceeding for which there was plenty of justification—and give it to Murdoch, his own eldest son. In spite of his former bellicose attitude, he consented to a fresh truce, to which France was party. It was originally for three years, but was carried on by renewals for the next ten.

A few months later, Robert II died, on the 13th of May 1390, at his own castle of Dundonald in Ayrshire, and was buried not at Paisley or Dunfermline, but at Scone. He had served his country well in his strenuous youth, and in age and weakness sought always her best interests. He did not, as King, succeed in ensuring them, but his failure, which deeply saddened his old age, deserves compassion rather than contempt. He was peaceably succeeded by his son John, Prince of Scotland, Earl of Carrick, and High Steward, now a frail elderly man of fifty odd.

APPENDIX TO CHAPTER III

THE precise grounds of Douglas's claim are now very difficult to determine, but so far as is known, they are these. His wife was Countess of Mar in her own right. Her mother, Isobel Stewart (*probably* a daughter of Alexander Stewart of Bonkill) had already before her marriage to Donald 8th Earl of Mar (the Regent killed at Dupplin) been married at least twice, and it is *possible* that there may have been a third previous marriage, to a Baliol, as a Thomas Baliol appears as ' brother ' of her son Thomas, 9th Earl of Mar, and consequently of Thomas's sister and heiress, Douglas's wife. Douglas *may* have considered that his wife was heiress to her half-brother as well as to her brother, and claimed on that ground. The pedigree of this Thomas Baliol is as uncertain as the rest of the business, but he would seem to be descended from Henry Baliol, Chamberlain in 1246. Henry *seems* to have been the father of Alexander Baliol of Cavers, and the grandfather of another Alexander, who *may* have been Isobel Stewart's husband, as he certainly had a son Thomas of Cavers, who sold the estate to Douglas, and who *may* have been the latter's half-brother-in-law. This very conjectural pedigree would run as set forth opposite.

Even if the conjectures are correct, Douglas's claim, or his wife's, would be inferior to that of the descendants of Eleanor Baliol, represented at this time by the co-heiresses of David 12th Earl of Athol. There was a Douglas assertion in the fifteenth century that William, 1st Earl of Douglas, besides his wife's claim, was son of a sister of Red John Comyn, called Devorgilla : but there is no trace of the lady's existence, and the only known wife of the Regent Archibald is Beatrice Lindsay. In any case, the Athol claim would still be superior if any Baliol one were admitted at all.

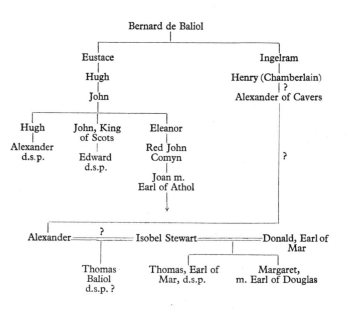

Bernard de Baliol
- Eustace
  - Hugh
    - John
      - Hugh
        - Alexander d.s.p.
      - John, King of Scots
        - Edward d.s.p.
      - Eleanor
        - Red John Comyn
          - Joan m. Earl of Athol
- Ingelram
  - Henry (Chamberlain)
    - ?
    - Alexander of Cavers
      - ?

Alexander ══ ? ══ Isobel Stewart ══════ Donald, Earl of Mar
- Thomas Baliol d.s.p. ?
- Thomas, Earl of Mar, d.s.p.
- Margaret, m. Earl of Douglas

HERE ENDS CHAPTER III

CHAPTER IV

ROBERT III : 1390-99

A Prince for Peace, that had for Mars no Mind,
    Abhorring Warrs and all Intestine Strife.
Noght to be Cross'd with Kingly Cares Inclined,
    Bot loving more a calme and quiet Life :
    A King indeed, and yet in Sho bott sitts,
    For to his Brother he the Care Committs.'
            Alexander Garden, *Theatre of the Scotish Kings.*

THE new King was crowned at Scone on the 14th of
August, the day after his father's funeral, the Queen
next day. His name of John had such ill associations
that he sought to cheat Fortune by taking that of
Robert. The goddess, however, still thought of him as
John : he had no better luck than the other unfortunate
sovereigns of that name. He had the faults of his
father's declining years, and his virtues also, except
for his youthful vigour : before his crippling he had, as
a very young man, done service in the clearing of
Annandale, when he cannot have been more than at
most eighteen : but the kick of a horse had lamed him
in early manhood, and he had never taken much part
in affairs. He was already older than his years—
gentle, courteous, dignified, and kind-hearted, with a
noble presence and a long snowy beard, but with
broken health and a lack of vitality that made him unwilling even to attempt to cope with the arrogant
turbulence of his nobles. Like his father he meant

well, sought to give Scotland peace, to achieve prosperity for the nation at large : the ' people ' knew that, and regarded him with affection. Like his father also, he failed to put his intentions into action, and suffered, even more bitterly, in the knowledge of his failure. He was deeply religious, but his religion of a type that made less for energy or even comfort than for the sense of failure in his responsibilities that breaks out in the famous cry to Queen Annabel, that the only epitaph she need put above him was ' Here lies the worst of kings and the saddest of men.' From the first years of his reign, the power was not his, but still wielded by his younger brother Fife : his own interests and those of his young heir as against Fife were guarded less by himself than by the Queen, an able, resolute woman, who had a hard task enough, for between Fife, greedy of power, and the succession, there was only a boy of twelve, her charming, headstrong, rather spoilt son David. His brother, Robert, had died as a baby, and the last son, James, who was to succeed his father, was not born till the latter had been King four years. There were four daughters besides. Egidia, the youngest, died as a child : the others, Margaret, Mary, and Elizabeth, were all to marry into the House of Douglas.[1]

The first act of the reign was to secure the continuance of the *status quo* by ratifying both the truce with England and the alliance with France. The

[1] Margaret married Archibald ' Tyneman,' 5th Earl of Douglas and 1st Duke of Touraine ; Mary, George, 1st Earl of Angus ; and Elizabeth, Sir James of Dalkeith, grandfather of the 1st Earl of Morton.

F

English truce was formally renewable from year to year, and the war party in England did their best to upset it, by proposing in 1391 that Robert should be required to attend an English parliament, do homage for his kingdom, and pay £2,000 a year for the lands of Edward Baliol. The English envoys, however, appear to have been wise enough to suppress the suggestion, and the truce continued unbroken till Richard's deposition in 1399. Indeed, all through the thirteen-nineties there was a steady improvement in relations with England : the Wardens, on both sides, policed the Border with vigour, and safe-conducts were freely granted to travellers. In 1394, there were even proposals, with the strong approval of King Richard, to turn the truce into a definite peace, and Queen Annabel was suggesting a marriage between the Prince of Scotland and a lady of the English blood-royal. Neither suggestion came to anything, but in the following March Scotland was party to a general truce of twenty-eight years between the Kings of France and England and their allies, the assenting parties also binding themselves to work to repair the scandalous schism in the headship of the Church, which since 1378 had presented the spectacle of two rival Popes, to the detriment of its influence throughout Europe.

There was no lack of unscrupulous individuals on both sides, who troubled the truce for their private interests. In 1396 we find Richard appealing to Charles VI, whose daughter he had just married, and asking him to remonstrate with his ally : Charles

replies somewhat curtly that if the English will state
their complaints in detail and give specific instances,
he will see what he can do. Whether he did intervene
is not known : if so, it was taken in good part. The
Scots government were in a conciliatory frame of mind,
and Robert appointed, the next year, a commission for
the better keeping of peace.[1] This commission led
to a very important one in the next year again, when Fife
and the Prince, with Bishop Wardlaw of St Andrews, met
John of Gaunt, Worcester, and the Bishop of St
Asaph's at Hawdenstank on the 26th October 1398, and
went thoroughly into the question of Border peace.
The spirit of the meeting was most conciliatory on both
sides, and the provisions are both wise and thorough.
Prisoners on both sides were to be released with horse
and harness : those who had been ransomed were to
have the money returned, and captured merchants
were to be set free with their goods. The slate being
thus cleaned, they went on to the prevention of further
disturbance. Apparently they came to the conclusion,
perhaps correct and certainly convenient, that much
of the trouble was caused by renegades who changed
their nationality in order to prey with impunity on
their ex-neighbours : they proposed that in future no
national of either country should be *ressaivit to the faith*

[1] The record is the first extant Scottish state-paper to use English,
except the famous Statutes of 1318 : in both cases, however, there is
still a duplicate in Latin. One observes that French is dropping out
of use as an official language, though Ayala remarks a hundred years
later how common a knowledge of it was in Scotland : Queen
Annabel, however, used it shortly before this in writing to King
Richard, though he spoke English and she was not of Norman family.

of (*i.e.*, nationalised in) the other, while of those already nationalised, Scots in England were to be deported south of Tyne, and English in Scotland north of Forth. The Wardens (normally three for either country) were made responsible as an international body for the fulfilment of duty by their individual members, and must hold regular days for the hearing of complaints, while extradition provisions were made for breakers of the peace, and the payment of blackmail or protection-money was forbidden.

The spirit, no less than the detail, of these provisions, shows a real *rapprochement*. Anglo-French relations were also greatly improved. The unlucky Charles VI had been stricken in 1392 with the first of his intermittent insanity, and the government was mainly in the hands of his uncles : but Philip of Burgundy, the most influential, was friendly to England, and Berry's sphere of influence was the South, while King Richard was wisely determined not to re-open the costly and unjustified French wars. The result of this double change in English policy is that all this decade shows an increasing friendliness between Scotland and England. It was more than political : trade relations were improving, and so were social ones. There was much coming and going between the courts : the age that saw the decay of chivalry had a passion for its externals, above all for tournaments of extravagant splendour, which were often great international sporting events. Wyntoun, who in spite of his cloth, loved a tournament as a Glasgow keelie loves fitba', tells a characteristic tale. (It is possible that he was actually present.) The most famous tilter of England was Lord Wells : he issued a challenge to any knight of Scotland, which was accepted by Lindsay of Glenesk,[1] and they met on London Bridge, before King Richard II and his court. Lances were duly broken, but Glenesk was so firm in the saddle that the mob began to shout that he was tied there, whereat he rode up in front of the royal box, leapt to the ground, armed in heavy plate as he was, and back again to the saddle without touching the stirrup, then set about his antagonist once more. The fight reached the dismounted stage at last : Glenesk got his man down, stuck his dagger into the fastenings of his armour, and using it as a handle lifted Wells bodily from the ground, let him fall with a crash, helped him politely to his feet again, and presented him bowing as a gift to the Queen.

Bower caps the tale with a more flippant one. At another English tournament one Sir Peter Courtenay, a gentleman who clearly thought well of himself, adorned his shield with the device of a falcon, and the motto

> I beer a Falcon, fayrest of flyth. [flight]
> Quhaso pinchez at hir, his deth is dith. [dight]

This, apparently, annoyed a visiting Scot,[2] who turned out next day bearing a magpie, and the rival motto,

> I beer a Pye, pykkand at a pese.
> Quhaso pikkis at hir, I pik at his nese. [nose]

[1] Husband of Princess Katharine, later 1st Earl of Crawford.

[2] Unnamed in Bower. An English chronicler calls him Sir William Da rel. (? Dalziel)

Naturally, they met. At the first course, both lances struck on the helmet. The Scot's flew off, taking the shock of the blow. The same thing happened at the second course, and Courtenay, who had lost a couple of teeth, lost his temper also (that magpie was hardly soothing) and declared it a foul, that the Scot had broken the rules by leaving his helmet purposely unlaced. The latter politely suggested that if Courtenay really thought the terms were unequal, they should run six more courses on precisely equal ones, either paying two hundred pounds if he broke the condition. The irate Courtenay agreed : he could do no less. Whereon the Scot removed his recovered helmet, put back his long hair, and revealed an empty eye-socket to the grinning judges, who told Courtenay (one suspects with enthusiasm) that he would have either to lose his own eye or pay up.

While foreign relations were better than they had been for a century, domestic affairs show a very different picture. Recovery was hampered, all over Scotland, by constant minor civil disturbances, and behind them the threat of a full-dress civil war. In the year of the King's accession his very brother, Alexander Earl of Buchan, the Wolf of Badenoch, began a feud with his neighbour the Bishop of Moray, sacked Elgin, and burnt the beautiful cathedral, while his son Duncan raided Aberdeen and Forfar. He had to do penance, appearing in sackcloth in the Blackfriars Kirk of Perth, before the King, and to pay a fine : but it did not restore Elgin, nor do very much to discourage the like-minded. The famous and mysterious fight between *Clanquhattanis* and *Clankayis*[1] on the North Inch of Perth in 1396, that Scott used effectively in one of his minor novels, appears to have been an attempt to regularise a similar feud in a less exalted quarter, by reducing a private war to a formal trial by combat, thirty a side in *champ clos*, before the King and an interested assembly of spectators, who included a number of French and English knights. Unfortunately, it was seldom possible to regularise proceedings even so far as this, and civil strife was constant, and not only damaging in itself, but a perpetual danger to foreign relations. So early as 1393, indeed, the restless and unstable Earl of March was being driven by his jealousy of Douglas into the tortuous course of intrigue with England that was to make so much trouble later on, while the all but independent principality of the Isles had definitely cut its moorings, and was using the regular tactic of a small state in like case—an alliance with the great power in the rear of the defied suzerain. In the treaties between France, England, and their allies in 1392 and 1394, and in the general truce of 1398, Donald of the Isles, although he was Robert's nephew,

[1] Clan Chattan was a confederacy of small clans whose chief members were the Macintoshes and Macphersons. The present writer, being a peaceable person, puts forward no theory as to which was the head. *Clankayis* would seem to be *Clan Dhai* or Davidson rather than Mackay : the Mackays at least were rather too far north to have a really convenient feud with Clan Chattan. Clan Dhai was a member of the confederation of Clan Chattan, but the members were often at odds with one another.

appears as an independent signatory on the *English* side, between the Duke of Gueldres and the Doge of Genoa.

The growing power of the nobles as against the Crown is seen in a new constitutional phenomenon, a number of bands made between the King and individual nobles, where the vassal promises service and support to the sovereign and his heirs, in return for a salary settled on him and his heirs. The device, as might be expected, proved inadequate : and Robert's attempts to deal with matters by kindness were meeting with no more success at home, where the Court was split into factions, one headed by his brother, the other by the Queen and his young son. He tried to pacify both by a new honour. Edward III of England had adopted for his sons the Continental title of Duke. It appears that the Earl of Fife, at some conference, was snubbed by John of Gaunt, who was Duke of Lancaster. He considered that if Edward could make Dukes by sealing a parchment, Robert could do the same. Certainly Robert, early in 1398, gave him the title of Duke, not of Fife, but of Albany, by which he is best known in history. The choice is an odd one. Albainn (which is still the Gaelic name for Scotland in general) was the old Pict kingdom above the Forth, united by Kenneth MacAlpin to the small western one of Dalriadic Scotia. The King probably saw in it something vaguely royal : the Duke, something a good deal more precise—perhaps a virtually independent principality, like that of David I in his brother's life-time. If he had such a scheme, he did not attempt to pursue it, for he won to larger rule in a few years' time. To please the opposite faction, his nephew Prince David was at the same time created Duke of Rothesay : the town is in the old Stewart patrimony, and was a favourite residence of the two Roberts. The King also offered the new dignity to the Earl of Douglas, father-in-law of Princess Margaret, but Archibald the Grim, when the heralds addressed him as *Sir Duke, Sir Duke*, merely quacked back at them with *Sir Drake, Sir Drake*, so his family had to wait for their strawberry leaves till his son gathered French ones in Touraine.

Albany's intriguings for power came to a climax in the next year, 1399—a climax, for the moment, incomplete. The Estates had been trying to restrain the disorder. Besides provisions for reform of the debased coinage, and a good deal of economic legislation which suggests a considerable, or at least promising, export trade in wool, salt meat, and salmon, the Parliaments of the later thirteen-nineties are much concerned with measures for internal peace. In 1399, perhaps aided by Albany, they determined at last on a very drastic measure—nothing less than the virtual deposition of King Robert. In January of that year, at Perth, they went about it. They did not actually call for an abdication, for the King was personally well enough liked : but they did affirm that the misgovernance of the realm was attributable to the King and his ministers, and declared that

' sen it is welesene and kennit that our lorde the kynge for seknes of his persone may nat trauail to gouerne the Realme na restreygne trespassours and rebellours,'

the government should be placed in the hands of a
Council General. The head, however, was not to be
Albany. He was too late. His nephew, Rothesay,
was twenty, and the heir. He, therefore, was made
Governor. Albany, naturally, was upon the Council,
which included the Bishop of St Andrews, a partisan
of his enemy the Queen, the Bishops of Glasgow and
Aberdeen, the Abbot of Holyrood, the Earls of Douglas,
Ross, Moray, and Crawford, also Douglas of Dalkeith,
the Constable, the Marischal, and certain others, one
of them the Ramornie who later on was to play a
sinister part in bringing the young Governor to his
death. Rothesay had to take the same oath as a king
at coronation, and there are detailed and elaborate provisions to prevent interference on the part of the King.
Robert, thus set aside, made no attempt to recover his
royal power, and the seven years of life that remained
to him were spent in a weary and melancholy retirement
on his family estates in the South-west.

HERE
ENDS
CHAPTER
IV

CHAPTER V

THE REGENCY : ROTHESAY AND THE ALBANIES :
1399–1424

' Le sang qui vous unit aux deux princes mes fils
Vous fait trouver en eux vos plus grands ennemis.'
J. Racine, *La Thébaïde*, I. v.

FOR the next quarter of a century Scots affairs were
dominated, with a curious weak tenacity, by the House
of Albany, though for three years the nominal head was
the young Prince. Rothesay had not the mettle in him
to stand. He was handsome, scholarly, charming, and
accomplished, but dissipated, spoilt, and irresponsible.
He had already his uncle's enmity, and was soon to
earn that of another powerful man. At first, however,
he was backed by the Queen and Archibald the Grim,
and the feud between himself and Albany was prevented from flaring into open discord by the sudden
pressure of events abroad.

Richard of England, for the first nine years of his
personal rule—that is, till 1397—had shown conspicuous wisdom in governing. Then the devil of his
house entered into him : he had already won enemies
by his virtues, and now he proceeded to make more by
his faults. The gentry were angry with his peace
policy, his refusal to sanction the brutal methods of
repression their panic found needful after the Peasant
Rising, and his independence of Parliament, their

organ. The Church resented his tolerance of heresy, the merchant class his illegal exactions. His long-delayed vengeance upon his uncles, for Suffolk's death and their early bullying, made him bitter enemies in his kinsmen also, not least his cousin, Henry Earl of Derby, son of John of Gaunt. No one, by now, had any liking for him, except his personal friends and the common people. The former had no power but from Richard himself : the latter could do nothing without leaders. He had no child, and his heir was a boy of six, Edmund Mortimer Earl of March, great-grandson of Richard's uncle Lionel Duke of Clarence, the next brother of Richard's father the Black Prince.

In 1399 Richard crossed to Ireland, in an attempt to reorganise matters there. Derby, whom he had banished, used his absence to return to England and depose the King, purchasing parliamentary support by his deference, and ecclesiastical by a promise to persecute. He made terms all round with the forces of discontent, walked over the rights of young Mortimer and his sister, and was crowned as the nominee of Parliament. It was a revolution, not only in the machinery of government, but in the very conception of the kingship . . . and the real beginning of nearly a century of civil and foreign war, both alike disastrous. A little later the imprisoned Richard died in Berkeley Castle : there were rumours of both his murder and his escape. Henry attempted to counter them by giving his cousin what was supposed to be a public funeral. The corpse was in fact carried through

London, with the face showing : but Richard's very conspicuous yellow hair was swathed from sight, and the body was not given over for public burial, but interred in private after the procession . . . while men said that Richard's chaplain had disappeared : and he bore a strong facial likeness to the King.

Now, the Scots government had been on increasingly friendly terms with Richard : in spite of dissentient nobles, the two countries had been heading steadily towards a real peace. Scotland was deeply shocked by the usurpation. At the same time she had no desire to renew the war. Neither had Henry. He was a hard-headed realist, so far as his notion of reality went : he wanted power, not his grandfather's or his son's conception of glory. He began by ratifying the current truces with both France and Scotland, and the odds are that he really meant to keep them. A usurper, however—and Mortimer, if not Richard, was still alive—is always in the hands of his supporters. Henry had to burn heretics to please his bishops : he had to make war on Scotland to please his nobles : and unluckily for the well-being of both countries, he soon had both incentive and excuse.

The initial trouble was in Rothesay's lightness. His early betrothal, to Euphemia Lindsay of Crawford, had either fallen through, or the lady had died. At all events, by 1399 he was again betrothed, to Elizabeth, daughter of the Earl of March. Now, whether he had some muddled notion of policy, of linking himself with Douglas against his uncle ; whether Douglas, whose

heir was married to a princess, desired to make his
daughter Queen of Scots; or whether from pure
levity, he jilted her for Douglas's daughter Mary,
whom he married in February of 1400.

The discarded bride took the veil. (She died
Prioress of the Hospital of St Leonards.) March,
furious, fled to England. There was already disturbance on the Border, but both governments had so far
been attempting to treat it as a mere matter for the
Wardens' police-work. Now March stirred up the
Percies, Henry Hotspur of Otterburn and his father
Northumberland. Hotspur had not forgotten Otterburn, and his sobriquet appears to have been deserved.
He and Talbot invaded Scotland. They were driven
back by the new Earl of Douglas, Archibald ' Tyneman ' : Archibald the Grim had died soon after his
daughter's unlucky marriage.

It was too much for the English war-party. Henry
had to yield to their urging, and in the late summer he
led an army to Newcastle. Apparently he gave them
their heads completely, for he issued thence a fantastic
document that is not in the least like his shrewd
ordinary—a summons to King Robert, in the oddest
mixture of truculence, unctuous piety, and a splendid
ignoring of historic fact. *Consideratis Christiani Sanguinis effusione aliisque periculis et dampnis*—' taking
into account the shedding of Christian blood and other
dangers and disasters ' if he does not obey, Robert
is ' required, counselled, and exhorted '—(*requirimus,
monemus, et hortamur*) to do homage for his kingdom

to the King of England. If he does not do so at once, *ad extendendum Brachium nostrae Potentiae Provocaremur*—' we should be Provoked to stretch forth the Arm of our Might ' : but Henry hopes piously that *in Clementia Summi Judicis qui tribuit unicuique quod suum est*—' by the Clemency of the Supreme Judge who gives to each his own,' he will not be compelled to the extension. It is significant of the new conception of dependent kingship (the point was not likely to be wasted on Henry) that a similar summons was despatched to the Scots nobles, who were adjured to compel the king to do homage, and if they could not, to come and do it themselves independently of him.

Robert, most probably, never saw the thing. At any rate, it was Rothesay who replied. Apparently the pious terms made him flippant, for the counter-reply to his, a fortnight later, says that he *asserit quod sicut et nos ita et ipse desiderat Christiani sanguinis effusionem evitare, et . . . cum trecentis aut ducentis seu centum nobilibus se offert nobiscum pugnaturum, quasi nobilium sanguinem Christianum non censeret*—' declares that he desires as much as we do to avoid shedding Christian blood, and offers himself to fight us with three, two, or one hundred gentlemen [presumably a side] . . . as if he did not think nobles' blood *was* Christian ! '

No one took this exchange of suggestions seriously. Henry marched on Edinburgh and burnt it, sparing Holyrood because it had sheltered his father. In spite of his epistolary manners, he behaved with a conspicuous moderation, sparing life whenever he could, saving the clergy, and giving safe-conducts to all who asked for them. The *Liber Pluscardensis* credits his conduct to his respect for Queen Annabel and his own grandmother, Alice Comyn : but though this might have been a factor, it is more than probable he sincerely regretted the spoiling of the good relations, and since, having yielded on the point of the war, he was now in command again, he determined to do as little as he could that might prevent their renewal in the future. Apart from the destruction of Edinburgh (which, to be sure, was a serious blow to Scotland) the invasion effected nothing. Rothesay. held Edinburgh Castle. Albany, with an army, came on to the English flank at Calder Muir. He has been blamed for not attacking, but in fact he showed wisdom in leaving the matter to the weather, which was vile, and to English politics. The English army were starving, and the Welsh were rising under Owen Glendower. Henry turned and took his men home without a battle, and by the end of November arranged a six weeks' truce in order to treat.

The brief renewal of the war had little immediately apparent effect, save on the unlucky burgesses of Edinburgh and the Englishmen who had died of disease or starvation. The next year, undeterred by it, and by another serious epidemic of plague, the Estates were hard at work, reforming land tenures and the law of debt, taking steps to accelerate judicial process, and making special provision for the hearing of complaints by churchmen, widows, orphans, and those under wardship. They took time, incidentally, to deal with the game-laws, and enforce close seasons for both hares and salmon.

These peaceful activities went on to an accompaniment of growing ill-feeling between the rival princes. Rothesay had already lost his supporter Douglas, and the new Earl, though twice his brother-in-law, appears to have sided rather with Albany. (The Duchess, in fact, had a good deal of cause for complaint.) In 1401, Queen Annabel died also, and the Bishop of St Andrews. Rothesay had now to stand on his own feet, and he did not manage it for very long. A certain Ramornie, who was one of the Council, appears to have precipitated matters. He had been a favourite of Albany, but friendly also with the young Prince, and was a type not uncommon in that age—a scholar, a diplomat, and quite without principle. The whole business, for obvious reasons, is obscure. It is said that Ramornie had approached the Prince, and suggested that he should safeguard his position by murdering his uncle. Rothesay was dissolute, but more from lightness than positive wickedness ; he was shocked, and said so, whereon Ramornie played for his own safety by going back to Albany and crediting the proposal of murder to the gentleman who had just declined to accept it.

Ramornie and Albany then made a band, drawing in with them one Lindsay of Rossie, whose sister Rothesay had seduced. Bower says that Albany's

G

youngest brother, Walter of Brechin, the Athol of
James I, was really at the bottom of the affair : and his
subsequent record makes it not unlikely. Rothesay
at once played into his enemies' hands. In the middle
of March 1402, he rode with a few followers to St
Andrews, in order to seize the castle. (The see was
still vacant.) Douglas and Albany, possibly with a
warrant from the King, who would certainly not have
approved his son's general conduct, caught him on the
road and shut him up in Falkland. In a fortnight he
died there, officially of dysentery. There were widespread and detailed rumours of starvation, so strong
that the Estates were forced to investigate. Albany,
however, was now very near the throne, with only a
failing old man and a small boy of seven between him
and kingship : the alternative heir was the wife of his
ally Douglas. Being weary, it would seem, of Rothesay's misconduct, the Estates were loth to risk a civil
war when a foreign one might be renewed at any
moment. They returned a canny verdict of ' Not
Proven '—that Rothesay *ab hac luce divina Providentia
et non aliter migrasse dinoscitur*, ' was decerned to have
departed from this light through the act of divine
Providence, and not otherwise.'

The cautious decision left Albany firm in the saddle.
He slipped again into the Governorship, for Robert,
weakened further by the shock, was less fit than ever.
Indeed, Albany was king now in all but the bare name.
He assumed the style of *Gubernator Dei gratia*, spoke

of his ' subjects,' gave charters in his own name, dated
by the year of his regency, not of the reign, and had his
own Great Seal, whereon he is shown in a canopied
chair of state, with for sole mark to distinguish him
from a king, a coronet and sword for crown and
sceptre.

He had hardly found himself in power again when
there was more disturbance on the Border. This time
the aggression was Scots. In June one Hepburn with
a small force of four hundred made a raid into England,
was chased back by Percy and March with a larger one,
and cut up at Nesbit Muir. They had, or Percy had,
considerable excuse, but technically they should have
complained to the Scots Wardens. Albany was
largely dependent on young Douglas : at any rate he
certainly could not control him, and Douglas and
March were of course at feud with each other, over
the Rothesay marriage. Douglas, with Murdoch
Stewart, younger of Albany, counter-invaded in force,
and near Wooler on the 14th of September suffered a
very serious defeat. Douglas was a fighter, like all his
house—a fighter, according to Shakespeare,

> whose high deeds,
> Whose hot incursions and great name in arms
> Holds from all soldiers chief majority
> And military title capital
> Through all the kingdoms that acknowledge Christ :

but he never was anything of a commander, and though
his personal courage was known over Europe, he bore,
and earned, the acrid by-name of *Tyneman*. He drew
his force up compactly on Homildon Hill. The

position was strong against cavalry attack, but made no provision for the archery that made up a large part of the English troops. Hotspur was no more a general than Douglas himself, and nearly made him a present of his cavalry by an impetuous charge : but the cooler-headed March contrived to restrain him, and bade the archers play on the massed Scots ranks. It was Falkirk over again on a smaller scale. The only chance was a desperate charge at the archers. Sir John Swinton begged to be allowed to lead one, and a squire, Adam Gordon, whose father he had killed, flung forward and asked for knighthood at his hands. Swinton hastily gave him the accolade ; they embraced, and galloped downhill at the head of a body of horse, both dying in the bitter flight of arrows as the English archers fell back, still shooting, on their own cavalry, which counter-charged then the shattered Scottish ranks. The English chronicler says that no knight or squire on the English side of the battle drew sword till then : it was purely an affair of archery. The slaughter was dreadful. Douglas, in plate of proof, went down with five wounds and was taken, with Murdoch of Albany, Moray and Angus also, and many more Scots knights.

The chain of causes in history can be a strange one. Had Rothesay been less light-hearted over engagements, March, who won Homildon, would have been with the Scots : and the repercussions of March's victory almost brought down the new English dynasty. Henry had been faced with a most inconvenient

complication. A man who might be the deposed
Richard II had appeared in Scotland—a poor half-
witted creature found in a castle of Donald of the
Isles, where Donald's sister-in-law, a Bisset of Antrim,
recognised him for Richard, whom she had seen in
Ireland. Whether or not he was Richard (they say he
denied it) the madman was a strong political card. He
was handed over to Albany, who kept him at Stirling
with shadowy royal honours, until he died there in
1419, and was buried in Blackfriars Kirk as the King
of England. It is uncertain yet if he was or not.
Many people, in both countries, thought he was : and
Henry, even in making truce with Scotland, never
requested that he should be handed over, as one might
have expected him to do if he could have been certain
of exposing the claim.

To Henry, therefore, it was no less than a godsend
to have Albany's son and heir in his hands as hostage.
He sent the Percies a peremptory message, ordering
them not to ransom or parole their prisoners. Now,
this was a clear infringement of recognised rights.
The son of the Scots Regent, the sons-in-law of the
King of Scots, were pieces of valuable property :
Henry, whom the Percies had helped to the throne,
had arbitrarily prevented them from realising on it, and
had given them instead, for the victory, a shadow-
earldom on the wrong side of the Border—Douglas's
own, no less ! And young Percy was uncle to that
Mortimer who had a better right to the throne than
Henry. Indignant, they did not take long to make up

their minds that if they could make one king they could make another, and persuaded Douglas to join them as an ally : it is practically certain that Albany was in the affair as well.

Percy formed his plans with some skill. He marched into Scotland with the whole Army of the North, but instead of trying to capture his ghostly earldom, he sat down before a little Border peel called Cocklaws Tower. Cocklaws gravely promised to surrender in six weeks if Albany did not relieve it. Albany set to work to raise an army, and meanwhile Percy and his late prisoner Douglas were marching amicably south together, to get into touch with Glendower, Henry's Welsh enemy. March, Percy's old associate against Scotland, had been involved in the affair as well, but he could not stomach being side by side with Douglas. He went over to Henry, and betrayed the plan. Henry and his son made a forced march to Shrewsbury, and gave battle before Glendower's Welshmen could come up. There was a desperate fight, long undecided. Percy was killed. Douglas struck down the English standard-bearer, and all but killed Henry, who was rescued by March, before he went down with one eye gone and a bad wound in the groin. Henry was left victor, and Albany, who had news of the failure before he could cross the Border, stayed where he was, allowing Douglas's action to remain, officially, unofficial.

There is small doubt that if Shrewsbury had gone otherwise, Albany would have either produced the

' mammet,' or backed the coronation of Mortimer.
Meanwhile, however, he had kept himself clear . . . and
the French, while these rapid affairs were in actual
progress, were negotiating another truce with Henry,
and insisting, as an essential condition of it, that the
Scots must be included if they wished, since they were
*alliez au Roy et à ses predecesseurs de long temps et y
peuvent et doivent estre compris se il leur plest.* Both
Albany and Henry seized the chance. Henry took no
official cognisance of a Scottish part in the Shrewsbury
affair, and Scotland became a party to the truce. The
provisions of the Convention of Hawdenstank were
renewed in July of the new year, 1404. The repercussions were not over, however ; the stone flung into
the political pool had been heavy, and the ripples it
stirred up had not yet ceased to spread.

Both governments had plenty of civil trouble.
Henry had to cope with incessant conspiracies and
fierce unrest among the labouring classes, Albany
with the inveterate turbulence of the nobles. As a
sample, there is the case of his own nephew. In 1404,
this gentleman, Alexander Stewart by courtesy, a
natural son of the Wolf of Badenoch, took a fancy to
se ranger. He considered that a very suitable wife
would be Isobel, Countess of Mar in her own right, the
sister of the second Earl of Douglas : she held not only
the earldom of Mar from her mother, but large lands
as well from her father and her brother. The lady had
one defect : she was married already, to Sir Malcolm
Drummond, the brother of the late Queen. Alexander

refused to let trifles stand in his way. Sir Malcolm
was murdered : his self-appointed successor besieged
the widow, in the most literal sense, in Kildrummie
Castle, forced her to marry him, and whether by con-
straint or his charm of address (he seems to have been
a most personable scoundrel) induced her to make
over the earldom to him in a formal public ceremony
before the Bishop of Ross, duly confirmed by an
immediate charter. Far from being made to suffer
for his conduct, he had a brilliant and successful career.
He did find it advisable, certainly, to go abroad for a
while after his marriage, served with distinction in the
Low Countries and as a privateer (he captured a ship
of Dick Whittington's, by the way) and lived for some
time in Paris, where his handsome face and graceful
courtesy made him popular among all classes. In
1410—his uncle still the Regent—he was recalled, to
serve against Donald of the Isles, whom he defeated
next year at Harlaw : the resulting odour of respecta-
bility allowed him to live in Scotland till 1435, escaping
the downfall of the Albany faction, and dying Warden
of the Marches for James I.

Besides such lawlessness, there was grave scarcity.
Between weather and war, Scots farming had suffered
badly : one observes that many prisoners are ransomed
in grain. Fishing suffered sorely from English privateers, who fell on anything in the Narrow Seas, no ship
that they could tackle being safe, not even those of
their own Genoese allies.

Early in 1405 there came the last backwash of the

Percy *putsch*. Northumberland and his grandson had fled to Scotland, and had been kindly received by the old King. They were given shelter at St Andrews, where they were on friendly terms with the young Prince James and his tutor Bishop Wardlaw, a brilliant scholar, nephew of the late Cardinal-Bishop of Glasgow. Albany decided to cement his imperilled friendship with King Henry by handing them over. Fleming of Cumbernauld, one of the Prince's gentlemen, learned it and warned them, and was murdered by the Douglases for his pains. The old King took fright. There was nothing but the little Prince's life between Albany or Douglas and the throne : he himself was King no longer, but he was still the boy's father. He could not protect him, but no one could contest his right to send his son where he should choose. He determined to send the ten-year-old boy to France, to Charles's court, ostensibly for the good of his education. In the early spring of 1406, accordingly, the boy sailed from North Berwick with the Earl of Orkney. Off Flamborough Head the ship was taken by English privateers : Orkney protested, but vainly. The Prince and his suite went prisoners to London, where Henry, in spite of truce, shut them in the Tower, returning to Robert's protest only the answer that as he spoke French extremely well himself, James might learn it as well at his court as at King Charles's. He did set Orkney free after a while, and most of the suite : but the Prince remained a prisoner for eighteen years. The loss of his Benjamin broke the old King, who was nearly seventy.

On Palm Sunday, the 4th of April, 1406, he died at Rothesay, his death hardly noted.

The death of the old King, the capture of the young one, left Albany still Governor. Except for the little James in his English prison, there was no legitimate male of the royal house but himself and his sons and grandsons, Walter of Brechin, his much younger half-brother, whom he made Earl of Athol in 1409, and the latter's son. Albany was his nephew's next heir, in fact,[1] and the Estates were in no mind to upset the lawful process of succession. In June of 1406 they met at Perth, recognised James as King, and confirmed Albany in his place as Regent, sending the customary embassy to renew the alliance with France.

Henry had, somewhat cynically, confirmed the truce, and Albany, as he had no doubt expected, did not refuse. Until shortly before the latter's death in 1419, Anglo-Scottish relations stayed tolerably quiet, in form at any rate, though often threatening, and with bursts of semi-official liveliness. In 1407, for instance, the people of Teviotdale rose, apparently of their own motion, and recovered Jedburgh, which had been in English hands since 1346, while in the next year the Master of Dunbar took Fast Castle from an English pirate Holden, who had used that almost impregnable position to make himself a serious danger to shipping :

[1] The exclusion of Marjorie Bruce in 1315, in favour of her uncle, would give precedent for a Scottish ' Salic Law,' and for other reasons a queen-regnant was undesired.

and about the same time the Admiral of England attempted to relieve an English famine by landing in the Forth and carrying off so much grain that his grateful country surnamed him " Robin Mendmarket."

Neither government took action—overt, at least. One of Henry's allies, however, grew dangerous. In 1408 that king renewed his league with Donald of the Isles, in a treaty of perpetual peace and friendship *inter nos et quoscumque ligeos et subditos nostros et praefatos Donald et Johannem* (Donald's brother) *et subditos suos* : and in 1411 Donald plunged the country into what might have been a ruinous civil war. We do not know whether Donald was actually aiming at supreme power, or even how far his ally was involved : but he was certainly bidding for mastery of somewhere between a third and a half of Scotland, and with a very respectable legal case.

The affair was, in its inception, a personal feud with the House of Albany over a question of succession. Donald MacDonald had inherited the Lordship of the Isles from his father John, son of Bruce's friend and ally Angus Òg, the great-great-grandson of Somerled : John, from his father, had the Lews, Islay, Jura, Mull, Coll, Tiree, and the smaller isles, with Morven, Lochaber, Duror, and Glencoe on the mainland. The dowry of John's first wife, Amy MacRuarie, was Skye, the Uists, and Barra, Garmoran, Kintyre, and Knapdale : and although he had put her away to marry Margaret, daughter of Robert II, he retained it.

Donald was the son of this second marriage (and therefore, by the way, Albany's nephew) but Amy's son Ranald, ancestor of Clan Ranald, had acquiesced in his becoming heir to the Lordship and its possessions, which included not only the Isles but a good deal of the western littoral. Now, Donald in his turn married, Mary Leslie, sister of that Alexander Earl of Ross who had married Albany's daughter Isobel. Alexander and Isobel had only one child, a daughter Euphemia, to whom the earldom of Ross passed in 1402. Euphemia, inconveniently for Scotland, took the veil, and thus becoming legally dead, was induced to bequeath her enormous estates not to her father's sister, Donald's wife, but to her *mother's* full brother, Albany's second son, whom his father made Earl of Buchan in 1408.[1]

This was a politic stroke for Albany, as it not only provided handsomely for his younger son, but prevented Donald's already enormous power from being increased by the addition of much of the North to

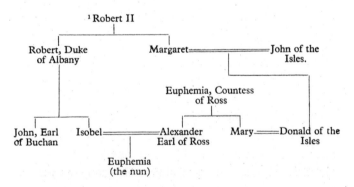

[1] Robert II
Robert, Duke of Albany
Margaret=====================John of the Isles.
Euphemia, Countess of Ross
John, Earl of Buchan Isobel=========Alexander Earl of Ross Mary=====Donald of the Isles
Euphemia (the nun)

the West. Donald, of course, was no less aware
of this :

> He waxit wroth and vowit tein,
> Sweirand he wald surprise the North,
> Subdew the Brugh of Aberdene,
> Mearns, Angus, and all Fife to Forth,

and summoning the men of Ross and of his Lordship,
he marched against the lands of his rival Buchan,
sacking on the way Strathbogie and the Garioch, which
belonged to their left-handed cousin the worthy Mar.
Mar had been recalled from the semi-voluntary exile
which had followed on his enterprising marriage : he
raised in his turn Mar, Angus, the Garioch, and the
Mearns, with the citizens of Aberdeen under their
Provost, Sir Robert Davidson : and on the 24th of
July of 1411, the two forces met ten miles from Aberdeen, in the fight that comes down in fame as the Red
Harlaw. Scots against Scots, it was one of the hottest
in our history, and though Mar's force won, the
victory cost them dear.

> The cronach's cried on Bennachie,
> And doun the Don and a',
> And Hieland and Lawland may mournfu' be
> For the sair field o' Harlaw.

It is commonly described as a fight between Highland
savagery and Lowland civilisation : the Eastern force
undoubtedly had the better armament—

> Yet they hae but their tartan plaids,[1]
> And we are mail-clad men—

[1] An anachronism : tartan comes later. Donald's men would have
been wearing the *leine chroich*, the voluminous ' shirt,' or tunic, of
saffron-dyed linen.

but neither the racial nor the cultural division is very clear-cut. Donald (who apparently was a Cambridge man) was probably no less civilised than his cousin, the bastard son of the Wolf of Badenoch and widower of the unfortunate Lady Mar; and as for racial divisions, Davidson is a Highland name, the North-east, whence Mar's force derived, was then Gaelic-speaking, and the Mackays and Frasers had opposed Donald's march. It would be more accurate to describe the battle as one of the earliest of the great clan fights, between Mac-Donald and Stewart, with the Crown as a directly interested party, for Donald's victory might well have meant a change of dynasty, purchased quite possibly on Baliol terms, and supported in the South by an English invasion.

Albany backed his nephew with unusual vigour : he raised an army, marched to Dingwall, and retook the earldom of Ross. In the next spring Donald, defeated again, surrendered. He gave up his claim to Ross and the English alliance, swore homage to the Crown, and gave hostages for his future good behaviour. He kept the oath till his death in 1423, though his son and grandson were to make trouble yet. For the time, at least, the Isles were quieted down, and Henry, seeing his ally thus defeated, consented in 1412 to a six-years' truce.

The truce should have done something to forward the return of the young King, who at its beginning was in his eighteenth year. In fact, it did not. Albany used the opportunity to treat with Henry, but not on behalf of his nephew : Murdoch Stewart Earl of Fife, his eldest son, had been a prisoner ever since Homildon Hill : he was now at last exchanged for Hotspur's son . . . and James, fretting in his prison, did not forget it.

Notwithstanding the various disturbances, national life was now recovering from the devastation of the past century. In spite of piracy on the seas, war on the Border, and civil strife or the threat of it endemic, trade was clearly mending, and with the increased material prosperity men found a leisure they had not had for long to think of more than existence and subsistence.

Literature, in the last generation, was already reviving. Mediaeval Scots literature is a puzzling problem, far more puzzling than most even of scholars are used to realise, because we have certainly only part of it, and we do not even know how large a part, or how small, or how it ranks, as to quality, with regard to the whole. We are apt to assume that what has survived is necessarily the best and most important. In fact, the poppy is nowhere more blindly scattered : the lovely lyric of Alexander Scott comes down by thin chance in a single manuscript copy . . . and Scott lived late in the sixteenth century, some two generations after the introduction of the press. We know, for instance, of nine poets of the fifteenth century whose works have perished down to the last letter : and some score of others between then and the early sixteenth are represented by one or two pieces that chanced to please Bannatyne or Sir Richard Maitland. It is probable that there is no country in Europe whose past is ploughed under as deeply as our own, nor is all the damage the work of a foreign invader.

The Gaelic literature of the high Middle Ages is less obliterated than that of the Lowland vernacular, and the surviving twelfth and thirteenth century work that is certainly Scots [1] shows an elaborate literary tradition : but the Scots-Gaelic MSS. of the fourteenth and fifteenth centuries are less concerned with creative literature than with theology, history, and the sciences of astrology and medicine. Some of these last are versions of Greek or Arabic originals (Greek probably through Arabic) and may be the work of the famous family of hereditary physicians, the Beatons of Mull and Islay. The philosophical work, incidentally, shows the use of Gaelic to provide technical terms—many now obsolete—for abstruse metaphysical conceptions.

The literature of what was becoming increasingly the Lowland vernacular and, after the accession of the Stewarts, increasingly the court and legal language,[2] presents even more difficult problems. Scotland undoubtedly had taken her share in its thirteenth century revival as a literary language, and in the great inter-

[1] In mediaeval Gaelic it is often difficult to distinguish between Scots and Irish.

[2] The original Stewart country was Gaelic-speaking until about the time of their accession. Up to Robert II all but their progenitor Fléald and the two English-born generations were probably bilingual in French and Gaelic, using French habitually and domestically. There is no sign that Robert II spoke English, though he may have done so : his surviving correspondence is French or Latin. It should be remembered that Richard II was the first King of *England* for over three hundred years who could speak English with any fluency.

national structure of the Arthurian Legend : Thomas Lermont's *Tristram* was known in Germany, and an Englishman of the following generation calls it the greatest of all *gestes*. The war that continued, with but small interruption, for a century after his death was no forcing time for literature, but South-east Scotland certainly shared the movement towards writing English romances on French models, and we know that there were many popular songs, though all but the names of some fifty of them have perished. But so far as Scoto-English work is concerned, the earliest extant remains that are not in modernised or anglicised texts belong to the time of the first Stewart kings, and even then what is extant is but a part : we have only a portion of the work of ' Hucheon ' and Barbour, and the latter's *Brus*, the best known Scots work of the later fourteenth century, survived precariously in one MS. of the late fifteenth and in part of another written a year or two later, while his companion epic of the Stewarts is lost completely. Both men—even if Hucheon did not write *The Pearl*—are writers of far more literary merit than one would gather from historians unaccustomed to reading Northern Middle English : Hucheon's certain work shows a definite and elaborate ' literary ' tradition, and Barbour's is that of a scholar with an excellent gift for forthright narrative.[1] Wyntoun, Prior of Inchcolm,

[1] Barbour died in 1395, under Robert III, and Hucheon probably earlier : if he *is* Sir Hugh of Eglinton, in 1381, under Robert II. I have discussed the remains of this Scoto-English literature more fully in my *Historical Survey of Scottish Literature to 1714*.

H

a generation later—he died, an old man, in Albany's
regency—takes up the tale in the tradition of Barbour,
or still more of the Latin chroniclers : but though he
was a scholar (and a sportsman) he has much less
literary quality.

Of a Scots contribution to the copious Latin
mediaeval literature we know very little. That literature was so completely international and so largely
anonymous that it is difficult to sort out at any time :
and the Scots scholar was decidedly mobile. The
greatest known figure in mediaeval Scoto-Latin is not
a man of letters but a philosopher and scientist, who
recovered Aristotle, by way of the Moors—Michael
Scott of the mid thirteenth century, Dante's lean
magician. The various monastic chronicles, normally
Latin, were of all forms of literature the most likely to
carry on an unbroken tradition through the worst of
the war, though even they would be affected by the
Black Death : but the Reformation turned the monastic
libraries into waste paper, and for practical purposes
Scoto-Latin literature, which is of uncommon brilliance in its kind, begins with Barbour's younger contemporary and probable colleague at Aberdeen, John
of Fordun, who like him wrote history, the *Scotichronicon*. He, like Barbour, was dead by 1400, but
his work was being continued, at first from his own
notes, by Walter Bower, the Prior of Inchcolm.

Of the other arts the fourteenth century must have
been almost barren, save, in the Highlands at any rate,
of music. Painting of course, was still primitive

throughout Europe, although there is superb mediaeval sculpture. Images suffered so badly in the Reformation that it is difficult to say what Scots mediaeval sculpture was like, though it existed : that of the Dark Ages ranks very high in its kind. There had been fine building before the war, but during the greater part of the fourteenth century the battering-ram replaced the hod and trowel. There were attempts at repair in the intervals, for the *Liber Pluscardensis* spares a curse in the by-going for certain *membra diabolica* who in 1336 carried off the magnificent new woodwork that was being erected in the Kirk of Dollar : and as soon as the clearing of the country allowed him, Robert I had built a palace at Cardross. But except for such things as erd-houses, brochs, and earth-works, there is very little Scottish secular building, unless mere fragments among later work, that survives from an earlier date than 1400. The century of ' the Jameses ' saw a wave of fine work, religious and secular : but by Albany's time it was hardly more than beginning, for even the nobles were desperately poor, and the country at large stripped almost to the bone : trade by 1400 had begun to recover, but not yet to its thirteenth-century level.

The education that is the nurse of the arts had, like everything else of any positive value, seen its progress checked by the ruin of the long war. What machinery had been in existence before that, in the monastic schools and the burgh grammar-schools, appears to have struggled through somehow or other, if none the better for the experience : but for a full century after 1290, any further development was impossible. Now, however, it was to come, and importantly. Scotland took her place in the forefront of the great fifteenth century expansion of university teaching. In 1400 there were fifty universities in Europe, of which two-and-twenty were in Italy : [1] by 1500 the number had nearly doubled, and the new ones included no less than three in Scotland.

Universities, in the modern conception of the word, are born of the great twelfth century renaissance : they come into being as it crystallises into the brilliant thirteenth, that organised the gains of its predecessor. To quote from the excellent summary of Professor Tout, in *The Empire and the Papacy*,

> The age that witnessed the culmination of the idea of the ' regnum ' under Barbarossa and Henry VI [1152–97] and the triumph of the ' sacerdotium ' under Innocent III [1198-1216] saw the establishment of the ' studium ' as a new bond of unity and authority. . . . The strong instinct for organisation that about the same period led to the association of . . . the French communes, that united England under the Angevins and South Italy under Frederick II,[2] that set up merchant guilds . . . and gave fresh life to . . . the ecclesiastical societies, brought about the organisation of the masters and scholars into the universities which still remain as the most abiding product of the genius of the Middle Ages.

The greatest of these early schools were those of Paris in theology and philosophy, of Bologna in law : and these, the *Almae Matres* of all Europe, attracted

[1] The rest were eleven in France, seven in Spain, six in the Empire, two in England, one in Portugal, one in Poland.

[2] And Scotland under the later MacAlpin kings.

from the beginning the wandering Scot. So did their earliest daughter institutions. The oldest of these in the British Isles is Oxford : and the oldest of its colleges, founded in 1266, within a few years of its claim to act as a fully constituted university, is the Scots one, Balliol, a relic of the Hundred Years Peace. It is reasonably certain that if the Alexandrine development had been able to continue unchecked, Scotland would have had a national university at least a hundred years before she did. Between continuous war and the Black Death, fourteenth century Scotland was no place for the scholar. He went abroad : before Bruce's War was quite over, in 1326, the Bishop of Moray founded a college in Paris, where there long had been a large Scottish colony : the Scots belonged to the *Natio Alemannica*, and when in 1378 it was divided into three *tribus*, these were *Germania superior, Germania inferior*, and *Scotia*, the latter including the English and Irish students.[1] Fourteenth century Orleans, the great school of law, had three foreign ' nations ' as well as the seven French : and they were Germany, Lorraine, and Scotland. The remoter ones had their Scots colonies also : there was a Scottish ' nation ' at Padua, that lasted into the eighteenth century, and at Vienna, where in the early fifteenth there was a Scots monastery, the Scots students are mentioned about the same time as being included in the Saxon nation.

[1] This division lasted to 1528, when the *tribus* were reduced to *Continentales* and *Insularii*. When John Major took his degree at Ste.-Barbe in 1494, ten of his twenty-nine fellow-graduates were Scotsmen.

The Scot who sought scholarship thus contrived to find it, even with his country trodden down by war : but as the chaos began to stabilise there was an increasing need for some national institution which could not only teach but qualify teachers—which had, that is, the right to confer the *jus ubique docendi* which was the hall-mark of the fully constituted university, and in an age when scholars used an international language, no empty phrase. Very soon after 1400, the pious and scholarly Bishop Wardlaw, tutor to the young Prince, decided the time had come for such a foundation, in his own see-city.   St Andrews was held the senior diocese, and its schools already had a high reputation : according to Rashdall, in the fourteenth century the sons of the nobles were commonly sent there.   It was also by far the wealthiest, and Wardlaw was famous for his open hand : the story goes that when a distracted seneschal suggested that catering would be simplified if his master would tell him who were to be his guests, the Bishop answered cheerfully, " Fife and Angus." It is probable that Albany favoured the scheme : he was, like so many of his house, a scholar.

In 1411, Wardlaw issued a foundation charter, setting up the machinery of a university, and staffing it with twenty-one doctors.   The students were divided into four Scottish nations, Fife, Lothian, Angus, and Albany : the general organisation was based on Orleans, though the first *paedagogy* or hall was founded on the German model of Leipsic : residence was

compulsory except for ' poor students ' or those living
with relations. Other ' masters ' might, and did, open
paedagogies of their own as private ventures : but in
1429 these were suppressed, and teaching outside the
original one forbidden, so that instead of the older
conception of a shifting body of graduates, all of whom
could teach as they pleased, there is from the beginning
at least the germ of a permanent professoriate. In the
February of 1413 the new foundation received from
Benedict XIII the bull conferring authority to admit
those duly qualified to the mastership which gave a
right to teach.[1] The town received it festively and
beflagged, and there was a solemn *Te Deum* in the
Cathedral.

Spiritual affairs were in a less hopeful condition than
intellectual. If Scotland shared vigorously in the
intellectual quickening of the age, she also shared its
moral decadence. The great impulses of the twelfth
and thirteenth centuries were fading, the results of the
religious reformations and the splendid conceptions
of chivalry in decay, the great social organisations had
ossified and crumbled : material values were swamping
the perception of spiritual, and the natural result

---

[1] The master's qualifications were strictly defined, even with a
certain canniness at times : my Aberdeen master's diploma is at
pains to state that in addition to satisfying the examiners after an
approved course of study, I have conducted myself modestly and
with decorum (*modeste et sobrie me gesisse*) *for the space of time required by the Senatus.* Aberdeen official terminology, even in
English, still carries traces of mediaeval custom : the successful
candidate for a doctorate is still told that ' his thesis has been sus-
tained,' a relic of the days when he would have qualified by defending
a *thesis* or proposition in open debate.

was a landslide in ethics. The age of Faith, of chivalry, like all others, had seen plenty of cruelty, treachery, and greed, but it had recognised them to be vices. The fourteenth and even more the fifteenth century took them for granted as normal human conduct : the latter indeed made greed and treachery into qualities so admired one may call them virtues. They were in fact, and quite frankly, an element in the Renaissance conception of *virtù*, which is not quite the same thing, but certainly amounts to a combination of desirable qualities.[1]

Corruptio optimi pessima. Just as man, being only part animal and the rest divine, can therefore be a grosser brute than the beasts, so the organisation that more than any other blended humanity with divinity was that which suffered most from the moral squalor. The Church, lopped by the Black Death, inoculated by the prevalent corruption, and poisoned by wealth diverted from its purpose, was rotten. Since she was now fourteen hundred years old, it was not, of course, the first time it had happened : and since human will can choose good as well as evil, can ally itself with the Eternal Spirit, these times had always stirred men to good resistance. The Middle Ages had seen three great reformations, those associated with Cluny, with

---

[1] The ὕβρις of the age, its arrogant self-assertion and self-suffic-iency, shows clearly in both its building and its costume—the intri-cate gorgeousness of the ' flaming ' Gothic or the English ' per-pendicular,' the costume whose fantastic exuberance is exemplified by the women's towering head-gear : both are far removed from the stately but simple structuralism of the true Middle Ages.

Cîteaux, and with the Friars, in the eleventh, twelfth, and thirteenth centuries. These reformations had each gone hand in hand with an intellectual quickening as well, but now there were signs of that very deadly thing, a divorce of the spirit and the mind its servant, with the inevitable consequence (though the thing in fact runs in a vicious circle) of the sinking of both in the interests of the flesh. One ugly, significant phenomenon, the cause alike and result of much corruption, was the scandalous schism in the Papacy, which was one of the strongest predisposing causes of the greater and more comminuted schism produced by the later attempts at reformation.

The exile of the Popes from Rome, the mother-city of the West, to a virtual imprisonment in Avignon, between 1309 and 1377, had lowered the prestige of the Church's central authority. The Great Schism, which sprang from it in 1378, with one Pope still in Avignon and one in Rome, was a further blow to the credit of the Church, and divided Western Christendom as well, France, Spain, and Scotland holding for Avignon, and the Empire and the other countries for Rome. The existence of anti-Popes was not a new thing : there were several such cases in the tenth, eleventh, and even twelfth centuries : but this was by far the most serious of such divisions. Apart from the harm to the Church's moral prestige produced by the unedifying quarrel, the whole organisation that was her visible and outward body was weakened by doubt as to which of the rival heads should count as the lawful successor of St Peter :

and just at a time involving the maximum danger the
financial urgencies of their opposition induced both
to be tolerant of gross abuses, and caused that vending
of indulgences that was one of the major scandals of
the day : and just as Christendom split into nations
whose unity in a spiritual whole was at once precarious
and immensely precious, the influence of the one unit-
ing force that stood above temporal princes was fatally
weakened.

   The Schism, of course, affected the Scottish Church.
At first she stood somewhat aloof from its debate.   It
happened in the reign of Robert II, and no doubt the
general effects were felt then : but it was not till his
son's Regency that Scotland took an active part in the
matter.   The great University of Paris had from the
beginning been eager to heal the breach : in fact, she
addressed her own Pope, Clement VII, with such
vigour that he proceeded to die of shock.   By 1407 she
had induced the rivals to undertake a meeting : but
although they set out, they refused the actual en-
counter.   Paris then tried a third expedient.   There
was one earthly thing above the Pope, the Church of
which he was head, but only head.   A General Council
of the whole Church, therefore, would have authority
to deal with him.   One was called, at Pisa.   It met
in 1409, declared both Popes deposed, and elected
another . . . thus succeeding merely in turning two
into three, the Empire, France, and England adopting
the new one, Scotland and Spain still faithful to
Avignon, and Italy to Rome.   And unluckily the new

Conciliar Pope had not the vigour to act effectually. In 1414 the Emperor Sigismund convened a greater General Council at Constance, to discuss both *causa unionis* and *causa reformationis*. Neither Scotland nor Spain would recognise it at first, for its heads were the Emperor and the Conciliar Pope, and in 1416 the Abbot of Pontigny was sent as its envoy to the Scottish Church, to induce it to abandon Benedict XIII. Benedict sent a counter-ambassador, and the Emperor added one to Albany, requesting him to persuade the Scottish bishops at least to send a representative. There was a storm in the Annual Provincial Council, the parliament of the Church : Bower, who no doubt was present, clearly enjoyed it. Albany wanted the Council to stand by Benedict. A learned English Franciscan stated his case, *contra quem tota Universitas Sancti Andreae* (rather ungratefully) *insurgebat*. Fogo[1] dealt with him *per naturas, figuras, scripturas, puncturas, et alia exempla*, and the Rector of the University and other distinguished theologians tore his conclusions to pieces, finding in them *conclusiones scandalosas et seditiosas de haeresi multum suspectas, schismatis nutritivas et unionis Sancti Matris Ecclesiae non inductivas*. The poor man went down before the withering blast, and in spite of Albany, the Scots Church decided to support the Conciliar movement for reform, and adhere to the Conciliar Pope, Martin V.

[1] Later Abbot of Melrose. Grub suggests that he was probably the Scottish abbot who at the later and more effective Council of Basel (1431) was one of the three persons chosen to nominate the electoral college who were to appoint a new Pope.

Causa unionis was a good deal advanced. But in Scotland as elsewhere, *causa reformationis*, the other branch of the Council's activities, was a wider matter, and far more intricate. There were, as there always have been in such times, men earnest to reform the Church from within : Bishop Wardlaw himself was working to that end, and his university part of the reform. There were also, again as always since the Apostles' day, men whose remedy for any given abuse was to destroy not only abuse but use, or who *chose* from the Creed or the practices of the Church certain parts which they emphasised to the point of distortion : the word *heresy* means a choice, a picking out. All men of course, in practice, lay more stress on some parts of a large intellectual whole than on others : it is a question of temperament. Often, however, as is always the case in many other things besides religion —in science, art, and politics, for example—such choosers were good men, but of narrow vision : at times they were men of twisted intelligence and possibly morals : and the results might be lop-sided or worse. They were sometimes, indeed, sufficiently lunatic, or led to an antinomian metaphysic that had extremely ugly moral issues. In fact, the teaching of the good narrow man might turn in his followers' hands into something not merely narrow but fantastic.

In the fourteenth century an Englishman named John Wykliffe had given rise to some examples of this, that were to affect our own country later on. He was a man of high character, great courage, and strong but very narrow intelligence. He is best known in popular tradition as a translator of the Holy Scriptures, to which, like most mediaeval theologians, he was deeply devoted : a new version was in fact part of his work, though hardly the novelty that tradition makes it : most of the Bible—all the New Testament—was already accessible in English.[1] Besides this work, he attacked, and very justly, the growing corruption of the Church, at first much on the principles of St Francis, preaching the doctrine of Holy Poverty : he founded, in fact, a sort of informal missionary order of Poor Priests, who went abroad as the first Friars had done, and whose devotion and self-sacrifice had the same reward of popular affection. His teaching, devout as it was, had one dangerous weakness : it was largely negative—sound enough negatives, as a general rule, but not always distinguishing abuse from use : and Wykliffe was at once no metaphysician and extremely certain of his metaphysics : if he could not imagine how a thing might happen, it could not happen, and that was simply that. Thus his followers' devotion to the Scriptures, in itself most excellent, produced some results that were rather disconcerting. When a quite untrained man with no philosophical background, no knowledge of the tradition which has both formed

[1] How well the mediaeval man knew his Bible is visible all through mediaeval art—not only literature, though that is full of biblical allusion, but such ' bibles of the unlettered ' as the sculptures of Chartres or the glass of Fairford. An audience of the thirteenth century could have grasped a biblical allusion, in fact, much more surely than that of the present B.B.C.

and guarded the canon of scripture, approaches, in a mood of uncritical fervour, the intricate metaphysics of St Paul or the domesticities of the Patriarchs, the result may be Muckle John Gibb as well as St Francis. And idolatry of the Scriptures, detached from their setting, at times leads simple minds to the conviction that anything not mentioned in them, such as surplices or chloroform, is wrong, while anything revealed as practised in them, as for instance polygamy, is virtuous.[1]

The regrettable result of this type of error was to cause the Church to fall into Wykliffe's own, and treat abuse and use as the same thing, an attitude made easier, of course, by the mediaeval insistence upon *training* : no age has had less regard for the amateur. The result was an unhappy opposition, in which the best and worst of both sides were involved. That most of Wykliffe's followers meant well is certain. That any attack upon authority, at a time when both the lay and the clerical were very largely corrupt and tyrannous, would be popular at once, was no less certain. Lollardy, as the movement came to be called, soon became as much political as religious, and linked with the peasant revolts against oppression that occur throughout the fourteenth century in nearly all the North except in Scotland : and along with its war against very real abuses there entered some other and more dubious factors. The doctrine of Holy Poverty, for

---

[1] Even the very learned John Milton used Scripture to prove (in the posthumous *De Doctrina Christiana*) that polygamy is incumbent upon believers.

instance, appears not only as applicable to individuals called to renounce the world, but as a denial of all *meum* . . . *et tuum* : and what is nowadays oddly called Free Love, a principle with a quite remarkable habit of invading the creeds of unbalanced enthusiasts, made its appearance also. And the natural reaction of the Church, for good reasons and bad, was profound disapprobation. Bad churchmen disliked being told how bad they were. Good ones viewed with a very well-based apprehension not only the craziness of the wilder spirits but the danger of those who in the vernacular phrase were trying to empty the baby out with the bath. The good men threw doubled fervour into their teaching : it is very probable that Lollardy assisted the founding of more than one university. And the age's scale of values being what it was, not only the bad but some of the best of the good adopted that fatal method of fighting ideas, repression by force . . . and nothing fertilises a creed like bloodshed.

Lollardy spread from England rapidly—at first, apparently, into Bohemia, through the followers of Richard II's Queen. It came to Scotland about 1400, and attracted converts. The authorities decided on an example, and an English missionary called John Resby was burnt at Perth in 1407. The movement does not seem to have been popular, or else the Church was very tolerant, for only one other martyr is recorded, and he not a Scotsman either but a Bohemian physician, burnt at St Andrews in 1433. But there certainly was a Lollard movement in Scotland, mainly, it would seem, among the poorer folk of the South-west : and towards the end of the century, under James IV, thirty Lollards from Kyle were tried, admonished, and dismissed unpunished by the King himself ; while in view of the developments of the next century, its beginnings in Scotland cannot be overlooked in even so brief a sketch of mental background, the more as the new English religious movements, from Lollardy on, were to reverse the traditional foreign policy, and lead to the breaking of the Auld Alliance.

Just at the time when they began, however, that alliance was reaching almost its closest point, and with immensely important results for Europe. The year 1413 witnessed an event that had repercussions upon several kingdoms—the death of the usurping King of England. He left his country distracted with discontent, yet powerful and wealthy, in much the mediaeval equivalent of the Hungry Forties of Victoria. His son had the makings of a brilliant soldier, no scruples, and an appetite for glory, and knew that a popular, profitable war was the best safeguard against following his cousin Richard. Nor was the opportunity to seek. England had never forgiven France for defeating her in the previous century : it was one of the charges brought against Richard II that he abandoned a lost and expensive fight. Now, France was in a different condition from her state in the time of Charles V and Guesclin. The King was mad, the

Queen, his keeper, bad, the Princes locked in an internecine quarrel. In 1407 Orleans, the King's brother,
had been murdered by his cousin Burgundy. Before
long all France was involved in a civil war between the
faction of the murdered Duke, headed by Armagnac,
his heir's father-in-law, and that of Burgundy. At
Henry's accession the war was at its worst. He saw
his chance and took it brilliantly.

He proceeded to lay claim to the French crown : he
had even less right, of course, than Edward III, but
it gave a convenient basis for recruiting. In August
of 1415 he landed at Harfleur. The town held out for
a month, but he took it, and marched on Calais. On
the wet narrow plain of Agincourt a larger French
army confronted him. Individually brave, they were
ill led, or rather not led at all. Their enthusiastic
cavalry masked their archers, and went on, no less
fatally, to choke itself. Henry's force was small, but
with excellent discipline, and he thoroughly understood
the use of his most admirable archers. The result was
a French defeat, with ghastly slaughter, increased by
Henry's subsequent massacre of the less valuable
prisoners. Seven princes were killed, and the Constable of France ; and Orleans, the nephew of King
Charles, was taken. As in all the battles from Falkirk
onwards where their archers could not be reached by
horse or guns, the English casualties were very slight :
but the military result, for the moment, was not great,
as Henry had lost nearly half his effectives at Harfleur,
and had to go home to England for fresh men.

I

Henry's aggression, and its comparative failure, caused, naturally, some apprehension in Scotland. The truce, to be sure, was due to last till 1418 : but Henry's claim on the French crown had shown how easily he might find excuse to break it . . . and King James, now twenty, was his prisoner. A few months after Henry's return to England, the Estates proceeded to a significant gesture : they ordered that the Treaty of Northampton, by which Henry's great-grandfather had under oath abandoned his claim to suzerainty over Scotland, should be transcribed and published in the chief towns. There was an attempt to get into touch with the King. Albany made some half-hearted negotiations for his *temporary* release, to visit Scotland, offering a bail of 10,000 merks, but the arrangement was never carried out.

Henry's next blow, however, was south again : but the war was spreading, and Scotland was soon involved. The ruinous French civil war continued. The Duke of Burgundy, in its earlier stages, had accepted English help, and now pledged himself to neutrality as between France and England, and induced the Duke of Brittany and the King's cousin Anjou to do the same. The opposite faction had already some close personal links with Scotland, that reinforced the traditional national friendship : the murdered Orleans had had Scots troops in his service, under Robert II's son-in-law, the Earl of Crawford,[1] and it is he who

[1] Crawford served with the Franco-Castilian fleet at Coruña. There is a glimpse of him giving an anchor and boat to the Norman Bethencourt, then about to sail on the voyage that discovered the Canaries.

made the famous retort to an English gibe at the little Scottish armies. His son, the prisoner of Agincourt, the poet, inherited the liking, and had a Scots personal guard : now, his father dead, he was the senior Prince of the Blood save King Charles's young son ; and he appealed for help to Albany, suggesting the latter should use the supposed King Richard, the poor 'mammet,' as figure-head for an attack on England, that should relieve the English pressure on France.

Albany did not act on the suggestion, but the last century had made very plain that an English conquest of either France or Scotland would have dangerous repercussions upon the other . . . and England already had all but conquered both, and allowed them the experience of her rule. In 1417 he broke the truce with a half-hearted attempt at a diversion, by an ill-managed attack on Roxburgh, driven back by Bedford, Henry's fighting brother, with so little resistance it was called the Foul Raid. The feeble threat of course irritated Henry, and by way of discouragement from further action, an English army swept over the South-east, wrecking Hawick, Selkirk, Jedburgh, Lauder, and Dunbar. Meanwhile, the French war went on, in Henry's favour. He himself, in 1417, returned, and took Calais, while Paris rose against the Armagnacs, who were the national party and stood for Charles : its new ruler, Burgundy, was the friend of England. In 1419, Henry carried out a masterly campaign in Normandy, which still is one of the classic feats of war, and took Rouen after a seven-months' siege, when

12,000 non-combatants, extruded from the town as
useless mouths, starved to death between the walls
and the English lines.   Vendôme, in the beginning of
the year, had come to Scotland and begged the Estates
for help, and popular pressure forced Albany to act.
He sent over seven thousand men under his son John
Stewart Earl of Buchan, and though Henry despatched
a fleet to cut them off, they got over and landed in
safety at La Rochelle.

They found France at one of the blackest moments
in her history.   Henry held all the North.   The rest
was in a chaos of armed disunion, the government
in the hands of the traitor Burgundy and the evil
Queen Ysabeau.   The Scots seemed to have come too
late to be of service, and they were, as result, extremely
unpopular.   They were broken up and sent to reinforce
the garrisons still holding out in the West : and
Buchan, having studied the situation, went home again
to raise a further force.   Burgundy tried to negotiate
a peace, but Henry would not consent on lower terms
than marriage to a Daughter of France with the whole
North and West for her dowry—Normandy, Brittany,
Maine, Anjou, Touraine, and Guyenne, about half the
kingdom and more than two-thirds of the seaboard.
Even Burgundy hesitated at that.   He swung towards
the Armagnacs, then quarrelled with them, and was
murdered on the bridge of Montereau in the September
of Henry's victorious year.   There was a landslide then
in the French fortunes.   At Troyes on the 21st of
the following May, Henry, Queen Ysabeau, and the new

Duke of Burgundy made a *magna et finalis pax* that gave the first even more than he had claimed in the previous year. He married Madame Catherine, he was ceded half France, and was made Regent of all for the King's lifetime, and his heir after that, the Dauphin being formally disinherited. France was where Scotland had been in 1305.

Henry's grip, however, was not so firm as it looked. He did not know of a ten-year-old girl in Lorraine who wept for King Charles as she sat and span by her mother : but the grim endurance of Rouen should have taught him something, and there were many lesser instances, like that young widow Madame de la Roche-Guyon, who rather than swear allegiance to the invader took her children in her hand and walked out of her château to beg on the roads. And in Scotland Buchan was stirring up his half-brother. Their father had died a few days before Burgundy's murder, and been quietly succeeded, without any formal election, by his eldest son Murdoch, a feeble and colourless man of fifty-seven, ' sair hadden doun ' by his three turbulent sons. Buchan got his men, though it took him a long time : it is very likely that the Peace of Troyes may have seemed at first sight to be the end of the war, and he waited to see if resistance would continue.

It did, in the West, with a sort of sulky and hopeless stubbornness, centring on the ungainly person of the Dauphin, not a man who could inspire a forlorn hope. In the first days of 1421, Buchan arrived again at La Rochelle, with another five thousand. No one received

him well except Charles himself : again he seemed to
have come too late to be useful.   Charles, however,
had faith in ' his Scots ' : he let Buchan gather the
troops of the previous force into one corps with the
new and march them inland, and the movement marks
the first turn of the tide of war.   Up to this point,
Henry had been consistently victorious, had become a
legend, a demon.   It seemed impossible to stand
against him.   Buchan dealt the first blow to that
paralysing prestige.

Since the nominal pacification of the summer, King
Henry had, in the military phrase, been ' mopping up '
the towns that still held for the Dauphin.   He knew of
Buchan's preparations in Scotland, and he sent for his
prisoner the young King of Scots—no longer *nostre
adversaire d'Escosse*, but, for a reason, *carissimus con-
sanguineus Rex Jacobus Scotiae*.   It was out of James's
power to refuse, of course, so he went with a good
grace : he was on friendly terms with his captor's
sons.   Half as a prisoner, half as a guest, he saw Henry
ride into Paris in December, a few weeks before
Buchan's landing at La Rochelle.   As soon as Henry
heard of that event, he commanded his prisoner to
order Buchan's return.   James replied politely that
since he was a prisoner, it did not become him to act
as King of Scots.   The orders were issued, none the
less, in his name : but his shrewd cousin declared that
he was not bound to obey a King who was not his own
master, and with Wigtown [1] and La Hire for his

---

[1] His brother-in-law and heir of the Earl of Douglas.

lieutenants he marched on Henry's brother Clarence in Anjou.

Clarence was giving siege to the town of Baugé. It was Holy Week, late March of 1421, so Buchan from Le Lude sent him a message, proposing an armistice till Easter Monday. Clarence agreed . . . and then on Easter Eve marched on Buchan, camped in the woods beyond Baugé Bridge. By one good chance, the rapid march of his surprise attack sent his cavalry on without waiting for the archers : by another, three Scots gentlemen, Robert Stewart of Ralston, John Smale, and Hugh Kennedy, were near the bridge with a few of their followers, and they saw lances moving among the trees. They sent back a warning at once to the main camp, then rode to the narrow bridge and held it dourly till Buchan could get his men under arms and reach them. Their small party was overwhelmed, but they had made time. Clarence, leading his men triumphantly across, was met by so fierce a charge of the angry Scots that his cavalry, lacking archers, was shattered to pieces, and driven in flight as far as the town of Le Mans. Clarence was killed in the action, by Buchan himself : the Earls of Kent and Ross and Lord Gray fell also, and many gentlemen were made prisoners.

It was the first success on the French side, and the moral effect of it was considerable. The Dauphin's despairing followers took heart, and he was delighted : he gave a dinner at Tours to the Scots officers and their prisoners, and challenged anyone about the court to

call 'his Scots' useless winebags any more. The
Sword of France—the badge of the Constable—was
given to Buchan, and his distant kinsman John Stewart
of Darnley was made Seigneur of Concressault and
Aubigny.[1] (He was later given the County of Evreux,
and other Scots the seigneuries of Oizon, Langeais,
and Châtillon.) Buchan went home again, and raised
fresh men, and induced his father-in-law the Earl of
Douglas to join him with four thousand followers : and
Douglas was given the great duchy of Touraine.

The English, of course, saw the Scots intervention
from another angle. Henry's estimate of its probable
effect appears in his order forbidding quarter to
Scottish prisoners. He himself hanged twenty Scots
knights at Melun, and at Meaux and other sieges the
Scots were expressly excluded from the terms of
capitulation. (Even after his death, when young
Somerset at St-Aignan took three hundred Scots, he
put them all to death.) Henry died soon after this
first blow at his conquests, on the 14th of August in
the same year : by curious chance the illness that
carried him off was that which was called *le mal de St
Fiacre* : he had looted a shrine of the saint a little
before . . . and St Fiacre had been a Scottish prince.
They say that when his physicians named his disease,
he cried out savagely, 'Wherever I go, I find these
Scots in my beard, alive or dead.'

---

[1] He founded a famous fighting house, which remained in France
but kept in touch with Scotland. Bernard Stuart d'Aubigny, the
great captain of the Franco-Italian wars, was his grandson.

Charles VI survived him by only a couple of months, and Henry's conquests fell to a baby son, whose uncles were Regents, Gloucester in England, the fighting Bedford in France. The Dauphin, now Charles VII, carried on the war, and began it ill, with a couple of defeats, in both of which the Scots were involved, and lost heavily. Towards the end of July 1423 a mixed force under John Stewart was cut up at Crevant by an Anglo-Burgundian one, and in August of the next year there was a more serious defeat at Verneuil. Bedford, Gloucester, and Salisbury were besieging Ivry, and Narbonne moved to relieve it with a force of French, Lombards, Genoese, and the Scots under Buchan and Douglas. Buchan's promotion to the Constableship had roused some jealousy : their command was at odds, and they failed in co-operation. (French and Italian have never mixed well, in fact.) The Scots, in front, drove in the English van : the Italians, in reserve, thought the day was won, and swung round the English rear to loot the baggage. Bedford, an excellent soldier, saw a gap between Scots and French, and thrust into it, using his archers too to good effect : it is the last great victory of the long-bow. The French and Scots troops both lost heavily, Buchan and Douglas falling in the field. The defeat was a blow to the rising hopes of France, but the breathing-space given by the Scots intervention had staved off surrender for just long enough. The war went on, and hung yet for four years in the balance : then a peasant-girl appeared before Charles at Chinon, and the tide ran

steadily to final success. Many Scots took a share in
the victories under St Joan, led by Hugh Kennedy who
had held Baugé Bridge : indeed, it was a Scot who
painted her banner. They fought under that flag at
Orleans (where a Scots bishop received her as she rode
in), at Jargeau, Patay, her last victory of Lagny, and till
her capture outside Compiégne. Buchan's shattered
command from Verneuil, having lost their leader, were
incorporated in the famous *Garde écossaise* :[1] a contemporary tapestry shows them leading the army on
the march to Reims for Charles's coronation.

Before St Joan had made her appearance, however,
King James had succeeded at last in gaining his freedom. He was, in spite of the war, on terms of personal
friendship with the English princes, who may have
been more mindful than their elder brother that their
father, on his death-bed, had bidden them release James
without ransom. Scotland wanted her King, and
Albany was dead, and the younger Albany, though
conceivably no well-wisher of his cousin, too weak
to oppose the popular demand. English policy also
dictated a release. England was finding her war very
expensive, and the French resistance stiffer than had
at first seemed possible : the friendly James would be
more convenient to have at the head of Scotland than

---

[1] Down to the Revolution the senior company of the *Gardes-du-
corps* was known as the *Compagnie écossaise*, and wore the Scots
colours, though its personnel had by that time ceased to be Scots.

the brother of the late Connétable de Buchan . . . and James, most obligingly, was falling in love with an English royal lady, a Lancastrian, grand-daughter of John of Gaunt. The sooner he was let go, in fact, the better, especially (Henry IV's dying request being forgotten) if his release could be made to earn some money. In July of 1423 the affair was set on foot, and the English envoys were given secret instructions, which survive. It is not possible to ask for a ransom, as James cannot be called a prisoner of war : but they are to claim as much as possible for the payment of his expenses while in England : they must propose this, without naming a sum, and let the Scots make a bid. If the latter offer *summas placabiles* they are to accept. If not, they are to ask for £40,000, and if the Scots refuse, reduce the sum by £1,000 at a time, but not on any account to go below £36,000. The Dutch auction being satisfactorily settled, the rest is of minor importance. It is probable that the Scots will offer peace : if they do not, the offer is to be made, —perpetual peace, *honestiori medio quo valeant*, on the most respectable terms they can achieve. If there is no time to work out terms then and there, they are to make a truce for as long as possible and try to induce the Scots to send out no more help to the Armagnacs (*i.e.*, the French nationalists, King Charles's party) and to withdraw those troops already in France. If the Scots suggest an English bride for James, they are to agree, and say that he himself knows all the eligible English ladies, and can make his choice, but if the

Scots do not raise the point they must not either :
English ladies are not wont to woo foreigners—*non
soleant ultro virorum connubiis se offerre.* If the Scots
make any mention of reparations, they are to do whatever seems best at the moment. The document was
not for the public eye, and it throws some amusing
side-lights on diplomacy.

In September, at York, they met their opposite
numbers, whose leader was the Bishop of Glasgow.
They agreed on terms. One observes that the *expenses*
are £40,000. The Scots troops were to be recalled,
the King was to marry an English royal lady, but
apparently they could not decide about a truce.

James was eager enough to keep the last condition.
He was deeply in love with the Regent's first cousin,
Joan Beaufort, daughter of the Earl of Somerset by the
niece of Richard II. He assented to the rest, but
delayed for his marriage. It took place on the 12th
of February 1424, at St Mary Overy, now Southwark
Cathedral, Gloucester, in the name of the child King
Henry, presenting the bridegroom with his wedding
finery of cloth of gold. The King and his bride made
a slow progress northward, and at Durham on the
28th of March he signed a truce for seven years from
May. There had been time now to consider terms,
and they are worked out elaborately to ensure peace
on the Border. There are careful extradition provisions for malefactors, who cannot escape by naturali-
sation. Naturalised criminals are to be tried by a
joint tribunal : offenders against the peace of the

other country are to be handed over to their own Wardens. Men of either country can pursue offenders into the other without safe-conduct, up to six days from the crime, or within that time can lay a complaint before the foreign Warden. These supplements to the careful provisions of the Hawdenstank Convention are illuminating as to Border life—in fact, the cold prose obverse of the ballads. With regard to France, James was in a very difficult position. His own personal sympathies were probably divided, but he refused to go against those of his people by reversing the traditional policy of his government. The most to which on consideration he would agree was a declaration that he would not be responsible for any acts of his subjects in the French wars, but that if any should return to Scotland, he would forbid them to go back to France while the truce lasted : till they did return, he would not answer for them.

With that, and the promise of £40,000, the English Government had to be content : and just ‘ betuene Mersh and Averill,’ James came home, and rode over Tweed a free man and a king, with Queen Joan by his stirrup.

HERE
ENDS
CHAPTER
V

II
1424-1513

ΑΤΟΣΣΑ.   ἔτ' ἆρ' Ἀθηνῶν ἔστ' ἀπόρθητος πόλις ;
ΑΓΓΕΛΟΣ.   ἀνδρῶν γὰρ ὄντων ἕρκος ἐστὶν ἀσφαλές.

Aeschylus, The Persae.

Atossa.   Then Athens stands a city yet secure ?
Messenger.   While Athenians live, she has walls no man can break.

CHAPTER VI

JAMES I : 1424-37

SAVE for one brief interlude of a spoilt boy, Scotland
had now been ruled, since the memory of all but the
elderly, by a succession of old men : it was in fact
almost a hundred years since she had known a ruler
of any vigour. She had one now. James was just
turned twenty-nine, and the ideal prince of the
Renaissance : he was one of the most accomplished
men of his time, handsome in person, of middle height
but thick-set and powerfully made, with auburn hair and
the vitality that is so often found with that colouring.
King Henry, who coldly politic as he was, was not
vindictive, had squared his conscience over the boy's
capture by giving him an excellent education, and all
James's fiery natural energy, deprived of other outlet,
had grasped at it. He was skilled in all athletic exer-
cises, and in the graceful arts—lettered, like most of
the Stewarts, and a poet : not much of his work in that
medium is left (even the *Kingis Quair* was nearly lost,
for it survives in a single English MS. made after his
time) but it shows a gift for very graceful verse, a
vision shaped indeed by current fashion, but fresh

notwithstanding, and a real emotion beneath the conventional forms. He loved music, and was famous abroad for his skill, and he loved all visual beauty (the *Quair* shows that) encouraging all the crafts that made for it : foreign artists and craftsmen were welcome at his court.[1] But he was no self-indulgent dilettante : his intense vitality was controlled by the essence of its own energy. He was deeply religious, and in all worldly matters his strength was fed and directed by two devotions, to his beautiful Queen and to his unhappy kingdom.

He returned there as no stranger, no David II. He knew to what he was going, the desolation of long war, the anarchy, the turmoil of arrogant nobles, the feeble rule that could not save the weak from their oppression. In his prison he had never lost touch with Scotland : his suite came and went freely, and doubtless brought news, and the boy turned it in his mind, applied to it the results of his reading, of his keen observation, and of his own passionate sense of himself as King. Nearly all the Stewarts had that : it was sometimes distorted in exercise, and oftener in the record of enemies, but at bottom in most, and in all the best of them, it is rooted in a profound and mystical sense of one man who is set by God to stand for the people, holding his kingdom as a trust for itself, and for all itself. It was the virtue, and the wreck, of the Stewarts, that none would ever endure an oligarchy, the government of a

[1] The history of the early Scottish drama is so obscure that it is of interest to note that they included a Flemish company of players.

class in its own interests : and few things are harder to overthrow than that, few harder to prevent. But it was the glory of the Stewart kings that they saw, and tried to rule, Scotland as a whole, Highland and Lowland, peasant, burgess, and noble : and the conception was founded by James I.

When he rode north, he knew what he had to do, and he had thought out the means of doing it. It is in these means that he shows the weakness of his age, and indeed of the Stewarts. In an age of craft and violence for selfish ends, they stooped to craft and violence for nobler ones. It brought James to his death. Yet the violence was certainly needed, and deserved. The craft, of the Inverness Parliament, is harder to justify, but the alternative was an exhausting civil war, that would have been a certain bait for England. Indeed, there is a case for considering that what seemed to those few who suffered to be injustice was rather impatience with the slow forms of process that checked his right to do justice to the many : like most of the Stewarts he had too much initiative, and impatience, to make a good professional civil servant. That impatience was the Stewart ἁμαρτία, the tragic failing that brought them their disaster : it gave the strongest card to their enemies, the nobles now, the middle class later on, who grew to power through the crushing of the nobles and replaced the oligarchy the Kings had broken with another that eventually broke them.

The reign so envisaged was tragically brief. It lasted a few weeks under thirteen years : he was barely forty-two when he was killed, in the full vigour still of maturity. But in that time he had changed, and for the better, every aspect of national life. He broke, and he builded. He broke the power of the nobles, restored that of the Crown, that stood for a central and national government. He made reforms in the Church, and achieved an immense amount of legislation, some of it economically unsound, but most of it beneficial, and touching every aspect of national life. He improved trade, agriculture, arts, and crafts. He kept peace till the end of his reign with Scotland's great enemy, yet strengthened the league with her most powerful friend, and made more friends, laying the foundation for the net of alliances that was to cover North Europe in the next reign. He set a standard of kingship that had been lost for over a hundred years. And the inveterate luck of the Stewarts found him. He died, struck down like a cornered rat, in a drain.

James rode over Tweed in the spring, and came to his kingdom. His first act, at Melrose, was to ratify as a free monarch the truce that he had signed as a prisoner. Then he set to work at that to which he was already consecrated in heart, and would soon be outwardly on a May day in Scone. It was at this time that as he talked with one of the men about him he broke out in that passionate challenge to Fate, ' Let God but grant me life, and there shall not be a spot in all my kingdom where the key shall not keep the castle, the broom-bush the cow, though I lead the life

of a dog in securing it.' And thereupon, still un-
crowned, barely in Scotland, he summoned the
Estates, and he struck his first blow . . . and already
in his beginning there is a colour of what was to bring
his end.

The business is not clear. We can guess well
enough at the general grounds of it, but behind them
is a more sinister suggestion. This first blow fell
upon his own kinsmen, the House of Albany. He
arrested the Regent's heir, Walter Stewart, and two
others, Walter's brother-in-law, Malcolm Fleming of
Cumbernauld, and Thomas Boyd, younger of Kil-
marnock. His probable general reasons are clear
enough. Walter is known to have been a type of the
arrogant selfishness that was James's first task to curb :
there is a significant tale that when his father refused
him a hawk he fancied, he snatched it from the elder
man's wrist, and wrung its neck. He was James's
own kinsman, and it is sound policy to strike the tall
weeds first : moreover, since his house was directly
responsible for the government, they had more guilt
than any for the disorder. Beyond these things,
perhaps, James may possibly have remembered that
neither Albany nor Albany's father had made any
serious effort for his release : and for all the amenities
of his prison life, he had not the temperament that
finds iron bars no cage. There are glimpses, too, of
another, and sinister, cause—the King's own uncle,
Walter Earl of Athol, the youngest of that long brood
of Robert II. Bower accuses him roundly of being

art and part in Rothesay's murder, and now of turning the King against Albany. It is probable that there was little need to do that. James had both personal motives and larger ones. It is known, however, that he dealt generously with Athol, and that Athol was guilty, most treacherously, in his death. And Athol, no more than a sixth son by birth, would if the house of Albany were destroyed—Duke Murdoch and his three sons and his brother Buchan, who was to die very shortly at Verneuil—be heir-presumptive, after his great-nephew, the boy Malise of Strathearn. If James should strike down the Albanies, and fall in the probable vengeance, or to the fear of nobles who saw their turn coming, Athol would have but a child between him and kingship. Bower's charge is not proved, but it is likely enough . . . and the most disastrous weakness of the Stewarts, far beyond, for practical purposes, their reckless impatience in the choice of means, was their fatal gift for trusting the wrong people.[1] James rarely showed it, but he did with Athol at the end of his reign, and conceivably may have done so in the beginning.

He went on now to Scone, and on the 21st of May his old tutor Bishop Wardlaw anointed him King, and his cousin, the ex-Governor Albany, being Earl of Fife, set him upon the throne. Queen Joan was

---

[1] Contrast Mary and Elizabeth. Elizabeth might lose her elderly head over a handsome face, but she took care to trust Hatton or Essex with nothing that mattered, beyond her dignity. For serious purposes she rarely made a mistake in choosing her servants. Mary, an intelligent woman, hardly, through her reign, did anything else.

crowned also, and five days after that—he was losing
no time—he met the first of his parliaments at Perth.
They passed twenty-seven statutes, and the country
tasted the mind of its new King. The Lords of the
Articles—*certae personae ad articulos*—had drawn them
up : most likely he chose them from those men on
whom he could count. The nobles, warned by Albany's heir's arrest, learned further what it was they
had to look for. The privilege of private war was
forbidden, and rebellion, which included refusal to
help the King, incurred forfeiture : to back that, no
man could take the road with an excessive retinue in
arms. And in addition, the King might summon all
vassals to show their charters, and justify their right
to their estates. These threats launched, he went on
to the more pressing financial problems : he had come
into a hornet's nest of those, for the long Albany
administration had been generous with Crown lands,
and done nothing to remedy the long-standing results
of King David's extravagance : and values had fallen
besides, for the King as for everyone else. James
was not extravagant, but he liked splendour and
beauty, he had a heavy debt, and apart from these
things, only a wealthy Crown power could cope with
the nobles. The Sheriffs were charged to investigate
the state of Crown property, and a tax of twelvepence
in the pound of values was laid on all lands, regalities
included, for the ransom. (This unpopular measure
was to be dropped very soon.) Others fell on cattle
and corn : the customs were voted to the King for life

—a usual grant—and gold and silver mines were declared to be the property of the Crown : no great one, but trifling amounts of both metals were found, and they may have hoped the yield might perhaps be larger. The burghs were to provide 20,000 nobles, English, for the King's ransom, a sixth of the whole. Following an English practice, they made the economically unsound decision to lay export duties on cattle, horses, and skins.

The country would have to be taxed, but it was to be taxed fairly, and made fit to bear taxation. There were elaborate provisions for the appointment of honest fiscal officials, men who had a stake in their own honesty, and a new valuation survey was set on foot, so that the taxes might fall with equity. Measures were taken for trade and agriculture. Gold was not to be exported : foreign merchants must spend their gains in Scotland. The debased coinage was to be reformed, on a parity with English—a measure again which was not carried out. Statutes were passed for the preservation of fisheries, an important basic industry, and two practical ones for farmers, for the destruction of rookeries and the prohibition of muir-burn between March and harvest. The problem of mendicancy was tackled : beggars in real need, who could not work, were to have the King's licence and beg unmolested—the origin of the Blue-gown : able-bodied idlers and sorners were to be set to work, and if they refused, branded and banished. Finally, James had an eye to the military situation : he knew what had happened at Homildon Hill to the brother-in-law who was to die a few weeks later at Verneuil, and he determined to improve Scots archery. All men were to practise with the bow and . . . football and golf were to be prohibited.

The country's feelings, no doubt, were somewhat mixed. Every class received something from the new legislation : but every class, also, came under discipline, and human nature being what it is, a number probably were inclined to regret the good old slackness of the Albanies. James spent summer, autumn, and winter, in quiet work. A daughter, Margaret, was born at the end of the year. In March he met his Parliament again : he had realised, watching Henry of Lancaster, how a King and a Parliament, acting in concert, could bridle the unruly Second Estate. If any monarch of that generation had thought of having cause to fear the others he would have feared the First and not the Third : James counted that Kirk and Commons would be on his side, and in fact he won them, and to the end they supported the House of Stewart : it was the new Kirk, and the new merchant-commons whom the Stewarts made possible, that overthrew them, with the surviving power of the harried nobles. The work of this meeting began, significantly, by demanding whether the new statutes were being kept. Relations between the Estates and the King they were coming to trust show in another, that public prayers and processions are to be made for the welfare of the King and Queen *in thair bairntyme* :

again Queen Joan was hoping for an heir. The most notable statute of that meeting is this, which expresses the whole trend of James's legislation :

> Gif thar be ony pur creatur that for defalte of cunnyng [knowledge] or dispens can nocht or may nocht follow his caus, the king, for the lufe of God, sall ordane that the juge before quhame the causs suld be determyt purway and get a lele and wyss advocate to follow sic creaturis caus. And gif sic caus be obtenyt, the wranger sall assythe [indemnify] the party skathit, and ye advocatis costis that (sal) travale. And gif ye juge refusys to doe the law evinly, as is before saide, ye party plenzeand sall haf recours to ye king, ye quhilk sall sa rigorously punyst sic jugis, yat it sall be ane ensampill till all utheris.

With this protective care for the weak went a heavy hand for the strong. He had waited a year : now he struck for the tall weeds. Albany's heir was still in prison. Now he was joined by Albany's father-in-law, the Earl of Lennox, and by a man who was to be heard of again, and very darkly, Sir Robert Graham, the Tutor of Strathearn. At the actual Parliament, there was a further *ensampill till all utheris*. Albany himself was arrested, his wife, his second son Alexander, who had been knighted at the coronation, and some nobles also, and the King seized Albany's castles of Doune and Falkland. James Stewart, the third of Albany's sons, escaped, and aided by the Bishop of Argyle, burned the town of Dumbarton, killed its Governor, Red John Stewart of Dundonald, the King's uncle by the left hand, and fled to Ireland. The King demanded his extradition, but although the English were looking for him so late as 1429, he was never taken.

James decided to bring the rest of the house to justice.

The Estates had adjourned. They met again at Stirling in mid-May, and the prisoners were tried before their peers, a court of twenty-one nobles . . . whose head was Athol, uncle alike of Albany and the King. The record, unluckily, has not survived, but the charge seems to have been *roboria*. They were found guilty. That same day, on the little spurred knob of the Heading Hill, that stands out from the Castle Rock above the river, Walter Stewart died. His father and his brother and old Lennox followed the next day, and five men were hanged. There was a good deal of popular sympathy, for both Lennox and the Stewarts were tall and handsome men, of a noble presence : but James refused to do justice in a corner, and if the Stirling mob howled and the nobles were apprehensive, he knew that the Church, the small gentry, and the solider commons were coming to his side.

The rest of his domestic policy is of a piece with these early specimens. His reign is like a Renaissance tragedy, with entr'actes and an orchestration of Bluebook. The course of the more spectacular events that followed on the Albany executions will be clearer if it is all taken together, and the legislation may be summed also in one place, since it follows consistently on what has been described. In his third Parliament, he tried to clarify the tangle of legislation by enacting that Statute Law should govern the whole realm, taking precedence everywhere of local customs. A committee of eighteen, six from each Estate, was set up to overhaul the legal code, and the same parliament enacted that copies of all new laws were to be sent to the Sheriffs and proclaimed. (One observes that the records of James's parliaments are no longer in Latin but in the Lowland vernacular.) At the same time, the legal machinery was reformed. As early as 1425, we have the first rudiment of the Court of Session. It consisted of certain persons named by the King out of the Three Estates, who were vested with the jurisdiction formerly lodged with the Council : the name of *Session* come from the fact that in place of being itinerant with the King's court (which like all mediaeval courts, was constantly moving) it was to hold annually a certain number of sessions at fixed places, appointed by the King. Forethought felony was to be prosecuted by the King's officers, not by a private pursuer who might not dare to take action, and due provision was made that the personnel of the legal machinery should do their duty : the whole arrangement is carefully thought out, down to the provision of badges for the Sheriff's men (serving as a police), who could be smartly fined for not carrying them when on duty.

James attempted, with less success, the reform of the Parliament itself. Attendance at it was becoming neglected. He tried to ensure that the prelates and greater barons should attend, and to relieve the smaller barons and freeholders by introducing an analogue to the English system of knights of the shire, allowing those of each Sheriffdom to elect two representatives. (Clackmannan and Kinross were to have one each.) These

were to elect a Common Speaker who could deal with
their rights and privileges, and they were to have the right
to deliberate alone, and send their Speaker to represent
them to a higher court. This would have given the
germ of a Second Chamber, instead of the old single one :
but it was never carried out. The single chamber, whatever its disadvantages, is more congenial to the national
temperament, as witness its pride in the largest modern
Scottish representative body, the General Assembly . . .
or the famous commentary of Andrew Fairservice :

> In puir auld Scotland's Parliament they a' sate thegither,
> cheek by choul, and than they didna need to hae the same
> blethers twice ower again.

James concerned himself also with the defence of the
realm. The strong places were rebuilt, and he tried
to bring the army—*i.e.*, all able-bodied men from sixteen to sixty—on a proper footing of preparation for
war. He had been concerned from the first to train
archers who could cope with those English ones who
were the chief danger in a conflict with England, and
as the French developed the new weapon of fire-arms,
he saw its value, not only in foreign war but to the
power of the Crown : in 1430 he imported from
Flanders his first great cannon, a bronze piece called
the *Lyon*. Other arms were not overlooked. It seems
that there was a certain scarcity (the metals were not
extensively worked in Scotland) for it is enacted that
all merchants carrying goods overseas must bring back
arms in their return cargo. In 1429 an elaborate
Arming Act was passed, on the lines of Bruce's Statute

of 1318. All gentlemen with a yearly rent of £20 or over must appear well horsed and armed from head to heel (*cap à pié*, in the full plate or ' white armour ' of the time) while those with a rent of £10 to £20 must have gorget, breastplate, greaves and legsplints, rerebrace and vambrace (' sleeves ') and gloves of plate. A yeoman worth £20 in goods must have a doublet of fence, iron hat, sword, buckler, and bow and arrows, special provision made for those who *can not deyll with a bow*. Those worth under £10 can please themselves about defensive armour. A citizen or burgess worth £50 had to be armed as a gentleman. To enforce these regulations, wapinschaws were to be held in each district four times a year. These became popular and festive affairs, but their essential basis was kit-inspection, backed by fines for the slackers. James knew also that land armies were not enough for a country with a huge coast-line. Like nearly all the Stewarts down to and including James VII and II, he was keenly interested in the navy : the war and merchant navies were as yet not differentiated one from another. All lairds of estates within six miles of the sea on the west and north and opposite the Isles (the locality is significant, but need not be over-emphasised, for the trading towns of the East would look after themselves) were to contribute the equivalent of one oar of a galley to every four merks worth of land.[1]

---

[1] James's practical sense of justice shows in his provision over wrecks. The cargo is, or is not, to go to the Crown, according to the laws of the country to which the ship belongs.

Defence and the machinery of legislation were not all. The legislation had content as well as form, and a very positive content. Besides the attempt to suppress violence, there was much encouragement for agriculture and trade, the former excellently sound, the latter sometimes involving some unsound but then widely prevalent economics. All land tenures, small and great, were to be investigated and registered. Smallholders were protected : husbandmen could no longer be turned out on less than a year's notice, while conversely, farmers and freeholders were forced to cultivate their land. Trees were protected by legislation. Wolves—a danger to flocks—were to be put down by general hunts four times a year, with a bounty for cubs. Fishing was regulated and proper tackle and close seasons enforced. As for the towns, regulations were made for the craft guilds. Prices and wages were to be fixed by the bailies. Weights and measures were standardised. Idlers, as has been said, were punished, the really helpless being given a licence to beg. Lepers were segregated. Provision was made for more hospitals. Elaborate precautions were taken against fire, a standing menace in towns of wood and thatch. Inns—which had to close at nine—were to be provided, and to be supported, for travellers had to use them : those who travelled in a party might stay with friends, but their horses and servants had to go to the inn for the good of the house, and incidentally, perhaps, for the benefit of the police. The sumptuary laws are interesting : historians treat them, by tradition, as a joke or a foolish reactionary measure, according to temperament, but in fact they had probably a more subtle reason. They show, as has been observed, the increasing prosperity of the ' non-gentle' class, but there is another point, a politic purpose. The Middle Ages, with their intensely systematic outlook, had a very sharp sense of social distinctions and their outward marks : that is why, as in Spain or in the Highlands within living memory, the intercourse between the different classes was as easy, intimate, and unaffected as it appears for instance in the Prologue to the *Canterbury Tales* : a man whose position in society is clearly defined is not self-conscious about it.   James, like Louis XIV, was wresting from his nobles many privileges that marked their estate, but were anti-social : to distract their attention, so to speak, he did what Louis was to do— laid heavy emphasis on trifling but conspicuous privileges, barred them round and gave them an adventitious importance.   He broke the arms, but embellished the uniform.   This, at all events, seems his purpose, for James, though a man temperate and self-controlled in his private life, loved splendour and encouraged it about him, as indeed shows in one comforting sub-proviso for the deprived.   Only those of at least the rank of knight and of 200 merks rent, and their heirs, might wear silk and certain furs, or embroidery of pearl and bullion, but the rest can *aray tham at thar awin list* [pleasure] *in all uthir honest aray, as serpis, beltis, uchis and chenzeis.* Burgesses were not to wear the aristocratic furs, unless they were bailies—an

exception which shows the dignity of municipal office.
No yeoman or landward commoner was to wear a gown
below the knee, or party-coloured clothes, unless as
livery, and the commons' wives and servants were
debarred from long trains, hanging sleeves, wide head-
dresses (the spread ' horns ' were coming in) or costly
curches of lawn . . . one recalls the Wyf of Bathe :

> Hir coverchiefs ful fyne were of ground ;
> I dorste swere they weyeden ten pound
> That on a Sonday were upon hir heed.

Nor was James only interested in material welfare,
or even in such manners as are expressed in dressing
suitably. Devout, and a devoted son of the Church,
he was deeply concerned for the attacks from without,
and for the dangerous corruption within. The former
do not seem to have been active at this time. A
statute against heretics was passed in 1425, and James,
like all Kings of Scots from David II until long after
the Reformation, was bound by his coronation oath to
extirpate heresy. The only man, however, who
appears to have suffered what is called the extreme
penalty was a Bohemian physician, already referred to,
by name Paul Craw or Crawar, a Hussite, who was
burnt in 1432 at St Andrews. He is usually regarded
as a forerunner of John Knox (who declared that the
Hussite theory of the Sacraments was deserving of
death) but if the points of his teaching are truly
recorded, they would scarcely commend themselves
to a modern Assembly, as he denied not only purgatory
and the priesthood but the resurrection, and preached

L

state control of the Church and the common ownership of all the property of believers, including wives : all points which undoubtedly were held by some of the wilder followers of Wykliffe.

James was clearly far more interested in the more vital and fundamental question of reform from within, and in fact he carried his vigorous measures to ensure it to a pitch that produced a quarrel with the Pope. It is interesting to observe his eye for the strategic points. Besides his backing of the Conciliar Movement, for the reformation of the Church at large—a point which can be taken later on—he dealt at home with the prelates, the Orders, and the university, supported enthusiastically by his old tutor Wardlaw, who both by see and by seniority was a sort of unofficial Primus. (There was as yet no Archbishopric.) The prelates were the ' officers ' of the Church, and James spoke his mind to them. The Orders were front line troops : he saw that a monastery that fulfilled its function should be a radiating focus of spiritual power, and that if the protection of its discipline were relaxed, *corruptio optimi pessima* was the result. He hounded his abbots to measures of reform, and brought in new blood by introducing Franciscans of the Observantine Reform of St Bernardine of Siena,[1] and the Carthusians: these latter were by no means a new order, but had maintained their original discipline and escaped the prevalent corruption that slack observance of rule had produced in the others. He founded the first Charter-

[1] A return to the full strictness of the original Rule.

house [1] in Scotland, on the South Inch of Perth in 1429, and gave it the name of *Valla Virtuosa*. He fully grasped the need of a scholarly clergy, and was from the first a protector of the new university, attending its debates and giving it every encouragement. Further, he dealt with relations between Church and State : an early parliament, of 1427, took measures to curtail the cost and abridge the forms of process in civil causes brought against churchmen in the Commissary Courts (those of the Church) and bade the Provincial Council, the annual convocation of Scottish Prelates, register the decree.   It was this that brought him in conflict with the Pope.   The Bishop of Glasgow had backed him in carrying it through, and the Pope, considering it an Erastian measure, cited him to Rome. James defended his ally, sending an envoy to excuse his appearance, since as Chancellor of the Realm (its chief Law Officer) he could not be spared.   Martin V, unappeased, sent back as Nuncio the Archdeacon of Teviotdale, to re-cite him.   The Nuncio, being a Scot, could be charged with treason : he was, and fled, was tried *in absentia* and his goods forfeited.   Martin threatened an interdict, and Bishop Cameron did go to Rome at last, and succeeded in making peace with Martin's successor, Eugenius IV, who sent the Bishop of Urbino as Legate.   The quarrel was at length formally settled only a week before James himself was killed.

This independent attitude towards the Papacy made

[1] Really *Chartreuse*, from the name of their mother-house in Dauphiné.

it natural for James to support the Conciliar Movement.   In 1431 Martin V summoned the third General
Council of that century to Basel, to reform the abuses
of the Church *in capite et membris*, deal with the Hussite
heresy, and promote re-union with the Eastern Church :
it did in fact arrive at a concordat with the Hussites, and
passed a good many reformatory decrees.   James, like
his chief ally Charles VII, was strongly in sympathy with
the Council's aims, and sent an embassy of eight, headed
by his trusted Bishop of Glasgow.   It is probable that
if he had lived a little longer the Scottish Church, always
independent in outlook, would have achieved some
parallel to the Sanction of Bourges, which the year
after his death founded the liberties of the Gallican.

James's relations with temporal foreign powers are
worthy of note, and show the same careful regard to
the peace and prosperity of his kingdom.   At the
beginning of his reign he revived old relations with
Norway, whose king, Eirik, now wore the crown of the
three Scandinavian kingdoms, as heir of his great-aunt
Margaret, ' the Union Queen.'[1]   An agreement was
made for free trade between the two, apart from the
ordinary customs duties.   Norway still had a sort of
shadowy claim to the Isles, as the old equivalent had not
been paid in full, and James diplomatically recognised
it by agreeing to a nominal rent of 100 merks a year.

[1] Princess of Denmark and Queen of Norway. Mother of Olaf,
who inherited Denmark through her and Norway through his father.
On her son's death she was elected Queen of both kingdoms, and the
Swedes, having deposed Albert of Mecklenburg, elected her also.

He fostered trade relations also with Flanders, and apparently there was trade with Italy also, as Bower casually mentions the wreck of a great Lombard ship in the Forth.

The chief foreign relations, of course, were with France and England, and in spite of their mutual hostility, James was able to keep on friendly terms with both for at any rate a considerable time. The two, as usual, were closely inter-related. James began, it would seem, by leaning rather to England. His love for the Queen, his personal friendliness with the English Regents, and the truce he had signed, all inclined him to that side, as well, perhaps, as the fact that an active pro-French policy had been sponsored by his uncle and cousin of Albany. To keep the balance was no easy matter. France wanted more Scots troops. James, by the terms of his truce, could not send them, though it seems that a good many Scotsmen went over unofficially and enlisted. The French were disappointed. The English wanted a more positive attitude. The question, in the later fourteen-twenties, was of great importance to both sides, as the balance of the war was oscillating rather violently. Gloucester, the Regent of England, made complications for his brother Bedford, the Regent in France, by antagonising England's chief ally Burgundy. Philip of Burgundy had married off his cousin Jacqueline, Countess of Holland, Hainault, and Zeeland, to another cousin, Anthony Duke of Brabant, thus keeping the Low Countries in the family. The lady and her husband did not agree, and she left him for Gloucester, who wiled a declaration of nullity out of the now deserted anti-Pope, Benedict XIII (whom neither England, the Low Countries, nor Burgundy recognised) and married her. There was an intricate quarrel, till Gloucester settled it by falling in love with pretty Eleanor Cobham, and abandoning his doubtfully married wife to Philip's vengeance. Philip, thereon, ceased his recent flirtation with France, and the English grip on that country seemed to renew its firmness. James was still, if anything, pro-English : in 1427 he had even sent the Bishop of Moray to England with the suggestion of a final peace, and an announcement that he would discuss it in person. Gloucester, however, was by then on bad terms with his Beaufort uncle the Cardinal-Bishop of Winchester, and Queen Joan was a Beaufort. Exactly what happened is not very clear, but he failed to take the opportunity, and threw James back on France. At the end of the same year Charles VII sent an embassy to ask help—the Archbishop-Duke of Reims, Alain Chartier the poet (not as poet but as Chancellor of Bayeux) and Sir John Stewart of Darnley, now Sire d'Aubigny et de Concressault and Comte d'Evreux, the captain of the Scots in French service.[1] They asked for a renewal of the Auld Alliance, to be ratified by the marriage of the Dauphin, aged five, to Princess Margaret, then rising three, with

---

[1] He was killed the next year at the Battle of the Herrings, but not before he had been given the signal honour of quartering the Lilies of France upon his shield.

the promise of a Queen's jointure if she came to the throne. The 'if' was a rather large one at the moment, and the 'King of Bourges' could not add more than a promise of the county of Saintonge and the seigneury of Rochefort. The dowry that was asked with the little Princess was to be not gold but six thousand Scottish soldiers.

A few months earlier James might have refused, but Gloucester had apparently set him thinking : if the English were to win France after all, there would be little security for Scotland, however many truces she signed with her neighbour. He therefore granted the French king what he asked, and the treaty was signed at Perth in mid-July of 1428, and ratified at Chinon in November. France was in serious need of fresh Scottish help, for in October the English had laid siege to Orleans, the key to South France : if it fell King Charles's position would be hopeless.

Gloucester, apparently, realised what he was doing. Bedford, who was no fool, had come home and patched up the quarrel between his headstrong brother and Cardinal Beaufort. At the end of the year, James's own earlier suggestion was renewed from the English side. He was invited to Durham to meet the Cardinal. He was willing no longer, however, and declined, apparently doubting whether he could go safely. Anglo-Scottish relations were badly strained as a result. James was in arrears with the instalments of ransom, and according to an English chronicler there was wild talk in England of making another claim to the suzer-

ainty of Scotland . . . when Orleans had gone, and
France was in their hands.

Orleans held, however. In May 1429 St Joan
relieved it, and in July Cardinal Beaufort came north
and met James at Dunbar. England had no desire for
a Scots war now, and James never wanted one on his
own Border. He renewed the truce he had made on
his return, to last now until 1431.

That summer saw the recovery of France under St
Joan, the victories of Jargeau, Meung, and Patay, where
Talbot was captured. Hugh Kennedy's Scots—he had
succeeded Darnley [1]—fought through the whole cam-
paign, as has been said : in July they marched to Reims,
where Charles was crowned. May of the next year saw
St Joan a prisoner, and the beginning of her year's martyr-
dom: but the spirit she had kindled burnt like a flame, and
Richemont, Dunois, and Kennedy carried on her work.
There was no more English talk of invading Scotland.

The Anglo-Scots truce was due to end in 1431, and
in November of 1430, the English offered not only to
renew it, but to make a permanent peace, with the
return of Berwick and Roxburgh, and the marriage of
their young King Henry to a Scots princess. James
was probably tempted, but he would not take such an
important step without his Parliament, and in the
meantime would only consent to a five years' truce from
May—*i.e.*, to May 1436. There is an anxious clause

---

[1] A fortnight after the siege of Orleans began, he broke his way
through the English lines and got a force of Scots into the city. He
was on St Joan's council when the decision was made to attack the
Tournelles, and later garrisoned Lagny after she took it.

that no aggression by a *subject* of either kingdom shall be considered as a breach of truce.   Parliament met at Perth in October (1431), James laid the new peace proposals before them, and they refused assent. According to the *Liber Pluscardensis*, some considered the terms attractive at first sight.   The Abbot of Melrose, however, raised the point that the offer was no more than a device to break the French alliance. He recalled past history.   *Ipsi Anglici multa promittentes nichil de facto propter hoc perimplere volebant. Nam semper dum velint occasiones ab amicis recedere invenire sciunt, et ex eorum antiquis actibus evidencia perpetrati sceleris et experiencia demonstrant.*[1]   The Estates agreed, and the glittering proposal was turned down, but politely : the Scots could not make peace unless that were agreeable to their ally France . . . and both countries knew it was the last thing France wanted.

As a counter-move to Charles's coronation, little King Henry was crowned King of France in December —but at Paris, not in the sacred place of Reims, and by Cardinal Beaufort, not by a French prelate.   Burgundy was uneasy : letters had come into his hands that showed that Bedford and Gloucester were plotting his death : his sister, Bedford's wife, tried to make peace, but she died before she could do anything, and the Breton Constable of France, Richemont, an able

---

[1] ' These same English promise much, but in fact they have no intention of keeping their promise.   For whenever they choose they can find occasions for deserting their friends : both experience proves that and the evidence of their own former conduct and of the shameful acts they have committed.'

statesman, set to work to detach the Duke from alliance
with England. Burgundy, however, disgusted as he
was, was a man of his word. The most he would do,
and that not until after long pressure, was to set on foot
negotiations for a peace congress at Arras in 1435,
which the Pope was already striving to bring about.
It met in August of that year, and the English demanded
first the full Treaty of Troyes, and then the *status
quo* : they were offered Normandy and Guyenne in full
sovereignty, but still would not compromise. Then
Bedford died, and Burgundy at last resiled from the
English alliance, and in September was reconciled with
Charles, by the Treaty of Arras, signed on the 21st.

Before the Congress had met, Charles had attempted
to strengthen his position by clinching his previous
agreement with Scotland. At the end of 1434 he sent
over Sir Hugh Kennedy and the Sieur de Bazoges to
demand the little bride. James received them courteously at Edinburgh in January, and they had a most
friendly welcome from the people : but there was a
difficulty. James, like most Stewarts, was a devoted
father, and he could not bear to part with the little
Princess, who does appear to have been an enchanting
child. The court went to Perth : the ambassadors
went on a tour of the chief cities, where all classes,
according to Bazoges, gave them a most enthusiastic
welcome : and the impatient Charles sent over another
embassy, with a fleet of three large ships and six
' barges.' In early autumn—that is, about the time
of the Treaty of Arras—they reached *Dompbertrain*

(Dumbarton) after a voyage of fifty-six days. Still James delayed, with the weather as excuse. In March he had to make up his mind at last to what was perhaps the deepest grief of his life. The marriage articles were signed, with a provision that the Scots were to help France, at French charges, against English aggression, and reciprocally, and that neither would make peace without the other ; and then the child—she was only ten years old—was handed over by her weeping parents, with touching commendations to the ambassadors, and set sail, escorted by a hundred and forty squires and a thousand men at arms, under the Earl of Orkney, the son of her father's old fellow-prisoner.

She very nearly shared her father's fate. In spite of the truce, the English sent out a fleet to intercept her : the French wine-fleet came out of La Rochelle, and they gave chase to it, and a Spanish squadron came up and scattered them. Princess Margaret, having been a month at sea, arrived at La Rochelle on the 17th April, and made a triumphant progress up the Loire. On the 25th June, 1436, she was married at Tours to her fourteen-year-old bridegroom, the future Louis XI. A month earlier, her father-in-law King Charles had ridden into his recovered capital.[1]

[1] It was a most unhappy marriage. Margaret grew up a gracious and charming personality, a poet like her father, beloved by Charles and his gentle wife Marie d'Anjou, but hated by her husband. His favourite set going scandal about her, and Margaret demanded an investigation, which cleared her : but she never recovered from the blow to her pride, and *l'étoile claire et fine*, as a contemporary calls her, set, broken-hearted, in August of 1445, her last words ' *Fi de la vie ! Qu'on ne m'en parle plus.*' She was twenty.

So far, we have considered the steady current of James's work, the course of his constructive policy, at home and abroad. It is time to return and take into account those violent events that flamed up time and again, interrupting it, but linked with it causally, for what brought them about was the need to clear the ground for that peaceful progress. James's whole policy, as has been shown, was Scotland's prosperity and security : and one of the chief impediments to those was the turbulence of certain men in high places. He smote such rebels with a heavy hand, and perhaps with some degree of personal anger for those who jeopardised his passionate labour : and although he knew the men with whom he was dealing, he was completely fearless, and never would go guarded, save for state.

We have seen how in 1425, almost at the beginning of his reign, he had dealt with the Albanies. He held his hand then, perhaps hoping the example would suffice. It did not. James, though he waited, was studying the situation. The Estates were to meet in the spring of 1427, and he called them not to Perth, which was practically the capital in his reign, but to Inverness. There he proceeded to a *coup d'état*. His method was not scrupulous, and laid him open to a hostility that had excuse : his own justification was presumably that the Highlands had to be pacified,[1] that

[1] At the clan battle of Strathnaver about this time, between MacKays and Murrays, the combatants are said to have been 1200 a side, and there were nine survivors. The actual figures vary with different accounts, but the gist is the same.

the Isles were a constant menace, and that in dealing
with chiefs who could some of them put four thousand
men in the field, he must strike without warning, or
find himself involved in a civil war that—since the
balance in France was swinging for the moment to the
English—might mean a ruinous foreign one as well.

He summoned the Highland chiefs to Parliament.
They came, and he arrested forty of them.   It had been
a risk, and he knew it, and seems to have shown some
excited exultation, with a grim impromptu couplet in
leonine verse—

> Ad turrim fortem ducamus caute cohortem.
> Per Christi sortem, meruerunt hi quia mortem.[1]

Three were tried and executed at once.   Others, including Alexander MacDonald, the young Lord of the
Isles, were imprisoned, pending investigation.   Their
cases were gone into in due course : some were
executed—one for the murder of Alexander's grandfather, King Henry's old ally, John Lord of the Isles.
The rest were released, among them Alexander.   He
was young, and a distant connection of the King : his
father in fact had been the latter's first cousin.   James
evidently thought he had had his warning : the young
man had been on the court which condemned the
Albanies.   He invited him to Court, and Alexander
came : but apparently Harlaw was too recent a

---

[1] John Major, who quotes it, remarks disapprovingly on the false
quantity, but adds that the Latin is good enough, for a king ! The
sense is

> Let us wile the gang to a castle strang,
> For by Christ's wrang they deserve to hang.

memory. Somebody mocked him, and he lost his temper and flung away north again, and in 1429 he raised ten thousand men and burnt Inverness. James chased him into Lochaber, and smashed his force. On the next Palm Sunday, as the King and Queen went to mass at Holyrood, Alexander appeared among the crowd, alone, and in his shirt, and kneeling offered the King the hilt of his sword. James would have headed him, but Queen Joan interceded, and he was sent to Tantallon, while his mother, the old Countess of Ross, 'a mannish implacable woman' according to Bower (who would have had charge of her) was sent to the island Priory of Inchcolm.

It was not the end of trouble in the Highlands. In the next year, 1431, Alexander's cousin, Donald Balloch of Islay, raised the clan again, joined by Alexander of Lochaber. The Earls of Mar and Caithness marched against him,[1] and he defeated them at Inverlochy, where Caithness was killed. James again took the field himself. Donald fled to Ireland, and Lochaber was forfeited, his lands being given to the chief of Clan Macintosh. Notwithstanding this rising, the young Lord of the Isles was soon released, though forfeited of his earldom of Ross. He kept the peace thereafter, though his son was to be a serious danger to later kings.

The Highlands were quiet then for the rest of the reign, but there was plenty of trouble farther south. A story is told which suggests the type of personality with

---

[1] The King's cousins, though the first was illegitimate. Mar was the victor of Harlaw, and Caithness was the son of Walter of Athol.

which James had to deal, and the methods he could use
to cope with disturbance.   In the actual council, in the
King's very presence, two nobles quarrelled, and one,
the King's own kinsman, struck the other.   James
made him hold out his hand across the table, gave his
whinger to the man who had been struck, and bade
him then and there smite off the hand.   Queen Joan
threw herself between them and interceded.   James
would not refuse her : the striker kept his hand, but he
was banished.   The story may perhaps be apocryphal,
but it is characteristic.   James had determined *debellare
superbos*, and to be master in his kingdom.   To achieve
that end, he had not only to break his insurgent nobles,
but to strengthen the Crown.   He struck at March—
not the March of the Percy wars, but his successor.
March's English connections and his Border earldom
roused the King's suspicions at least, if nothing more :
in the beginning of 1434 a committee of three from
each of the Estates was charged to deal with him.   They
forfeited the earldom.   James gave March, as compensation, that of Buchan, vacant by the death at
Verneuil of his cousin the Connétable, thus, as Drummond puts it, ' setting Tay and Forth between March
and his kind friends of England '—and the Earl refused
it and fled to the said kind friends.

In the next year, the death of the Earl of Mar, the
victor of Harlaw, allowed his earldom to revert to the
Crown.   By 1436, forfeiture and reversion had buttressed the Crown with the earldoms of March and
Fife in the South and East, Lennox on the Highland

Line, Mar and Buchan in the North-east, and Ross in the North. Athol and Strathearn were held by the King's uncle, whom he believed his friend, and the only great independent earldoms left were those of Douglas, Angus, Moray, and Crawford, the two former being held by nephews of the King, while the other two earls were related to him. The Crown was above the nobles now with a vengeance : and the rest of Scotland was thriving, in spite of the plague and the terrible weather of 1432, when even ' beasts of chase ' died all over the country. There was prosperity and comparative peace, and abroad there was still continued truce with England, and a closer alliance than ever with the recovering power of France, friendship with Flanders and the Scandinavian kingdoms. Further, after six years' reign and the birth of several daughters, Queen Joan at last had given the King an heir. Twin sons, Alexander and James, were born on the 16th October of 1430, and Edinburgh blazed with bonfires and ran with free wine. Their cousin Douglas stood their godfather, and the fifty knights made at the christening included two boys, both called William, his son and nephew, of whom one was to be dragged not many years later from his godson's presence to semi-judicial murder, and the other to be stabbed by that godson's hand. No one, however, could see that stormy future, and all through these busy years of the early 'thirties, James's power rose and his achievement increased. In 1424 he had come to restore a wrecked kingdom. In 1436 he could look round him, and see the foundations on which he might build a new Scotland, indeed a Scotland that was already rising : and since he himself was only forty-one, he might well hope to consolidate his work.

It was the last full year he was to see. Already three men were plotting. Two were kinsmen and friends, old Athol and his grandson, Robert Stewart. Drummond calls the latter ' a riotous young man, gaping after great matters,' but James had been kind to him, treating him as a friend and making him his Chamberlain, to which honour had just been added the Constableship. Perhaps he and his father, to whom the King had given a second earldom, might have been loyal but for Robert Graham, the uncle of young Malise of Strathearn. He is a fantastic and terrible figure, like something in a play of Chapman or Webster, of reckless courage, an all but insane power of hate, and a legal training to shape that hate to an icy flame like a blade. James had arrested him with the Albanies, in 1425, but unhappily for Scotland had let him go : and two years later he had made Graham his mortal enemy.

At the root of the matter, without any Not Proven this time, is the old Earl of Athol, James's uncle. Athol's elder full brother, David, the elder son of Robert II's second marriage, had been Earl of Strathearn. He left only a daughter Euphemia, who had married Robert Graham's elder brother, Sir Patrick Graham of Dundaff. Sir Patrick and Euphemia were dead now, and their young son Malise bore the title of

M

Earl of Strathearn, and had for guardian his uncle Robert Graham. Now, Strathearn was a male fief. As such, it had fallen to the Crown on the death of the last earl of the old line, though he had a daughter : and Robert II had given it to his son, Euphemia's father and Walter of Athol's brother. The next heir, accordingly, should have been not Euphemia, but her uncle.[1]

Whether at his own motion or Athol's, James gave it to the old man, giving Malise as compensation the earldom of Menteith, vacant by the forfeiture of the Albanies.[2] Robert Graham had been furious at this, and James, very likely to prevent the boy from being used as figure-head for an armed rising, sent the latter to England as hostage for the ransom.

Robert Graham bided his time for years, nursing his hate and sowing disaffection as the self-constituted

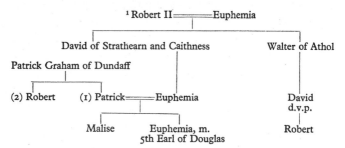

[1] Euphemia in 1390 had already parted with the earldom of Caithness to Athol, who was then only Lord of Brechin. It is possible that he had a grievance then over the other earldom.

[2] It is interesting to note that the usual account of historians is simply that James, without any sort of reason or compensation, ejected young Malise from his earldom.

champion of the nobles. Then he struck at last . . .
and the blow missed publicly and made him look a
fool. Rising before the Estates he made a wild speech,
denouncing King James to his face, then striding to
the King laid hands on him, crying out that he arrested
him as a traitor. James looked at him without moving,
and no man stirred. Graham swung on them with a
shout. ' Is it not as I say ? ' But still James was
silent, and no man would answer. Graham looked at
them—no doubt but some had spoken loud in the past
—spat contempt in a curt sentence, and strode out.
James let him go, but banished him to the Highlands,
whence he wrote a defiance glittering with hate, and
renounced his allegiance : and at last the King, having
spared him twice, put a price upon his head . . . and
perhaps comforted Graham's pride a little.

The open attack had failed. He tried other means :
the man's legal training comes out in the choice of them.
The King had favoured Athol and his grandson, but . . .
Graham cast back his mind to Robert II's marriages.
Going to Athol he reminded him that doubt had been
cast on the first, whose son was the King's father. He
contended that the sons of Elizabeth Mure were
illegitimate, and the lawful heir the son of Euphemia
Ross, Athol himself. Hate works queerly. Graham's
ostensible reason for hating the King was defence of the
rights of his own nephew Malise : but Malise was also
descended from Athol's mother, and in an elder line,
and Graham put him aside now to gain his ends,
unless he intended to ' double-cross ' Athol later. In

the summer of 1436 they made their plot : and a Highland seeress foretold Athol's coronation within the year.

It was the year of Princess Margaret's marriage, and there was ill-feeling between Scotland and England. In February, just before the Princess sailed, the English attempted to extend the truce, which was near its end. James's response must have been unfavourable, for in March there is an anxious letter from Henry, expressing a hope that it will yet be extended : he had just sent out a fleet to capture the Princess, who was at sea at the time when the letter was written. James protested against the attack on his daughter, but got no satisfaction, and apparently the truce was allowed to end. It closed in May : an English force crossed the Border, and were driven back at once by the Earl of Angus. At the end of July, James himself marched to Roxburgh, and gave siege to it. When he had been before the town a fortnight, the Queen came suddenly. What news she brought was never clearly known, but James left the siege, and called the Estates to Edinburgh. It was his last Parliament. After it was over, the Court went to Perth to keep Christmas, and at the Forth they were met by a Highland woman who sought the King, and told him she saw the shroud about his breast : if he crossed that water he never would come again. Whether she knew of the conspiracy and dared not speak out, or simply had the Double Sight, is not known : but James, being doomed, would not heed her, and held his way.

They kept Christmas at Perth, at the Blackfriars, and stayed there after into February, for the Council of the Church to which the Legate, the Bishop of Urbino, brought notice of the Pope's reconciliation. A week after James had received it, Graham struck. It was a wild night, the twentieth of February. James, they say, was playing chess with one of his gentlemen, a young man whose by-name was the King of Love, and reminded him, laughing, of a prophecy that a King should die in Scotland in that year, saying that since they were the only kings in Scotland, it behoved them to look to their safety : and Athol and Robert Stewart the Chamberlain, standing there as the King's friends and kinsmen, of his household, heard that. One of Graham's men, Christopher Chambers by name, who knew the plot, tried four times that evening to have speech with the King, and whether by design of men who knew also, or the mere chance of James's own orders against disturbance, could not win to him : and the woman who had warned him by the Forth came to the door, so urgent they brought a message to the King. But by that time it was late, and he was weary, and said he would see her in the morning.

The night wore on pleasantly with song and talk, and the voidé-cup came at last, the signal for parting. They say that Athol and Stewart were last to go, and the King, already in a chamber-gown, was left with the Queen and her ladies by the fire. The ladies began to make their mistress ready, and he stood and talked to them : then they heard a clatter of arms below on the stair. There was only the one door and the windows were grated : they ran to the door, and found that the lock was spoilt, and the great bar gone from the staples below the curtain : and there were no arms in the place, not so much as a knife. Then they remembered that underneath the floor was the vault of a sewer : James snatched the tongs from the fire and levering at the boards made a hole and dropped : he could have got safe away three days before, for the vault had an opening into the tennis court, but playing there he had lost his balls in it, and bade them build it up, and it had been done. The Queen and her ladies wrought at the loosened boards, and before they could smoothe them and scatter the rushes again, the sounds were close, and they say that one of the ladies, Katharine Douglas, ran to the door and thrust her arm through the staples of the bar. She held it there till the bone broke, and fell back, but she had made time : Graham and his men, as they rushed into the room, found none there but the women—no sign of the King. There was wild confusion then as they searched the place. One man put his sword point to the Queen's breast, and threatened her with death if she would not tell them where her husband was, but a son of Graham's struck aside the blade.

They ransacked the place, and found nothing, and went away. The ladies, thinking the danger had gone by, lifted the boards, and James called to them to let him down the sheets, and draw him up again from his filthy refuge : they tried it, and one slipped into the hole beside him, dragged down by his weight. The scuffle made a noise : perhaps someone cried out : and one of the conspirators remembered the vault and called the others back, and again they crowded up the stair and in, and found the loose boards and the women about the hole, and below in the darkness the King unarmed and alone. Only a few minutes more would have saved his life, for the place was rousing now. They were not given. The King saw Graham's face above in the light, and asked for a priest, for he knew it was his end : but they had no time for the niceties of murder, and two men leapt down to him. He fought with them, striking aside the blades with his bare hands : he was strong, and when they were taken a month later, they still had the mark of his grip upon their throats. But they were armed, and mad with fear and hate : he had fifteen wounds on him when he was lifted.

They did their work and fled, and got away, all but two. Dunbar of Cockburn, the brother of exiled March, killed one of them as they ran, and wounded another. In a month they were captured. Queen Joan took a bitter vengeance. Athol was crowned, as the spaewife had prophesied, but the crown was paper, and the head lacked a body. The rest died in torture, Graham with black defiance to the last, affirming that since he had renounced allegiance he was not the King's subject and had a right to revenge—that the murder was no wrong, but he took his death as the judgment of God on him for his *other* sins. He told his tormentors as the red hooks tore his flesh that if he blasphemed at his pain, the sin was theirs, and they would bear Heaven's wrath.   It sums the man.

Their deaths could not give life to the King they had killed.   He was buried in his Charterhouse at Perth, which was wrecked, with his tomb, at the time of the Reformation ;   and his heart went on pilgrimage to Palestine, whence a Knight of St John brought it back six years later.   The country he had served had for its King a little boy who was not yet seven years old, and whose heir, since his elder twin Alexander was dead, was either his young sister the Dauphine or the head of the towering ambitious house of Douglas.

HERE
ENDS
CHAPTER
VI

CHAPTER VII

THE MINORITY OF JAMES II : 1437–49

' 'Tis much when sceptres are in children's hands ;
But more when envy breeds unkind division ;
There comes the ruin, there begins confusion.'
Shakespeare, *I Henry VI*, iv, 1.

ON the 25th of March the child was crowned, not at
Scone, where the crown had been given from time im-
memorial, but in the safer place of Holyrood. The beginning of the reign shows an effort to continue the dead
King's policy. The best of the Churchmen, the ' civil
service' that James I had chosen, the burgesses whom
his strong rule had enriched, and the common people
whom it had protected all desired that it should go on.
Bishop Cameron was still to be Chancellor. Queen
Joan had the custody of the royal children. The fifth
Earl of Douglas, the little King's godfather, Archibald,
son of James I's eldest sister, and therefore the next
male in the succession, was made Lieutenant-general
of the kingdom. The records of the coronation parliament are mutilated, but we know that laws were passed
for the protection of shipping that was essential to trade,
and for the peace of the Marches that was essential to
good relations with England. In November a new
truce was ratified, and a few months later it was
reconsidered, and renewed for a further nine years,
that is, till the 1st of May 1447. The desire to

protect the stability of the Crown, the sense that such stability was vital, shows in a highly significant proviso, that it is

ordanyt be maner of statute that na landis nor possessionis pertenyng to the king be gewyn nor grantit till ony man without the avisioun and consent of the thre Estatis of the Realme, on to the tyme of his aige of xxj zeris.

But, says Pitscottie, looking back at the record of Stewart minorities, ' so lang as the king is young, great men reignis at their awin libertie, oppressand all men, as they, without doubt, will be punisched thairafter.' ' Thereafter as they be : ' an historian's job is this world, not the next : but so far as this world goes, Pitscottie was certainly speaking to the facts, and the facts of the minority of James II show one of the most notable examples.   The most conspicuous element in that time, and in the early manhood of the King, was perhaps the most dangerous of all the mediaeval renewals of strife between the central government and one section or element of the population—that between the Crown and the great House of Douglas, who were to Scotland through much of this century what Bur-gundy was to France across the water.

Their name has already echoed through this book, as it did through the pages of its predecessor. In that, the record was wholly one of honour, of Sir William le Hardi and the Good Lord James, great names in the defence of Scottish freedom. Since their day also the Douglases had shown what was never less than a magnificent courage : but darker and wilder colours

were entering. Their own great services in the recovery of the Border from Baliol's alienation had increased their power, with their royal marriages, and the
fall of their only rival in the South, the Earldom of
March : two-thirds of South Scotland was theirs, broad
lands in the North, and the great and rich French duchy
of Touraine. They were coming to feel themselves
above the Law : it is not without significance, perhaps,
that in the later fourteenth century both the third Earl
and the first Earl of Angus, the founder of the Red
house, were born out of wedlock, one indeed in what
that age would have called incest : yet both were earls
and one married a King's daughter, while the other
espoused his two sons (and one of these two was again
a bastard) to princesses, and his daughter to the eldest
son of the King. The double fact is not only expression
of their *superbia*, but something perhaps of cause too :
one may seek explanation for some of the Douglas arrogance at least in the second scene of the first act of *Lear*.
Now their huge power and their high marriages [1] had
brought them to a place very near the throne . . . and
near the temptation that sent Walter of Athol to stare
unbodied under a crown of paper, and James I to his
grave in the Charterhouse of Perth.

It was with smaller men that the storm began : indeed, Earl Archibald, the King's Lieutenant, son of the

[1] Of the twenty-three Douglas earls before 1600, five married
daughters of a King of Scots, one the daughter of a King of England,
and three others ladies who were closely connected with the Scottish
or the English royal house.

Earl who had fallen at Verneuil, lived till his death in 1439 without other expression of his arrogance than a lofty refusal to be concerned with strife, even to check it as his place required. The first bid for power was made by Sir William Crichton, a curious, somewhat enigmatic figure. James I, like most kings trying to form a strong government and break anarchy, had chosen his own servants largely from men whose greatness in place depended on himself : it was the policy of Louis XIV. He had used Crichton on diplomatic errands, employed him on his Privy Council, and in time made him his Master of the Household and the Governor of Edinburgh Castle. Now, within two years of his old master's death, Crichton seized on the royal revenue, and denied the Queen access to her young son.

It is somewhat difficult now to gauge his motive. It may have been a mere personal ambition : but James II's attitude, when he grew to manhood, suggests that Crichton may honestly have thought that the Queen's connection with England was a danger. There is no evidence that he was right in so thinking, if he did : but in his somewhat Machiavellian way he was certainly loyal to the little King. His motives, like those of many politicians, were probably mixed : if self-interest was strong, he at least inherited enough of the general policy of his dead master to identify it with the broader interests of Crown and kingdom, at any rate as he conceived them.

Queen Joan's reply to him was to steal the boy. She

announced her intention of going from Edinburgh by sea on a pilgrimage to Whitekirk of Lothian.[1] The little King went through Edinburgh gates in his mother's luggage, and the ship turned west, not east, and went up the Forth, to the Queen's jointure-house of Stirling Castle, whose governor, Sir Alexander Livingstone of Callendar, had again been a chosen servant of the boy's father.[2]

At first it seemed she would have Douglas at her back. A council held at Stirling on the 13th March of 1439 strengthened the hands of the Lieutenant against Crichton. *The Kyngis chosyn consal*, with Douglas for head, was to meet twice yearly, and provision was made that he might raise the country against rebels or *vnrewlful men* holding fortalices. Douglas, however, refused to act against Crichton, and it was Livingstone who marched on Edinburgh. Crichton tried for a band with Douglas, and the Earl shrugged his shoulders and told them to fight it out. The big man's indifference alarmed the small ones. They hastily made peace. Bishop Cameron was extruded from the Chancellorship, which was given to Crichton, and Livingstone became Guardian of the King. These things had happened by the end of May : before the next month was out, Douglas died of a fever, and left his huge power to a headstrong boy of fourteen. It was not yet two years and a half since King James's murder, and already his

---

[1] Of Brechin or Buchan, say other chroniclers : but the White Kirk of Our Lady in Lothian was a famous place of pilgrimage.

[2] He had been on the Court that tried the Albanies.

work seemed breaking into pieces. Livingstone and Crichton each now proclaimed himself chief in authority—a godsend to *brigants* who could oppress their neighbours under pretence of being of the opposite faction. The right of private war and *deidly feid* revived : and many of the men who practised them might have sat for Scott's description of Hell-in-Harness. Already in this year the failure of harvest *throw the tumultis and cumberis* made a famine in places, and a plague that was called ' the pestilence without mercy ' because its victims died on the day they were stricken added a deeper terror to fire and steel. In short, no sooner was the supporting arch of the government broken by the removal of the King its keystone, than it seems, as Drummond put it looking back, ' as if the heavenly Influences were sometimes all together set to produce upon this Ball of the Earth nothing but conspiracies, treasons, troubles, and for the wickedness of the Inhabitants to deprive them of all rest and Contentment.'

Queen Joan, left unprotected by Douglas's death, made a sudden desperate marriage a few weeks later, to Sir James Stewart, ' the Black Knight ' of Lorne. Instead of protection, it increased her danger by allowing Livingstone an excuse to act. On the 3rd of August, in spite of the armed resistance of her household, he arrested her, with her husband and brother-in-law. The men were straightway *put in pittis and bollit*, the Queen warded, though less drastically, in Stirling. At the end of the month Livingstone had the audacity to

do something very like bringing her to trial, before a
kind of Convention of Notables—the Bishops of Glasgow, Moray, Ross, and Dunblane, the boy Douglas,
Seton of Gordon, a great man in the North, Crichton
the Chancellor, his uneasy ally, Lord Dirleton, and
burgesses from Linlithgow, Edinburgh, and Inverness.
They professed to judge between Livingstone and the
Queen, informing her that what Livingstone had done,
with Crichton's concurrence,

> thai dide it of gude zele and motifs and of grete truth and
> leaute that was in tham both to our soueryne lord the king and
> his sawfte and to the said princess in her worschip. [honour]

The last clause must have fired the Queen, as well it
might, and they had to add that although Livingstone
was *doand that thing as trew liegeis aw to do*, it was not
for any light conduct of hers.   It was the only concession they would make her.   She had to give formal
pardon to Livingstone, to abandon him the custody of
the King, and—a curiously ugly touch of meanness—
her jointure of 4000 merks for his expenses, and to *lend*
him her dower-house of Stirling, which of course was
one of the vital strategic points in controlling the
kingdom.   She might have access to her son, but not
speak to him alone, while her suite must be appointed
by Livingstone, and had to take an oath to do him no
harm.   Her husband and his brother were released
then, which rather suggests that a woman of her fierce
spirit and known courage had stooped to these humilia-
tions as their ransom.
   The business ended her as a political factor, though

she was to live for another six years yet, bearing her
second husband three sons,[1] and dying in Dunbar in
1445, at the news of his capture at sea by Flemish
privateers. She was buried by James in the Charterhouse of Perth.

Crichton and Livingstone were now at the tiller,
with Livingstone in charge of the little King. Each
now attempted to clear his path of the other. Crichton
ambushed the boy and his suite in the dawn by Stirling
as they rode to hunt, and with courtesy to cover violence
took him to Edinburgh. Bishops Lichtoun of Aberdeen and Innes of Moray, whom Pitscottie describes
as ' good men, wise, and prudent ' (one can believe him
when he praises a bishop !) intervened in time to prevent a civil war : the antagonists met unarmed in the
Kirk of St Giles, and came to a concordat of some kind,
and the poor little pawn of a King was handed back.
There was even an attempt to use their understanding
as a basis for stable government again. In August of
1440 (the same year) the Estates at Stirling endeavoured
to put down violence. The Justiciars North and South
of Forth were to hold justice ayres twice a year, as old
custom was. So must lords of regalities in the said
regalities, and the King's bailies in his. Where there
was *rebellione, slauchter, byrning, refe, forfalt, or thift*—
the current amenities of social life—the King himself

---

[1] John Stewart of Balconie, created Earl of Athol by James II
(d. 1512), James Stewart, Earl of Buchan, called Hearty James
(d. *c.* 1500) and Andrew Stewart, Bishop of Moray. All played
considerable parts in the next two reigns.

was to ride through the realm and to call upon the Sheriff to do justice, whom all local barons were obliged to assist.

Besides the general menace to law and order, both Crichton and Livingstone, in this same summer, were clearly becoming conscious of another, that might trample down both themselves and the young King. This was William, sixth Earl of Douglas and Duke of Touraine, no more than a boy yet in his later teens, but with the power of his house and their arrogance, and with blood in him to make that last strong danger. Drummond says that he was ' of good inclination if he had been well accompanied ' : but the lad's counsellors may have ministered to his enormous sense of what he was, and certainly did not succeed in disciplining it. He rode his lands at the head of a thousand horse, and proclaimed himself sovereign within his marches, where his vassals need not obey the King's officers. Moreover, his defiance of the Crown might end not merely, like March's, in an alliance with its foreign enemies, but in an actual attempt for itself. It was not four years yet since that of Walter of Athol, and young Douglas had a nearer claim than he : he was descended from *both* Robert II's marriages, and as it happened, he was the next male to the senior representative of each line. His grandmother was the child King's eldest aunt : his mother the sister of Malise of Strathearn,[1] still an unmarried hostage far south in England : she was niece to the dark figure of Robert Graham, with a

[1] See genealogy on page 178.

N

blood-feud against Queen Joan if she so chose. By
blood he was thus the next man in the realm to the
King, whether one thought the king was James or
Malise : and he had more wealth than the Crown and
enormously more power than a child of nine or a
prisoner in a foreign and hostile country.

Douglas had the power : but he was a violent boy
(and not ungenerous for all his arrogance) against a
couple of crafty politicians. Crichton, in his own name
and that of Livingstone, wrote begging the greatest
magnate of the realm to give his counsel in the difficulties of the Commonweal. The lad swallowed the
bait and rode to Crichton Castle . . . and insisted on
taking with him, against all advice, his inseparable
younger brother David, who was his heir. Old Crichton
entertained him splendidly, and they rode on through
the autumn weather to the court, which was then at
Edinburgh. Douglas's suite observed many men of
Crichton's coming and going, and begged their young
lord to turn back, or at the very least send home his
heir : but the boys, afraid of being thought afraid,
refused, and rode on, their train after them *with sad
drearie and.quyet countenance*, to royal entertainment in
Edinburgh. For some days they were the guests of the
little King, who was within a fortnight of his tenth
birthday : the harried small boy admired their accomplishments and almost-manhood, and they con-
descended to his adoration, and sunned themselves in
the Chancellor's flattery. Then—the detail comes
from Boece, fifty years later, but it was tradition by

then, and true to the popular vision if not to fact—as the two lads sat at meat at their King's table, there was laid down before them a black bull's head. They were dragged away : the hot-tempered child, their host, tried to protect them, and Crichton flung him back with a curt phrase and forced him to preside at their ' mock trial.' (Was it such a mockery ? It was treachery in the manner of the capture : but without more record, even to say *Not Proven* would sway justice a little to the Douglas side.) The issue at any rate was the expected : the lads went straight to the courtyard, and the block; and three days later Fleming of Cumbernauld, their tutor and adviser, followed them.

It was effective, for the immediate moment : and like so many other things that are that, it was to exact a bitter vengeance later, and come very close indeed to a bitterer still, and the ruin of not only King James, but Scotland. For the time, it seemed to do what was intended, and break the danger of the Douglases, certainly their power. Touraine, as a male fief, re-turned to King Charles, Annandale, for the same reason, to the Crown : the rest was divided. Galloway and Bothwell, which were unentailed, went to the dead boys' sister Margaret, a child of eight, and the great entailed lands to their great-uncle James the Gross, Earl of Avondale, the Tyneman's brother, who had lands of his own in the North-east and Linlithgow, and now became the seventh Earl of Douglas. He was an elderly man of enormous bulk (' thai said he had in him four stane of talch [tallow] and mair ') which may have had something to do with his supineness. But his record is not remarkable for scruple : in his earlier and less encumbered days it was he who had been the Douglas of Balveny who murdered Cumbernauld in 1406 ; and it is probably not unjust to suspect at any rate a *post factum* collusion with Crichton. At all events, he did nothing while he lived. There was nothing to be feared from the Black Douglas while James the Gross sat peaceably to his dinner : and the Red house had been linked to the Crown that summer, for the young Earl of Angus, son of the King's cousin, had been betrothed then to the Princess Jean, the King's third sister, who was likely to give him a quiet life at least, for the poor child—she would be fourteen or so—was dumb.

Her elder sister, Princess Isobel, had been already demanded in marriage by John the Wise, Duke of Brittany, for his son, as ratification for a Scots alliance. The Breton ambassadors had described the lady as beautiful but singularly silent, and not, they thought, from discipline of wit so much as its lack : and John was delighted, for his ducal wisdom was of the kind that prefers its women stupid[1] : but he had only a younger son to offer, as his heir was married. The Scots refused the match. Then his daughter-in-law conveniently died, the Bretons tried again, and John died himself : and in October 1442, Princess Isobel

---

[1] His comment on the description was that a wife would have all the wit she needed if she could tell her husband's shirt from his collar.

was crowned Duchess of Brittany, her bridegroom gallantly postponing his coronation until his bride should arrive to share it with him. The alliance was one, just then, of some importance to both France and Scotland, for the Breton interests of the time were divided. Duke Francis was pro-French, but his brother Giles was actually Constable of England, to which the duchy might easily serve as a bridge-head. To have it in the hands of a friend of Scotland, brother-in-law of both King of Scots and Dauphin, was thus a useful stroke for the Auld Alliance.[1]

All through the 'forties, indeed, foreign relations were steadily being strengthened. By the middle of that decade, an embassy headed by the Provost of Edinburgh had straightened out a quarrel of some standing with the Hanse Towns, who had been not unjustly annoyed at the depredations of certain Scottish pirates. They negotiated with Bremen, Lubeck, Hamburg, Wismar, Stralsund, and Rostock, to the considerable advantage of trade. The Bishop of Moray's mission in 1441 drew closer Scottish relations with the Low Countries, and three years later these were ratified by the marriage of Princess Mary, the King's fifth sister, to Wolfaert von Borselen, Count of Grandpré and Lord of Campvere, the nephew of the

---

[1] Duchess Isobel was widowed four years later, with two small daughters. The elder, Margaret, married the next Duke, Francis II, and became the mother of the Duchess Anne, whose marriage to two French kings in immediate succession brought Brittany into complete union with France. Isobel lived to see her grand-daughter's marriage to Charles VIII, for she did not die till 1495.

Duke of Burgundy. Relations with the Holy See were friendly : in 1443, in fact, the Estates reversed the old policy of James I by congratulating Pope Eugenius IV on his triumph over what was left by this time of the Council of Basel. The reversal, however, was not unreasonable, for the Council had gone to pieces, had lost all the prestige of its early achievement, and was threatening the Church with another Schism.

Domestic politics were a less heartening sight. The anarchy continued and increased, and the Government could do very little to check it. Towards the end of 1443 the Estates at Stirling attempted to order matters. Perhaps on the motion of Bishop Kennedy of St. Andrews, who now comes to the fore, they proclaimed a general cursing of the *spulzearis* of the Kirk, backed by formidable temporal penalties : government service was henceforth closed to them, and they should be incapable of pleading in law. At the same time, they outlawed the Chancellor, Crichton, and put in his place the Bishop of St Andrews, who was to be the good genius of the King. He was son of Princess Mary, Countess Dowager of Angus, by her second marriage to Sir James Kennedy of Dunure, and was thus brother of Gilbert, first Lord Kennedy, cousin of the young King, and uncle, by the half-blood, of the young Earl of Angus, Princess Jean's betrothed and head of the Red House of Douglas. Born about 1406, he was a brilliant scholar, deeply learned in both theology and the law : his scholarship evidently took a practical turn, for we know that he wrote *Monita Politica* and a

Historia sui Temporis whose disappearance at the Reformation was an irreparable loss to the historian of two difficult reigns. He had been made Bishop of Dunkeld in 1438, and showed himself at once a zealous reformer : the wise Bishop Wardlaw died in 1440, and the young Bishop was chosen to succeed him, saying his first mass as Bishop of St Andrews in September of 1442. It was an excellent choice. He combined a statesman's grasp of politics, both secular and ecclesiastical, with a love of beauty and magnificence and a very deep sense of his responsibilities : in fact, he bears a strong likeness to his uncle James I, whose policy he endeavoured to carry out. For over twenty years he was a powerful and beneficent force in public life, both at home and abroad. In 1450 he founded and richly endowed the College of St Salvator in the university of his diocese, equipping its chapel splendidly at his own cost, with magnificent furniture, vessels of gold and silver, and a silver image, two cubits high, of the Saviour, while his tomb and his marvellous ship the *Sanct Salvator* were among the ' sights ' of Scotland.[1] Yet he was no mere Renaissance scholar-politician, but a true Father in God to his diocese, where he preached four times a year in each parish kirk, and personally examined its affairs.

[1] In the seventeenth century the wrecked tomb was opened, and there were found in it six magnificent maces, probably hidden there at the Reformation. Three of them are still among the treasures of St Andrews University : the other three, by a graceful and sisterly gesture, were presented to the Universities of Glasgow, Aberdeen, and Edinburgh.

Such a man, at the time, was needed, though his influence, beyond his own diocese, was slow at first in making itself felt. The Douglas menace was raising its head again. James the Gross died in the spring of 1443, leaving the earldom to a fiery lad of eighteen, the eighth Earl, William, with an arrogant mother and four active brothers. Neither Livingstone nor Crichton was at ease. The child King they had bandied between them was growing up : his mother they had harried was still alive, and they may have realised that the new Primus was likely to prove a formidable force. Both played for the rising powers. Livingstone won. The boy King, now thirteen, was strongly attracted by the brilliant young Douglas, five years his senior : it was not difficult to have the young man, as next male heir to the throne, set in his father's old place as Lieutenant-general : then Livingstone and Douglas, acting in concert, set Kennedy in Crichton's Chancellorship, and Douglas was paid for his help by being allowed to reunite the Douglas lands again, by marrying his cousin once removed, Margaret of Galloway, the eleven-year-old sister of the lads who had been beheaded at the Black Dinner. The marriage bound him to Livingstone and his faction, for Margaret's mother, Euphemia of Strathearn (known to distinguish her from the other two Countesses Dowager of Douglas, as Duchess of Touraine) had married Livingstone's grandson : but the immediate help for Livingstone was purchased by fresh danger to the realm, for Douglas, besides being next male heir to the King, was now in a position to raise through his wife the opposite claim as heir to Robert II's second marriage. The factions were in open war again. Douglas, in the King's name, took a Crichton castle, and Crichton, forfeited and charged with treason, burnt Douglas's castles of Abercorn and Blackness, and harried his lands, whereon Douglas in return besieged him in Edinburgh for eleven weeks, until he surrendered on terms, and was outwardly reconciled to the Livingstone faction. Meanwhile, there were more sinister complications. Douglas had made a band with the Earl of Crawford, and Crawford was not only the most powerful man in the North-east and the father-in-law of the beheaded Earl William : he had married the sister of the outed March, so that both his wife and his daughter had tangible grounds for a feud against the Crown.

Bishop Kennedy took alarm, and made a counter-alliance then with Crichton, giving back to him the Chancellorship—an action which, Kennedy being the man he was, tells considerably in favour of Crichton's motives. The common amenities of political opposition followed at once. Crawford and young Livingstone made a raid on Kennedy's lands in Fife and Angus : in retaliation the Bishop *continyually a year cursed solempnitlie* Crawford and his allies, *quhilk the erle highlie vilipendit.* But it was observed none the less that the curse came home, for a year to the day from its first laying on, Crawford was killed in an attack on Ogilvie of Inverquharity, whom the Abbey of Arbroath had made its justiciar, over the head of his son, the famous Beardie, who comes down in tradition as the Tiger-earl.

Crawford's feud with the Bishop, however, was merely a bye.   By the latter part of 1445, the two parties were once more in a dubious accord, that might break into civil war at any moment, with perhaps an attempt to bring down the dynasty.   At this point, however, two new factors entered.   The truce with England was ending, and the young King was ceasing to be a child.

The truce was to end in May 1447, and the politics of England at the moment were in as uneasy a state as those of Scotland.   King Henry's marriage in 1444 to a dowerless princess, daughter of a charming but out-of-work king,[1] had pleased no one except himself, Suffolk, who had contrived it, and perhaps the lady. Henry, though now a man in the middle twenties, was a gentle, devout, and learned nonentity.   Gloucester, his uncle and sometime guardian, had kept the real power, and was now fighting to hold it against the young Queen and her supporter Suffolk, who was generally assumed to be her lover.   Behind the two factions was rising a third figure, the sufficiently threatening one of the Duke of York, who was not only grandson of John of Gaunt's younger brother, but through his mother, Anne Mortimer, was heir of line of Lionel Duke of Clarence, John's *elder*, and thus with a senior claim to that of King Henry or any of the House of Lancaster.   Over against York, and like him

[1] René of Anjou, titular King of Jerusalem and the Two Sicilies, and brother of the French Queen, Marie d'Anjou.

on the second plane as yet, was the Duke of Somerset, John Beaufort, brother of Queen Joan. So long as King Henry had no son, either York or Somerset was heir-presumptive, and that without upsetting the legitimacy of the Lancaster kingship. Somerset was a grandson of John of Gaunt, York only his grand-nephew : but Somerset came of a legitimated line, whose heirship to the throne had been specifically barred at legitimation. The stage, in fact, was being set for the civil war that was not only to wreck the Plantagenets but to have powerful effects on Scots politics and bring the Stewarts at last a second throne.

In 1447 Gloucester died, perhaps by poison. He had been friendly to Scotland, so Suffolk's party were naturally hostile : and the latter very probably considered that a remedy for the national discontent with the inglorious issue of the French war, and for the dangerous tension of rival factions, would be a successful war with France's ally. And the state of Scots affairs made this seem feasible.

The truce ended, and in the spring of 1448, Northumberland and Salisbury, the English Wardens of the East and West Marches, swept over the Border, burning Dunbar and Dumfries. The war, if sharp, was a short one. The Douglases returned to the tradition of Good Lord James and the days of Otterburn. John of Balveny, the youngest of the five brothers, a mere boy, drove south and burnt Warkworth and Alnwick, and Douglas himself met Percy and Huntingdon with a larger force than his own, and scattered them. The

French alliance was renewed, and it was proposed to ratify it by the King's marriage. No French princess of suitable age was available, to Charles's great regret. There was a tentative suggestion from France that a dispensation should be procured for the marriage of the Dauphin to Princess Eleanor, who with Princess Jean had been sent to the French court at their mother's death, on a visit to the Dauphine Margaret, who died a little while before their arrival. The Pope, however, refused a dispensation for such near kinship, and Eleanor, early in 1449, was married to the Archduke Sigismund, the Emperor's cousin, whose lands included much of the southern Germanies.[1]   Charles, on the refusal, suggested another match, that should link Burgundy to the Franco-Scots alliance—that King James should marry Mary, daughter of the Duke of Gueldres, whose Duchess was sister of Philip of Burgundy. The lady was to bring with her as dowry not only 60,000 crowns in cash but a treaty of perfect peace, mutual defence, and intimate commercial relationships with Burgundy, Brabant, Holland, Zeeland, and Flanders, the richest states of North Europe, the rivals of the Hansa as its commercial centre, and the holders of the balance of power between France and the Empire, while Burgundy and (although less recently) Flanders had been traditional allies of England.

The match was agreed to, but before the arrangement

[1] Princess Annabel, in 1447, had been married to the heir of the Duke of Savoy, the southern buffer-state between France and the Empire, and conveniently on the flank of Burgundy.

could be implemented, war between France and England broke out again. England was still mistress of Normandy and Guyenne, but her garrisons were neglected and unpaid. One of them, near the March of Brittany, indemnified itself for its arrears by sacking the Breton city of Fougères. This threw Duke Francis definitely towards France, but before Charles could act, the whole of Normandy rose of its own accord to drive out the foreigner, and twenty towns were retaken in two months. In mid-October, Somerset was forced to surrender Rouen itself, the capital, to Dunois ; and though an expeditionary force was sent over the next spring, the Connétable de Richemont destroyed it, on the 15th April, at Formigny, and the whole of Normandy was French again.

The Scots, at the time when the Anglo-French war was renewed, had shown themselves willing to make peace with England. On the 10th of May, 1449, a commission were actually appointed to treat as plenipotentiaries, to go to London and make a fresh truce on the old terms, or on such others as they might think suitable : one observes that the Provost of Edinburgh is one of their number. The English, however, failed to take the chance : it is possible that they were exasperated by the threatened Scoto-Burgundian alliance, and did not yet grasp the trend of affairs in Normandy. They refused to treat, and in the middle of summer there were hostilities upon the Marches. A brief truce, for purposes of negotiation, was made in July —from 10th August to 20th September—and renewed then till the beginning of November. Just at the time of the renewal, a formidable English force was assembled, under Northumberland and a hard-fighting Governor of Berwick, Sir Magnus 'Red-Mane.' In October they tried for the West March, and Hugh, Earl of Ormond, Douglas's third brother, encountered them at the passage of the Sark. His force was out-numbered, and looked like being badly defeated, for the English archers were doing heavy damage : but William Wallace of Craigie, who led the left wing, changed the luck with a desperate charge on the English right. They were driven back on the Sark, where the tide was rising, and thrown into confusion. Sir Magnus was killed, and Northumberland's son taken prisoner in a gallant attempt to cover his father's escape. Some fifteen hundred English fell in the field, another five hundred were drowned in Solway Sands, and the rest driven back in disorder across the March.

Before that time, the King's marriage had been accomplished. On the 18th of June 1449, the beautiful sixteen-year-old Mary arrived in the Forth with a squadron of thirteen ships and a guard of three hundred men, made her devotions on the Isle of May, and, escorted by her uncle Philip of Burgundy, rode pillion to Holyrood Abbey behind her cousin Wolfaert of Campvere, the husband of her new sister-in-law, Princess Mary. The actual marriage took place with much pomp on the 3rd of July, the Archduke of Austria, Princess Eleanor's husband, the Duke of Brittany, Princess Isobel's, and the Duke of Savoy,

Princess Annabel's father-in-law, being represented by their ambassadors. The bride was crowned, as her husband had been, at the Abbey. And James, now nearly nineteen, with the wise Bishop Kennedy behind him and his new dignity as a married man, resolved to take his place as King of Scots.

HERE
ENDS
CHAPTER
VII

VIII

JAMES II : 1449–60

'The sons of Belial shall be all of them as thorns thrust away.
. . . But the man that shall touch them must be fenced with iron
and the staff of a spear.'

II Samuel, xxiii, 6-7.

JAMES's brief kingship showed him his father's son. He was no poet, nor had he James I's love for letters and music, that had passed to his sisters, though he was not without pleasure in the arts, for like all the rest of 'the Jameses' he was a builder. But he had his father's vigour of mind and body, and in part perhaps through Kennedy's influence, his father's devotion to his duties as King, and resolve to keep Scotland free and to make her prosper, to bridle the violent forces of disorder, and rule a united country, at peace with herself and if possible with her neighbours. In his brief reign he succeeded amazingly : he renewed his father's alliance with Church and Parliament, his father's hostility to the turbulent nobles, his foreign policy, of a close union with France yet peace with England, and a nexus of trade alliances over the North. One fierce and sudden crime stains his memory : but James of the Fiery Face —the broad red birthmark that disfigured one cheek— had a fiery temper, and those historians who blame its loss on one famous occasion, and the wild stroke that followed, sometimes fail to remember that the man he struck was not only a traitor but a murderer, and a most active menace to that Scotland to whose well-being James, as her King, was pledged. His people loved him, and he them : he went among them careless of state and even of his own safety, accessible to any man who sought him, and friendly to any who aimed at the country's good : in time of war—so John Major says of him—he was the comrade of the common soldiers, sharing the rations and quarters of his troops.

His position at his assumption of active kingship somewhat repeated his father's, in its contrast of affairs at home and abroad. Abroad, indeed, Scotland's prestige stood even higher than it had done a quarter-century before. She was the intimate ally of France, who had recovered her losses, all save Guyenne, which had been English so long men had almost ceased to think of it as French, and whose power and whose prestige were again at the level they had reached under Charles V or the later Capets. Besides the French alliance, there were the rest—with Burgundy, the great central power, then at its zenith, that held the balance between France and the Empire ; with the Empire itself, and with that Prince of the Imperial House who held the frontier states of Alsace and the Breisgau and the Border over against Italy ; with Savoy, that completed the long central March ; with Brittany, the key to the balance between France and England ; with the great commercial powers of the Hansa and the Low Countries. Relations with England had just been

o

sharply strained, but James after all was the son of an English princess, and Somerset, who might any day be appointed heir-presumptive, was his uncle : besides, England's stock at the moment was standing lower than it had ever done since Henry III, and was to sink yet. Relations with Scandinavia were doubtful, but she was not formidable just then, for the death of King Christopher the previous year threatened the Union of Kalmar with dissolution, and Christian of Oldenburg and the Swede Karl Knudsen were quarrelling which should wear the Triple Crown.

Domestic affairs were a very different matter. The framework of James I's legal organisation apparently still held, but was almost powerless. To the tall weeds he had lopped had succeeded others, that choked what should have been the country's harvest. In face of the young King now were Crichton and Livingstone, who had overshadowed his life since he could remember— or could he perhaps recall some remote golden age, in the last year or two of a kind father ? Their quarrels might at almost any moment bring a renewal of the civil wars : and rising now in the foreground of affairs there were the handsome, fascinating Douglas, still a young man in no more than the middle twenties, and his brothers, who had newly won laurels in the English war. Nevertheless, the young King did not stand alone : beside him was the wise and magnificent Bishop who recalled his dead uncle and loved that uncle's son : and possibly too the young wife whom James seems to have loved, and who was a woman of courage as well as beauty, may have helped to sharpen his sense of his new manhood.

His immediate policy, on this first assumption of an active kingship, was to recover peaceful relations with England, which he could do now without being disloyal to France ; to keep on good terms with Douglas, still heir-presumptive[1] ; and to check the possible civil war at its root. The truce with England has already been mentioned. The commissioners for it were appointed a few weeks after the King's wedding, Livingstone, now Justiciar, and the Treasurer (the Abbot of Melrose, who was the King's confessor) being added to the original ones of May. The English commissioners were in a truculent temper. They greeted the Scots with a solemn protestation that the proceedings were without prejudice to King Henry's rights as overlord of Scotland. The protestation, which is inserted in English into the Latin records of what was arranged, was no doubt a gesture for the English public, who were not pleased with their own government, on account of the recent *dégringolade* in France. The Scotsmen, at this rattling of the sabre, may have glanced at each other : but they permitted the discharge of emotion, and eleven days later consented to a truce of fourteen months between the most terrible and most Christian prince (*metuendissimum et Christianissimum*) Henry and his illustrious kinsman the King of Scots.

[1] Princess Margaret had died childless : Princess Isobel's children were two very young daughters, of a foreign house, and none of the other sisters had any yet.

Neither James nor Henry, in fact, desired a war. James needed a longer breathing-space in which to tackle domestic difficulties, and Henry, or rather Somerset, realised that with Normandy slipping from under its garrisons, and Dunois in Rouen, a Scots war was inopportune. On the 3rd November the same commission was re-appointed, and on the 15th of the month—there can have been but a very brief discussion —the terms of the truce were altered and enlarged. It was now to be indefinite, for as long as should please the two Kings, each agreeing that if he wished to break it he would give the other a hundred and eighty days' notice. Various detailed practical provisions were made—forage and fuel for the garrisons of Roxburgh and Berwick, and free passage through the Debateable Land (all ' without prejudice ' to either's claims), the protection of shipping, including wrecks, and the usual extradition clauses, with the extremely significant proviso that neither government should grant any office to a rebel or criminal fleeing from the other.

Both the contracting parties then settled down to deal with their disturbances at home : and both found plenty of work. James, it seems, had been considering affairs. At the end of the year, he struck his first blow. Livingstone was Justiciar : for twelve years he had been more or less continually at the head of Scots affairs, and he had been a commissioner for the truce. Now, in mid-winter, only a few weeks later, the whole family of the Livingstones was arrested. We know no details, only that in six weeks their whole power was broken, their castles held for the King. On the 19th January, 1450, they were tried at Edinburgh before the Estates : again we know almost nothing of what happened. The attack on Queen Joan in 1439 would seem to have been one of the charges, at least, and *roboria*, probably, would not be hard to prove, with a few of Kennedy's tenants to bear witness. Old Livingstone was imprisoned at Blackness : his younger son Alexander went to the block. James, the elder son, was pardoned, and won the King's favour, becoming later his Master of the Household and being raised to the peerage as Lord Livingstone.

It is probable that the blow fell barely in time. Somewhere before this—the date is rather vague— Livingstone's ally Douglas had made a fresh band, with the new Earl of Crawford, the Tiger-earl, and with John MacDonald, son and heir of James I's enemy Alexander, then newly dead. John, as the Lord of the Isles and Earl of Ross, had a place in the Highlands on a level with that of Douglas in the Lowlands, and he had a personal grievance against the King. He was then but sixteen, and in the previous year the King had made his marriage, to Livingstone's daughter : now the fall of that house had cheated him of her dowry. The King may or may not have suspected the band—one cannot even be sure it was made just then —but he certainly had no solid proof of it, and perhaps he still felt Douglas's brilliant charm, while the Douglas services in the recent war might possibly suggest a change of heart. He tried to win Douglas peaceably, at least, showing him favour, and giving him some of Livingstone's forfeited lands, which the latter's late ally accepted without demur. Douglas and Crawford, indeed, served on the Marches, in positions of trust. It may have been Kennedy who a little later hit on the tactful device of paying the Earl a conspicuous compliment that detached him at the same time from Scots affairs and kept him conveniently out of mischief. The Papal Jubilee fell due that year : Douglas was sent as the head of an embassy to convey the courtesies of the Scottish nation. He went without protest. He had business of his own at the courts of both France and England—at that of King Charles to procure the restoration of Touraine, and at that of King Henry to form an alliance with the enemy of both James and Henry, York. He left his youngest brother John of Balveny to watch his interests, and went, in princely state, accompanied by the others, Archibald Earl of Moray and Hugh Earl of Ormond, and joined in Parsi by Archibald's elder twin, James, a brilliant young scholar intended for the Church, who was, in fact, to die a monk at last, but not until after a variegated career.

The King had taken Crichton into favour, and it is to the credit of the old politician that now his dead master's son had asserted himself he followed him loyally for the rest of his life. Kennedy's influence meant the support of the Church, and now James renewed his father's alliance with the Estates. The first parliament of his majority—that which tried the Livingstones—is remarkable for the scope and vigour of its legislation. The primary task was to end the state of violence by making its machinery illegal. The King's Peace was proclaimed throughout the realm, as surety under which *al men mycht trauel sourly and sikkerly in merchandice and vthir wayis*, thus outlawing at a stroke the prevalent system of what is nowadays known as racketeering. Those who were threatened were not to look to safe-conducts issued by private individuals for gain, but to the King's Sheriff, who was bound to protect them on their complaint of being in dread. Even justices and the King's officers were to *ryde bot with competent and esy nowmer. Oppin and publist reyssis and spoliaciounis* of peaceful men's goods must be put down : the party injured should complain to the Sheriff of the spoiler's district, who must deal with the *spulzeour* : if he would not disgorge, the Sheriff should put him to *the Kingis horne*, and if he did not, the pursuer should carry his case to the King's Lieutenant, who should treat the Sheriff as he should have treated the *spulzeouris*, while legal officers who had been deforced were given the right to invoke the Privy Council.

Other protective statutes were also passed against the less openly violent forms of oppression : one important one is *for the sauftie and fauour of the pure pepil that labouris the grunde*, and bears that on transfer of land, all extant tacks should run to the end of their term at the original rent. Other provisions were made against oppression by equals and from below. The holding up of *vittale* was penalised, and there were vigorous measures against *okkiraris* (usurers) and the rabble of the roads : *sorneris, ouerlyaris, and masterful beggaris with horsis, hundis, or vthir gudis, and ony that makis thaim fulis that ar nocht,*[1] and alas, *bardis,* were to be imprisoned at their own charges while their funds lasted, then to have their ears nailed to the tron and cut off, and finally to be banished under penalty of hanging.

Besides all this outlawry of oppression, the machinery for enforcement of law was examined, and some of James I's provisions were revived. A register of infeftments was to be drawn up, going back to 1424. The Court of Session was re-enacted, to be drawn from all three Estates, and sit thrice in the year. Judges were to be of good character, and learned in the law. The Arming Acts were to be enforced, under penalty of a sliding scale of fines according to the culprit's social position, the said fines to be payable in sheep. Statutes were passed against false coining and the export of gold, and finally, a committee drawn from the Three Estates was appointed to examine all Acts and Statutes of James I, and to report before the next Parliament.[2]

It must have seemed as if James I had returned. And

[1] That pretend to be mentally deficient.

[2] Unfortunately, all that has survived of the proceedings of this Parliament is what must be one of the earliest Dangerous Drugs Acts, a prohibition of the import of poison, whether by natives or by foreigners. One would like to know what stirred them to legislate: poison does play a notable part in that age as both a political and a domestic convenience : but the Scot has generally preferred cold iron.

men may have thought it also a good omen for the revival of saner national life that while this very Parliament was sitting, affairs were in train not only to enlarge the resources of the university, by Bishop Kennedy's College of St Salvator, but to give Scotland a second. Glasgow then was a place of no civic importance, but its bishopric was accounted the Second See : it was anxious to be on level terms with St Andrews, and to uphold the dignity of the West by forming a centre of higher education conveniently accessible to the Highlands. In January of 1450, Bishop Turnbull received the Bull of Foundation from Pope Nicholas V, who conferred upon the new institution all the accustomed privileges of Bologna. On Trinity Sunday (that is, in June) of the succeeding year, the foundation was proclaimed at the Cross of Glasgow, though the King's Charter was not received until 1453. The see of Glasgow had only half the revenues of its rival,[1] and the new university was ill endowed : there were no buildings until 1460, and for a while it had something of a struggle, though one of its first students, the future Bishop William Elphinstone, was to rank among the greatest of its sons, to become the founder of Scotland's third university, and succeed Bishop Kennedy in the nation's councils.

There was a small foreign breeze about this time, for in 1450 Princess Isobel was widowed, and her late

---

[1] The unequal revenues of the dioceses were one of the difficulties of the mediaeval Church. St. Andrews had eight times those of Aberdeen, which came next after Glasgow, and thirty times those of the poorest, which was the Isles.

husband's subjects tried to marry her again, to the Prince of Navarre. She had two small daughters, heiresses to the Duchy, and wished to stay with them and guard their interests, so she appealed to her brother, who intervened, with success.

Before long, the promise of peace and prosperity was gravely threatened by further trouble with the Douglases. John of Balveny, left in charge of their lands, was a spoilt and turbulent lad, of not much past twenty. To use an expressive modern idiom, he began now to throw his weight about. James acted, and promptly, in defence of his new statutes : he sent an armed force, which took Lochmaben and razed Douglas Castle. Young John of the Isles proceeded to implement his band with Douglas by seizing Inverness, Urquhart Castle, and Ruthven in Badenoch. There was the threat of a violent blaze in the North, but again James acted promptly and with vigour. Douglas returned in 1451 to find comparative peace throughout the country . . . but on his journey from France by way of England, Garter King of Arms had been sent to meet him at sea, and had waited upon him while he was in that country very much as if he had been a sovereign prince. James still endeavoured to win him over by kindness. (His own position, as against the Douglases, had been strengthened by the birth of a son, James, on the 10th of July of that year.) He did withdraw the Lieutenancy, but with a major king there was the excuse that the office was not needed : and

Douglas was made Warden of the West and Middle
Marches, and received a fresh entail of his lands and
several new charters.   The King's friendliness, however, was unavailing : it was cancelled out, in Douglas's
estimation, by the loss of his position as heir to the
throne, and the Earl used his office as Warden of the
Marches to carry on a fresh intrigue with England.
That country just then was not in case, however, to
do much against James.   Cade's rebellion in 1450 had
embarrassed the government, and Suffolk had gone
to the block in the same year, leaving Somerset in
alliance with the Queen, and York's power increasing
steadily against both, for the loss of Normandy had
badly tarnished Somerset's reputation : and before
Douglas's return to Scotland, Dunois was leading an
army against Guyenne, which had been English for
almost three hundred years.   On Midsummer Eve
he rode into Bordeaux, and England concentrated her
resources for a counter-invasion in the following year.

Douglas, however, felt little need of York's help.
The ὕβρις of his house had seized him again.   He took
on himself the circumstance of a king, holding something like a Parliament of his own, and forbidding his
people to attend King James's.   More, he defied the
King by open violence, taking pleasure, it seemed, to
shatter the new laws.   Herries of Terregles, a friend
of the King's, tried to recover stolen property from a
man of Douglas's.   Douglas captured him, and in face
of the King's direct order for his release, hanged him.
Sandilands of Calder and two other gentlemen of the

name of Stewart, again the King's friends, were murdered on the road by Douglas men ; and Douglas himself, in the very streets of Edinburgh, fell on the Chancellor Crichton : Crichton escaped . . . and so did Douglas, flagrantly unpunished. Then King James received definite evidence at last of Douglas's band with Crawford and John of the Isles, which he probably had suspected by this time, and knew that unless he acted very promptly half the armed force of the kingdom would be against him : and Douglas chose that moment to fill his cup, by his most cynical audacity.

He called up his vassals to resist the King. MacLellan, the Tutor of the young laird of Bombie, refused, and Douglas, having taken his castle, carried him as a prisoner to Thrieve. Now MacLellan was nephew of Sir Patrick Gray, the Captain of the King's Guard. Gray was sent by the King to Thrieve, with a royal message, requesting Douglas to hand over MacLellan. He rode to Thrieve (it must have required some courage) and presented himself. The Earl received him with civility, quoted the old proverb about its being ill talking between a full man and a fasting, hospitably refused to discuss any business until his guest had eaten . . . and gave orders that were not all for refreshments. Gray ate his dinner, and produced the King's letter : Douglas replied with ready courtesy that the prisoner should be put at his disposal, led him out to the courtyard, and offered him MacLellan—wanting the head, which had been removed while his uncle sat at meat. Gray kept his own, and civilly withdrew, but his self-control broke as the gates swung to behind him. He flung his gauntlet at the walls of Thrieve, cried his opinion of Douglas, and rode for his life.

He saved it, for luckily his horse was good. But Douglas had forced the King to a reckoning now. Still James continued to act with a curious patience for a young man of his fiery disposition. It may have been mere prudence, but all through his life he showed himself willing enough to face a danger. It is probable that, desiring the good of Scotland, he was holding back as long as he could contrive from plunging the country into more civil war, and trying for peaceful measures to the last ; and it is more than possible as well that he still felt a certain personal affection for the brilliant young Earl whose charm had dazzled him when he was a harried and bewildered boy, and recalled the horror of the October day when his new delightful friends were dragged to their death, in his name, and he had tried in vain to save them.

He sent for Douglas to Stirling. It was mid-winter. They say that the Earl demanded the King's safe-conduct, which was given, and on the 21st of February, he rode into Stirling Castle and supped with the King. For a while there was outward courtesy on both sides. After the meal was over, the two young men—the King was twenty-one, Douglas five years older—went to the King's cabinet with a little group of royal intimates, and James made a last attempt to win loyalty. Douglas replied with his common arrogance, and James played his last card. He revealed at last his knowledge of the band with Crawford and John of the Isles, and bade Douglas break it. The Earl curtly refused, and thereupon James's temper, fierce and deeply troubled for all that he cared for most, gave way of a sudden, and crying, ' If you will not break the band, my lord, this shall,' he drew his dagger, and struck. It released the anger of the rest : Gray, standing on guard by the door, and thinking no doubt of the last time he had met Douglas, flung forward and struck also with his pike, and the rest saw red and fell on with their drawn swords. Douglas's body was thrown from the window into the little garden on the ramparts, that looks out through high space to the greater wall of the hills, and there he was buried in haste, in an unsained grave.

James's immediate reaction was cold horror. They say, indeed, that he was so filled with it that he even spoke of giving up the struggle and flying as a refugee to France, for the war that he had striven to avoid was inevitable now by his own action, and he felt that by that same action, he was cursed. It was Kennedy who stiffened his resolution, brought him back to a sense of his duty as the King, and dispelled his hopelessness with the old apologue of the sheaf of arrows, unbreakable so long as they were tied, but easily snapped if one took them one by one.

James pulled himself together, and went to Perth to deal with the Earl of Crawford—the first arrow. Douglas's heir was his next brother James, the handsome stickit priest : he took up the feud. On the

17th of March he and his brothers rode into Stirling, where they fired the town, and dragged the King's safe-conduct, or so they said, at the tail of an old grey horse through the steep streets. Scotland was blazing now, and the war was a sharp one, but the King had allies. The Gordons of the North-east, where Albany had given them lands in Strathbogie, took arms for him against Crawford; and Gordon of Huntly (who had been made Earl half a dozen years before) was made the King's Lieutenant in the North. In May he defeated Crawford on Brechin Muir, so thoroughly that the Tiger as he fled vowed that he would take gladly seven years' hell for such a victory as his enemy's. Archibald Earl of Moray, the twin of the new Earl of Douglas, raided Huntly's lands. Huntly counter-raided Elgin, the chief town of Moray, burning that half of it which held for Douglas, and causing the proverb, 'Half done, as Elgin was burnt.' The two met at Dunkinty, and Huntly's force was cut up as the song bears witness :

> Faur left ye yir men,
> Gordon sae gay ?
> In the Bog o' Dinkinty,
> Mawin' the hay.

The Black Douglases tried to get Angus, the chief of the Red, to join them : he would not, and they besieged him in Dalkeith, while Countess Beatrice rode into England and offered the homage of her sons to Henry, as the price of his assistance against James.

It looked ill for the King, but when the Estates met

in June he found the soberer elements of the country were solidly and cheeringly behind him. Douglas's followers posted a defiance and an indictment of the King as traitor on the door of their hall the night before they met, and very probably it stiffened them. They were bidden to judge between the King and Douglas : and each Estate, meeting alone and with the King not present, exonerated James from breach of his safe-conduct, on the grounds that Douglas, the day before his death, had in public and with contempt renounced its protection . . . which is not by any means improbable. They also affirmed, in support of James's action, that the Douglases were in open revolt and guilty of conspiracy and oppression, wherefore he had a right to put them to death.

Many of the barons now were in arms for the King, whether from feuds with the Douglases and their supporters, or from real appreciation of his purpose. These were rewarded. Crichton's son and heir, James, was given Archibald Douglas's earldom of Moray, which was fair enough, as his wife was the elder daughter of the last earl, while Archibald, who had married her younger sister, had been given it over his head through Douglas influence. Crichton of Cairns received the earldom of Caithness, Hay the Constable was created Earl of Errol, and others had proportionate rewards. The King then—it was now the late summer of 1452—assembled an army on the Muir of Pentland, and marched by the easternmost of the Douglas lands to Dumfries.

James Douglas, finding most of Scotland against him after all, and solid for the King, surrendered now. He formally forgave his brother's death, gave up his claims upon the earldom of Wigtown, and undertook to dissolve all illegal bands, to pay compensation for the goods he had seized, and to execute his duty as the Warden. The rebellion being thus broken in the South, James at once showed a surprising leniency. He not only gave Douglas back the earldom of Wigtown, but actually agreed as well to forward the granting of a dispensation enabling him to marry his brother's widow, Margaret, the Fair Maid of Galloway, and her lands. (The Papal dispensation was granted at the end of the next February, the grounds being non-consummation of the first marriage.) Margaret, apparently, was unwilling, and all Scotland was scandalised by the ugly match, for since she was by this time about twenty, the grounds of the dispensation were not believed : but the poor young Countess was not allowed a choice. The great Douglas lands were duly united again, and Earl James might now revive, by right of his wife, the claims of Queen Euphemia's descendants. King James's consent to the marriage is in fact, on several separate grounds, so very strange that one can only imagine it must have been granted on some hot penitent impulse of reparation for the death of Douglas's brother in the past spring.

The early months of 1453 saw the King north of Tay. The Douglases were the backbone of disaffection, and now they were gone he had an easy task.

P

John of the Isles made terms, and was well received : the King was fair-minded enough to admit frankly that the lacking dowry gave him a real grievance. The Tiger-earl, left alone, surrendered also : he came to James humbly in rags, and begged for pardon, and his old enemy Huntly interceded. James had sworn a vow to take Finhaven Castle and make the highest stone of it the lowest : he kept his vow, but by climbing the castle tower and throwing a stone from the coping into the moat, and Crawford was pardoned and gave no more trouble for the few months of life that were left him thereafter.

Since the drive against Douglas in the previous summer the affairs of the kingdom had been fairly quiet. The Estates met, and went about their work, the administration was getting into harness. It is possible that the *tumultis and cumberis* had again caused some scarcity, for in 1452 there is another statute against hoarding food to wait for a rise in prices, and in July of 1454 the rather suggestive clause appears in another, that *strangeris that bringis in wittalis be fauorably tretyt and thankfully payit for thair wittalis.* Foreign affairs had been quiet for some years now, except that in 1452 James had had to intervene once more—though only by peaceful diplomatic means—in Brittany on behalf of his little nieces. Now the English situation took a turn that threatened serious disturbance in that country, or as a possible alternative, the resumption of war abroad, which would almost certainly mean war with Scotland. During James's conflict with the Douglases the régime of his uncle Somerset in England had been growing steadily more unpopular, for the Guyenne expedition of 1452 had ended in absolute failure, and the next year the defeat and death of Talbot, the best English leader, at Châtillon, completed the reconquest of that great province. Thrice in three hundred years, once by marriage and twice by war, half of France had been English, and now there was nothing left but the town of Calais . . . and one heritage more from the conquests of Henry V, which was to become apparent in this year. The conqueror had married a daughter of mad King Charles : and within a few months of the loss of his last conquests, the taint of that madness darkened his son's mind. In August the gentle and devout young monarch became, quite suddenly, helpless and witless as the infant son who was born to him two months later : he had to be fed with a spoon and lifted to bed. With the King gone, Somerset went down at once. York, made Protector, had him impeached and imprisoned in the Tower. The birth of the Prince had cut York out of that line of the succession that admitted the King's own claim legitimate : it sharpened his personal feud with Queen Margaret, who left alone, was fierce for her son's rights, and it threw him back on his claim through Anne Mortimer, which allowed him a senior place to King Henry himself, with no need to wait on the latter's death for his heirship, no ambiguous place in relation to Somerset.

At this point Douglas renewed the intrigues of his house.   He sent Lord Hamilton[1] into England to propose some kind of agreement now with York : the Duke offered help if Douglas would swear allegiance ; and Hamilton, who was kin to Kennedy and nephew of the pardoned Livingstone, and, as events were to show a little later, inclining nowadays to favour James, refused to promise anything of the sort.   Perhaps eventually through Hamilton, whose uncle was his Master of the Household, James came to hear of the matter.   He had forgiven, and forgiven again.   Now he determined that he would make an end.

He promptly raised the forces of the North, stormed and destroyed Inveravon, marched to Glasgow, and reinforced by a strong body of Highlanders, swept through Douglasdale and Avondale, while Orkney and Angus besieged the Douglas strength of Abercorn. The whole power of the Black Douglas blazed up against him, from Thrieve by Solway to Darnaway in Elgin.   Douglas collected what is said to be a force of 40,000—a quite impossible figure, but he was certainly in apparent great strength—and marched to relieve Abercorn.   Perhaps through the influence of Livingstone or Kennedy, or both, Lord Hamilton now attempted to check Douglas, who told him he could do

[1] The husband of Douglas's mother-in-law, Euphemia Graham, Countess Dowager of Douglas, sister of Malise of Strathearn.   He was one of the earliest benefactors of Glasgow University, leaving it a gift of property on the condition that the masters and students should pray daily for the souls of himself, his wife, and all from whom he had received any benefit that he had been unable to return.

well enough without him. Hamilton took him at his word, and went, and the King received him and offered mercy to others who should surrender. They remembered then how he had treated Crawford, John of the Isles, the Earl of Douglas himself, and the brother he was claiming to revenge : few men trusted James Douglas, and many were coming to trust and like James Stewart. They chose for the Lion Rampant against the Heart, and Douglas's force dissolved like snow in the sun. He fled west, and his brothers : the three latter, all of them young men still in their twenties, and Ormond once the victor of the Sark, rallied broken men and tried to make a stand. Angus sought for them with troops from the East March (that time begins the rise of the Scotts of Buccleuch) and on the May Day of 1455 he came on them in the smooth glen of Arkinholm, and the Red Douglas had put down the Black. Moray fell, and his head was sent to the King as token. Ormond, wounded, was captured, and his wounds patched up till he was able to go in form to the scaffold. Balveny got off, joined his brother in Argyle, and went to seek a refuge with John of the Isles.

On the ninth of June, the Estates condemned the two, and their mother Countess Beatrice, as traitors, to death and forfeiture. Douglas, still in the Isles, attempted a last wild throw. He had won over his old ally again. John raised five thousand men and a hundred galleys, and sent them, under Black Donald Balloch of Islay and the Glens of Antrim, to raid the west coast. The raid was unsuccessful, and Douglas left the Isles for a shelter in England, where he was pleasantly received by York. He made trouble, on and off, for thirty years yet, but the power of the Black Douglas was broken for good, and King James, in token of his thankfulness, offered a candle containing a stone of wax in St Mary-in-the-Fields by Edinburgh, where in the reign of his great-great-grand-daughter, another more famous fire was to be kindled.

A little while after, the last of the Black Douglases, the unhappy young Countess Margaret, took refuge also, but at King James's court. He helped her to an annulment of her marriage, and married her instead to his half-brother, Sir John Stewart, whom he now made Earl of Athol; and her rejected spouse consoled himself with York's grand-daughter, Anne Holland of Exeter. Another unlucky lady, about this time, Elizabeth Livingstone, wife of John of the Isles, appealed to the King, and he gave her an honourable pension, and secured her from molestation by her husband.

The Estates met at Edinburgh in early August. They repeated their condemnation of *James umquhill Erle of Dowglas*, his mother and brother, correspondence with them being declared an act of treason. Then they took order to prevent a recurrence of the recent danger, and it is significant of popular feeling that the primary means they chose was to strengthen the Crown. The young King, it is clear, had made himself trusted.

Forsamekill as the pouerte of the crowne is oftymes the cause of the pouerte of the Realme and mony vthir inconuenientis, certain castles and lands, in strategic positions from Galloway to Inverness, were attached to the Crown, and the King had to swear that he would not alienate them.[1] The customs were granted to the King for life. To prevent a repetition of the Douglas ' Burgundian problem,' the Wardenship of the Marches was no longer to be hereditary, a clause to which one polite exception was added, in favour of one newly appointed Warden, Alexander Earl of March (later Duke of Albany) the King's second son, who was then about two years old. The Wardens were not to judge in cases of treason, nor any others that were in the dittay of a justice-ayre, and no regalities were to be granted in future, unless with the consent of the Estates. It is clear that Scotland was aiming at a strong central government, of Crown and Estates working in harmony, and in mutual responsibility, at the apex of an administrative structure responsible to the national authority, and not to any sort of local power.

Certain other provisions have a peaceful air, as of men settling cheerfully to reconstruction. The black and menacing shadow of Douglas was gone, the greater rebel lords had been taught a lesson, many ruffians

---

[1] They included Galloway; Ettrick Forest; the castle of Edinburgh with the royal domain in Lothian; Stirling Castle and the neighbouring Crown lands; Dumbarton Castle; the earldom of Fife, with Falkland; the earldom of Strathearn; the lordship of Brechin; the castles and lordships of Inverness, Urquhart, and Redcastle in the Black Isle.

were the better by a hanging, and peaceful people might carry on with their work. An embassy was appointed to the Pope. A sort of small debt court was devised for the burghs, to expedite justice for the poorer pursuers : eight or twelve men were to be appointed by the Privy Council, in burgh towns, to deal, within a week, with all matters involving under the sum of £5. They even took time to discuss elaborately the ceremonial for the Estates, arranging seating and appointing robes for the members and the officials, according to their rank.

Then a bomb burst suddenly on this peaceful scene, a splash out of the hell-broth then brewing in England. The summer there had been no less stormy, and without the promise of a settlement. Henry had recovered his wits on Christmas Day and the Queen procured the release of Somerset. In May, York had taken arms, and at St Albans he and his brother-in-law Salisbury, and Warwick, defeated the royal troops. King Henry's madness returned on him again, and York was once more in the saddle as Protector. Douglas fled to England shortly after that, and York proceeded to throw out a *ballon d'essai* by granting him a pension of £500, until he should be restored again to the lands ' taken from him by the man who calls himself the King of Scots,' *captas per ipsum dicentem seu vocantem se Regem Scotorum.* James, still endeavouring to keep peace with England, protested to Henry, with whom he had always been on friendly terms, that this treatment of another king's rebel vassal was unsatisfactory.

The reply was received while the August parliament was still in session : it may or may not have been dictated by York, but certainly he was responsible for it, since it bears the Great Seal of England : it is not signed, but is written in the name of Henry himself, who certainly had nothing to do with it, as his madness was a mere collapse into stupor, and showed no paranoiac elements. ' The King greets the illustrious Prince James, who calls himself King of Scots (*se pro Rege Gerenti*). It is true and notorious that the supreme and direct dominion over the kingdom of Scotland belongs by law to the Kingdom of England. . . . In the same way, fealty and homage are due from the King of Scots, as a vassal, to the King of England as his overlord, since from times whose beginning is outside man's memory even to the present, we and our ancestors the Kings of England have possessed such rights.' James's letters, *plenas Jactantiae, Levitatis, et Contumeliae* (the use of capitals all through is amusing) have been presented by a certain person ' who calls himself your Lyon Herald and King of Arms.' James is informed that he and his subjects, ' disregarding the Sacred Obligation of an Oath, the Law of Nations, and the Faith of a Truce,' have injured ' Us and Our Subjects by more Crimes, Wrongs, Rapines, Thefts, and Insults than can be easily numbered '—*vos vestrique contra Religionem Jurisjurandi atque contra Jus gentium et Fidem Treugarum Nos et Nostros tot Dolis, tot Injuriis, Rapinis, Latrociniis et Contumeliis quae facile numerari non possunt.* ' We assure you as a fact ' (*illud autem ad Notitiam vestram pro certo deducimus*) 'that We are not merely not Frightened by such Boasting and Insolence, in which Cowards and Sluggards are wont to take great delight, but altogether Despise them : wherefore, since we are wounded by vast Wrongs and Insults, we mean strongly to repress and severely to punish your Insolence, Rebellion, Arrogance, and rash Attacks, of which the Highest is witness (*savente Altissimo*). We hope, none the less, as becomes a Christian Prince, that Our Lord Jesus Christ will turn you from Error to the path of Truth and Justice, and give you a Spirit of more wholesome Judgment.' That is the end, except for the Great Seal of England.

What the Estates said to it is not on record. James adjourned them, to meet again in mid-October, sent the Bishop of Galloway to Charles of France to suggest simultaneous attacks on Berwick and Calais, and apparently appointed a commission to overhaul the defences of the Border. Charles, who was having trouble with his son, that was to make more with Burgundy very shortly, declined to act. The Estates, meeting again, dealt vigorously with the question of frontier defence. An elaborate system of beacons was established, to run from the fords of the Tweed as far as Fife, each lighting at sight of the other across the country.

' A baile is warnyng of thair comyng quhat powere that evir thai may be of. Twa balis togidder at anis thay ar coming in deide. Four balis ilkane besyde vthir and all at anys as four candillis salbe suthfast knalege that they ar of gret powere.'

(Can one not see men standing at their house doors and watching a sudden spark light in the hills—' One . . . two . . . three . . . four, by God ! Gudewife, rax me my spear and cry to the lads to saddle.') Other provisions were made at the same time. Three garrison posts were arranged, one for each March, presumably as *points de ralliement* for royal troops. Berwick and Roxburgh were no longer to be supplied with provisions. No Scot was to cross the Border in time of war without the King's leave, and no Englishman without a Warden's passport.

After it all, the threatened war came to nothing. James led a force into England in the next autumn, but Henry recovered as suddenly as before : York had to let him go, and James, who was fighting York rather than England, offered truce, which after a certain amount of delay was concluded in the following July, of 1457, to last for two years. One observes that again one of the envoys is a burgess of Edinburgh.

The Estates had met at Edinburgh once more, in the previous October, of 1456. They were still concerned with defence, but the tone is cheerful : they report on the Border provisions described above, but think that the Borders now are better *cornyt* than when the arrangements were made. At the same time, they revived the Arming Acts : all men from sixteen to sixty are to be ready at need to march to the Border, but no *pure man na unbodyn* (*i.e.*, not fully armed) is compelled to cross it. The standard of accoutrement is much that of the earlier acts, but it seems that they had observed the notable achievement of the French artillery under the brothers Bureau, at the taking of Cherbourg and at Châtillon. Certain of the great barons are to provide *cartis of weir*, with two cannon of two chambers on each, and to see also to the training of the gunners.

Most of the work, however, was significantly peaceful. The clergy brought forward a revision of the Plague Regulations : stricken men who had means of subsistence were not to be turned out of their houses by force, but to be isolated at home if they preferred. The Court of Session was reported on, and a great deal of work was done about the coinage. The Estates had already, in 1451, drawn up an elaborate scheme for a new issue, and for regulation of the rate of exchange. A new silver grote was to be struck, twice the value of the old : the English grote was to circulate at par, but the English penny was not legal tender unless the recipient chose. A new gold *lion* was struck, worth 6s. 8d. in the new coinage : the old *demy* was to circulate at a reduced value. The French *réal*, *salute*, and *écu* equalled a lion ; the English noble, two lions; the Flemish noble, 12s. 8d., etc. Now they revised this, having found that the values had been fixed too low : the new lion, in fact, was worth more than its face value as bullion, so it was raised to 10s. and the grote to 12d., with a corresponding revision of rates of exchange. The elaborate detail of the statute suggests a serious attempt at helping trade.

James's position by now had changed markedly

from that he had occupied at the time of his marriage. He was still only twenty-six, but his power a vigorous reality : he had brought his nobles to order, was loved by the commons and trusted by the Church : a Provincial Council, under the Bishop of Aberdeen, took the very significant step of admitting his right to present to benefices. Since the Burgundian treaty at his marriage he had done all he could to foster foreign trade : the merchants of Bremen and Dantzig were under his protection, and the municipalities of the East Coast were in constant communication with these cities, and with Koenigsberg, Stralsund, Elbing, Lubeck, and Hamburg, while the recovery of France and her peculiarly intimate and friendly relation with Scotland no doubt helped trade there, the more as the wine-ports were in French hands again. The increasing prosperity that marks the fifteenth century is shown in the wave of fine building, religious and still more secular, that repairs the desolations of the fourteenth : a characteristically Scottish architecture, of severe and masculine beauty that lifts into an arrogant crown of adornment, has developed, akin to French, but graver and more harsh, between the climate and the hard local stone.

During the later 'fifties the balance of foreign relations had altered a little. James put forward a claim to Saintonge, which had been one of the terms of his sister's marriage. Charles yielded it, and intervened to smoothe down relations with Scandinavia, which were somewhat strained, as not only was the rent for the Isles in arrears, but a son of the Lieutenant of

Iceland had been seized by the Scots authorities and imprisoned : the matter was peaceably adjusted, however, and led to a close rapprochement in the next reign. A treaty with Henry, King of Castile and Leon, brought the Scots alliances over the breadth of Europe. There was some tension between Savoy and France : the Duke took offence, and as a gesture against Charles, the sister of his ally was divorced and sent home. Princess Annabel had no liking for her husband, and Savoy, except as an ally of France, was unimportant : James assented, securing her a jointure of 25,000 crowns, and married her to the heir of the useful Huntly, Princess Jean, who returned with her, sharing a stormy crossing, being bestowed at the same time on James Douglas of Dalkeith, who was made Earl of Morton.[1]

There was occasional strife yet with the nobles. John of the Isles surrendered in 1457, and gave no more trouble for the rest of the reign. Crawford was dead, and Douglas was in exile. Robert Erskine, however, who laid claim to Mar, had died in 1453, leaving a son, and the latter now proceeded to press the claim. At the end of 1457 the case was heard in Aberdeen, before a jury who decided for James : and Erskine withdrew, and made no attempt to take arms.[2]

[1] He represented the younger line of Andrew, brother of that William Longleg who was ancestor of the Black and Red Douglases.

[2] Mar had reverted to the Crown on the death of Alexander Stewart in 1435. Erskine claimed it through his mother, who was declared to be great-grand-daughter, by an entirely female line, of Earl Gartney, brother-in-law of Robert I. In 1440 the government promised an investigation, but Crichton postponed it till the King should be of age.

By the time he reached his twenty-seventh birthday, King James was in an even stronger position than his father had been the year before his death. The dynasty seemed secure : he had already three sons and a couple of daughters. (There seems to have been a third, who died an infant.) The young Prince David, Earl of Moray, died, but another son, John, created Earl of Mar, was born to the King in 1459. Both the Crown and Scotland were stronger than they had been since the death of Bruce. James, having taken up his father's task, and succeeded brilliantly on one side of it, now set to work at the other, to increase the prosperity of a pacified Scotland. The parliament of 1458 shows a great deal of vigorous legislation. Both internal and external defence are considered : the nobles agree that no bands are to be made, and no burgesses either are to *ride nor rowt in feir of weir*, save with the King or his officers, while wapinschaws are to be held, and archery is eagerly encouraged. Bowyers and fletchers are to be established in every county town, and butts set up at every parish kirk, and used after service on Sunday, when every able-bodied man is to shoot at least six rounds, the absentees being fined at least twopence, which fines shall be spent in drinks for the law-abiding : and *the fut ball and the golf* are to be *vttirly cryit downe and nat vsit*. Most of the measures, however, are more peaceful. The regulations for the Court of Session are gone into, and its duties and powers defined. Freeholders under £20 are excused from attendance at the Estates. Land tenures are overhauled, and farmers given increased security. There are many statutes for the encouragement of agriculture. The planting of trees and hedges is encouraged : all fences are to be quickset. A standard minimum is set up for cultivation of the acre. Muirburn is regulated. Wild birds are protected in the nesting season, except the destructive ones, such as crows : war is declared on these, and on wolves also, and close seasons enforced for fish, hares, and rabbits. A commission was appointed for the inspection of hospitals, the terms of the remit including inspection of foundation deeds with a view to seeing whether their terms were kept. Uniformity of weights and measures was enacted, and all goldsmith's work must be inspected and stamped by the Dean of Guild. Prosperity was sufficiently recovered for the nobles to feel the need of a sumptuary law. Silk, scarlet, and marten's fur were disallowed to the commons, unless they were bailies or other officers, an exception which shows the rising status of both the civil service and the municipalities. Their wives were to wear short curches or little hoods, and no trains. Labourers on working days must wear grey or white, though on holidays they might prank in green, red, or light blue : and women who appeared in public with covered faces were to lose their coifs. The whole record ends on a note of cheerful hope, an appeal to the King to go on as he has begun,

> sene gode of his he grace has send our souerane lorde sik progress and prosperitee that all his rebellys and brekaris of his

Justice are removit out of his realme and na maisterful party remenand that may cause ony breking in his Realme.

In well under three years from that cheerful parliament, James was lying in Holyrood where he had been crowned. The incessant menace of England was renewed : about the time when this parliament was sitting, York and Henry, who had again recovered his wits, effected a brief and hollow reconciliation, and the weak Henry was easily swayed by the Duke. Although the last truce had still more than a year to run, a strong English force, whose leaders included Douglas, raided the Marches. Angus defeated them, with considerable slaughter, and before York could force Henry into a war, the two of them had quarrelled again. York raised his standard at Ludlow, and was joined by his allies, Salisbury and Warwick, and Henry hurriedly renewed the broken truce.

James accepted, and agreed to extend it now for four years longer. There may have been secret negotiations also, for he had already shown himself willing to support his mother's family against York, whose accession was certainly not in Scottish interests : and Henry was in bitter need of help. Bishop Leslie affirms that he offered James Northumberland and Durham for assistance : there is no contemporary evidence, and the Bishop was writing over a hundred years later : but he had access to official documents, so there may be a certain basis for the statement. At all events, James moved, and clearly in concert with the Lancastrian party. All through the summer of 1459,

Q

the Yorkists, in spite of the official truce, had been creating disturbance on the Border. James crossed with an army in August, and marched to Durham, capturing seventeen fortalices in a week. Meanwhile, however, Henry's luck was turning. The indecisive action at Bloreheath in early September was followed by the desertion of much of York's army. He fled to Ireland, and Warwick and Salisbury to France, so that Henry, now apparently triumphant, called off his ally. James agreed and withdrew, sending an embassy with congratulations.

It was the unhappy Henry's last good fortune. Next June, the rebel earls landed in Kent. The county rose for them, and they entered London. At Northampton the next month the royal troops were heavily defeated, and Henry was prisoner. Queen Margaret, with the little Prince of Wales, got away, and fled for safety to King James.

He received her kindly, and took immediate action. It is probable that he had mobilised as soon as he had heard of the Kent landing, for he was able to move at once. Northampton was fought on the 7th of July, and by the 3rd of August, though he had not actually crossed the Border, he was in front of the town of Roxburgh. It had been held by the English, except for brief intervals, since Neville's Cross, and the Governor was Lord Fauconberg, a strong Yorkist. James decided not to leave it in his rear. He sat down before it. Huntly and Angus were with him, and he was joined there also by John of the Isles, who offered to lead his men a mile in advance of the rest on the road into England. The siege-train of artillery had come up, and on the 3rd King James went to look on at the firing of a great Flemish piece of his father's. It burst, and a fragment struck him in the groin, breaking his thigh. When they took him up, he was dead. It was some ten weeks before his thirtieth birthday.

HERE
ENDS
CHAPTER
VIII

CHAPTER IX

THE MINORITY OF JAMES III : 1460–69

'O navis, referunt in mare te novi
Fluctus. O quid agis ? '
Horace, *Odes*, I, xiv.

THE news of King James's death was sent to the Queen, and she received it with courage and resolution, acting at once, and boldly. She brought her nine-year-old son, now King, to where the army lay before Roxburgh, and so inspirited her dead husband's troops that the town was taken, and the army passed on to storm and demolish the strong place of Wark.

On the 10th of August, a week from his father's death, the little King James was crowned in Kelso Abbey. Perhaps the hundred knights made on the occasion may have thought that this coronation in the field augured a king who would follow his father's course. The child's guardianship was given not to Kennedy, as might have been expected, or to Angus, but to Queen Marie, an able, strong-willed woman, still in her twenties : and it seems that she took upon herself at once to act not only as guardian to her son, but, with Kennedy behind her, as the Regent. There was immediate discontent. Marie was young and foreign and feminine, and according to the Asloan Chronicle, the lords declared that *thai war litill gud*

244

worth, baith spirituale and temporall, that gaf the kepyng of the kinrik till a woman—a woman whose first act was to dismiss the governors of Edinburgh, Stirling, and Dumbarton, and replace them with men chosen by herself. Through the first winter of the new reign, however, the most pressing questions were foreign, not domestic. The condition of English politics had given a new twist to an old problem. Apart from James II's kinship to Henry and Somerset, and their always friendly attitude to Scotland, York's accession would be a very positive menace. It was York who had been responsible for the wild communiqué of 1455 : and two years later its claims had been supported, perhaps at York's instigation, certainly with his approval, by an extraordinary series of forged documents intended to give a colour of legality to a new English attempt at the conquest of Scotland. Their actual author was one John Hardyng of Kyme, writer of a famous *Metrical Chronicle* of English history.[1] He produced no fewer than eight *pièces de conviction*—a homage of Malcolm III, an admission by David II of homage by Alex-

[1] He had also composed a rhymed description of Scotland, addressed to his sovereign and written avowedly as a guide-book for English troops. ' Good country,' ' pleasant grounde and fruitfull country,' ' plentifull countrey,' and so forth are explicitly given as indications of the best places to loot. East of Brechin is ' a goodly porte and haven for your (the English) navye.' Another district is ' a good countree for your armye and plenteous.' Another is ' a pretye town alway, And plentifull also of good vitayle For all your army,' while another section begins ' And when ye have that lande hole conquered, returne agayne unto Strivelyne.' It is filled with loving anticipation of *Der Tag.*

ander I, four acknowledgments of David's own, and two more of Robert II's : he clearly had taken pains to make a really artistic job of it, for not only did he attempt archaic language and calligraphy, but declared he had brought the documents from Scotland at the risk of his life and a cost of 450 marks, and supported the tale by forging a safe-conduct from King James, who, he declared, had offered him 1,000 marks for the papers! The forgeries are in fact sufficiently clumsy, as he was not scientific enough to fake either the language or the writing, and had muddled the dates and the heraldry of the seals. But the English Parliament, not being antiquarians, had quite sufficient grounds for sincerely believing what it seemed in their interest to believe. Whether Henry believed or not, he refused to act, pensioning Hardyng for his pains, but doing nothing further. It was probable that he would continue to do so : but if York should be victor, the documents had explosive possibilities.

He was : by the end of October he forced Henry to a form of reconciliation, and to accept him as heir. Queen Margaret, with the young disinherited Prince, fled to Dumfries, and at Lincluden Abbey was entertained for twelve days as a guest of King James. There was discussion : the record has disappeared, but it seems that Margaret attempted to marry her son to the elder of James's sisters, Princess Mary. The match was refused, but the Scots gave some promise of help. Margaret returned, raised the North, and marched towards London to set free her husband. On almost the last day of 1460, her army met York's at Wakefield and broke it to pieces. York and his young son Rutland both were taken : the boy fell to Clifford's dagger and York to the axe, leaving his claim to his son Edward Earl of March.

In three months, Edward met Henry's army at Towton and defeated it bloodily in a raging snow-storm. Henry, set free by Wakefield, fled to Scotland with his Queen, and offered Carlisle and Berwick for Scottish help. On the 25th April, the St Andrew's Cross flew over Berwick once more, and a Scottish force set about the siege of Carlisle. Edward coun-tered by the old expedient, sending Douglas and Balveny to John of the Isles. The siege of Carlisle was a failure, but the threat induced Edward, at the beginning of August, to appoint the Earl of Warwick to treat for truce. Nothing was done at the moment, and a fresh appointment was made in early November ... and in between these two dates, on the 19th October, the Bishop of Durham and the Prior of the Hospital had met John of the Isles and Donald Balloch of Islay at Ardtornish, and the latter had signed a treaty drafted in England,[1] to which the Douglases were consenting parties. They undertook to serve Edward in any Scots war, John receiving a retainer of 100 marks a year *for Fees and Wage in tyme of Pees*, to be raised to £200 sterling during war service, while Donald was granted a fifth of these sums. If the war should succeed, they were to receive the whole realm

[1] This is clear from the language, which is ' English English.'

beyond the Scottishe See (*i.e.*, the Forth) to be held, in equal shares, of the English Crown, while Douglas, on similar terms, was to regain his old lands in the South. And there is a very significant proviso that John shall have the option of standing out of any Anglo-Scots truce.

The threat of dismemberment was made more serious by the growth of differences at Court. Tension between France and Burgundy, which was friendly to the Yorkists, and perhaps some reluctance to spend men and funds in supporting what was plainly a lost cause, were inducing the half-Burgundian Queen Marie, though scandal coupled her name with Somerset's, to a rapprochement with Edward : and a party of the younger nobles backed her. In April of 1462, Queen Margaret sailed from Kirkcudbright and went to France, to beg the support of the new king, Louis XI, who had acceded in the previous summer, and whose secret, intricate and able mind presented to the politics of Europe a series of difficult new problems. She offered Calais, and he gave her two thousand men under Pierre de Brézé, who landed at Bamborough. A Scots force moved to their help, commanded by Angus, but before he could get in touch, Edward and Warwick drove the Queen back to her ships, and shut Brézé up in Alnwick. Angus cut him out under the noses of Edward's men, but nothing effective was done, and Margaret had to return to France again. Douglas harried the Marches, in company with his brother : the latter was caught and executed, but there was a worse danger in the North, where John had come out and was claiming sovereign power, taking Inverness and proclaiming through the Sheriffdoms of Inverness and Nairn that Crown rents and customs were to be paid to himself.

His action may have helped to bring down the Queen. Her coquetting with York—it was said that Warwick proposed she should marry Edward—was proving dangerous, and her personal reputation was affected by further scandal (whether true or false does not matter much in practice) which made Adam Hepburn, Master of Hailes, her lover.[1] In July of 1462, rather less than two years after her husband's death, the Estates decided that the King and she should in future have separate households : he might remain with her, but she was not to interfere in the Government, where Kennedy succeeded her as Regent. She took no further share in politics, and died towards the end of the next year, being buried in Trinity College that she had founded.[2]

Kennedy had continued the policy of his uncle and his cousin, of friendship with Lancaster : but even he was loth to embark by now on a war on two fronts to help a clearly hopeless foreign cause. In the autumn

---

[1] The great-great-grandfather of Mary's Bothwell.

[2] In Edinburgh, the architect's name being commemorated by Halkerston's Wynd. It was one of the collegiate churches in which that century was prolific, with a provost and eight prebendaries, and a ' hospital ' attached for thirteen poor. It survived the Reformation almost unharmed, and was razed at last to make room for the North British Railway.

of 1463 he was decided. France and England made
truce. He decided to follow King Louis's example,
and to acknowledge the *status quo* in England, making
a brief truce for negotiations. Before it was over, the
indomitable Margaret had made another landing, and
in May had been defeated again at Hexham. A
month later there were suggestions of an English
marriage for the little King, and by autumn commissioners had been appointed to treat for a *perpetua
et realis Pax et Concordia*. This was not achieved, but
the truce was extended to autumn of 1479.

This staunching of the war and the establishment
of at least nominally friendly terms with the new
English dynasty was the last work of Bishop Kennedy.
He died on the 10th of May 1465, and even Buchanan,
that bitter foe to bishops, declares that the country
wept him like a father. The King was not quite
fourteen, and there seems to have been either slackness
or suppression in the matter of appointing a new
Regent : one can scarcely say whether it was or was
not good fortune that there was no one outside the
royal house to stand in Douglas's position in the last
minority, for the heirs presumptive were the King's
two young brothers.

For a little the boy ruled nominally alone, but the
situation was too tempting. In the February after the
Bishop's death, the usual features of a minority
began to develop. The dead bishop's brother, Lord
Kennedy, Keeper of Stirling, made a band with Robert

Fleming of Cumbernauld, and with Alexander Boyd, Governor of Edinburgh Castle, and Military Tutor to the young King. Fleming agreed to uphold the other two as custodians of the King : and closely linked with them were Crawford, Montgomery, Hamilton, and a churchman, Lord Kennedy's half-brother, Patrick Graham. In July the alliance went into vigorous action. The King was at an Exchequer Court at Linlithgow. Boyd, in arms, with Lord Somerville, Hepburn of Hailes, and Ker of Cessford, invaded the court and forced the King to mount, and carried him, virtually prisoner, to Edinburgh.

Boyd's raid was technical, if not actual, treason. His first move was therefore to put himself right with the law. It is probable that the retiring and gentle boy who was his pupil was easy to influence, by either coercion or cajolery, and that the episode which ensued had been well stage-managed. The Estates met in Edinburgh in early October, with James presiding. Boyd appeared, threw himself at the King's feet, and begged him then to declare before the Estates whether he was displeased by the raid on Linlithgow. The lad said that he had gone with him of his free will : and a formal pardon under the Great Seal was drawn up at once. More, Boyd was made the Regent, was given the custody of the royal children, and the castles also were delivered to him.

For a little while he was at the head of affairs. His brief rule, while it lasted, was not oppressive, though some of the statutes of this parliament, for which his party were presumably responsible, were of dubious wisdom : and he achieved the final exorcism of the last ghost of the old Norwegian danger.

The parliament which settled him in power had an active session, touching many aspects of the national life. A committee of lords was appointed, with full parliamentary powers, till the next meeting of the Estates, to judge all who held castles against the King and his brother. There was an attempt made to prevent abuse of the practice of giving bail against breaches of peace, *borrows-breaking* to be punished by an amercement of £100 for a lord or prelate, £50 for a knight or great clerk, and so on downwards. A statute of Robert I was re-enacted, forbidding the holding of any benefice, whether ecclesiastical or secular, by an Englishman. Another, forbidding the holding of ecclesiastical ones *in commendam* (*i.e.*, by an absentee, perhaps a layman, who drew the revenues) strikes at a growing abuse, whose scandalous increase was one of the causes of the Reformation—and strikes, unfortunately, in vain. Hospitals were to be reformed, and due provision made for *failzit creatouris*. There was also much of the currency legislation that was one of the major pre-occupations of Parliament all through this reign. The usual scarcity of specie shows in a fresh prohibition of the export of money, and an enactment that merchants of hides and wool-fells exported abroad must bring home two ounces of *birnt siluer* for each sack, to be sold at a fixed price to the Master of the Mint. The exchange rates of certain new English coins were fixed, and an innovation was made : the coinage had hitherto been of gold or silver, of varying finenesses, but now they decided to issue copper farthings, *for the eise and sustentation of the kingis liegeis and almous deide to be doune to pure folk*—a foreshadowing of the collection threepenny bit, familiar to churchwardens and elders ! This suggests there had been a decided fall in prices, requiring coins of a lower value than the silver pieces.

The parliament of the following January is again much concerned with commercial legislation, which is discussed in great detail. The growing power of the burghs shows in a statute that foreign trade is now to be restricted to free burgesses resident in burghs, and their factors and servants. Even a burgess, to engage in it, must be *famouse and worschipful* (*i.e.*, of good reputation) and own at least half a last of goods. An exception is made in favour of barons, prelates and clerks, who may set ventures on foot,[1] but no handicraftsman or artisan is to trade unless he renounces his craft. Specialisation, of course, and to a high degree, was one of the main notes of mediaeval civilisation : the purpose of these restrictions, probably, was to prevent the compromise of Scottish credit by wild-cat ventures insufficiently backed with capital, but it is obvious that such a statute might lead to the forming of a close and exclusive merchant class, who would make a solid *bloc* in the body politic. The

---

[1] Some of the Border abbeys were among the chief exporters of wool.

machinery of foreign trade received a complex mass of regulation. There is much on the subject of the ' staple ' goods : a close season was enacted for their export, and they were forbidden to be sent to Sluys, Bruges, the Swyn, or ' the Dam,' but must go to Middelburgh, which was to act for the time as the staple town (*i.e.*, the Continental clearing-house for certain major exports) until a new staple could be fixed, by a commission appointed for the purpose, at the port which offered the most satisfactory terms. General trade, outside the staple commodities, was to be free to all French and Norwegian ports. To regularise the business of distribution, none of the King's lieges might freight a ship without formal charter-party (the word is used) or agreement with its owner as to terms : and shipmasters were obliged to provide their passengers with fire, water, and salt.

It is clear that Boyd was thus continuing the domestic policy of the two previous reigns : the comparative absence of attempts at disturbance by the greater nobles shows the increasing power of the central government, as these statutes reveal increasing prosperity. His own power seemed well established, and likely to last : a few months after this parliament, about Easter, it was apparently consolidated by the marriage of his son and heir Thomas, then created Earl of Arran, to Princess Mary, the elder of the King's sisters, while Boyd himself, already Justiciar, was made Chamberlain. He had raised himself from a country gentleman to a position at the head of affairs, and a

close connection with the royal house. His brilliance
was meteoric, and to go soon and suddenly into darkness, but before it ended he was to achieve one notable
matter, in a settlement of a very old dispute and an
alliance with an old enemy who appeared at the moment
to be rising to a place of great power in the North of
Europe.

The Union of Kalmar in 1397 had peacefully fede-
rated the three Scandinavian kingdoms under the
brilliant Margaret, 'the Union Queen': her death
had nearly brought about a disruption, but by 1457
Christian of Oldenburg had drawn the Triple Kingdom
together again, and three years later had peaceably
added Schleswig and Holstein to it. Scots relations
with Norway had been actually quiet for two hundred
years now, but with intervals of tension that might
more than once have led to another Norse war, and
perhaps an attempt at recovering the Isles. Just about
this time there was what is politely called ' an incident ' :
the Bishop of Orkney, who was a Scot, was imprisoned
by the son of its Earl.[1] Protests were made : King
Christian raised the old question of the ' annual,' the
blench rent for the Western Isles arranged by James I,
which had been allowed to fall into arrears. The sum
involved was not considerable, but questions of
prestige made for ill-temper : there had already been
somewhat strained relations in the last years of James II,

[1] The earldom of Orkney had been for three generations in the
hands of the Scoto-Norman house of Sinclair : but they held it as a
fief of the Crown of Norway.

when Charles VII, that steady and grateful friend of
Scotland, had intervened to smoothe the matter over.
Now Boyd returned to Charles's old suggestion of a
Scandinavian marriage. The young King was seventeen, and Christian had a daughter of thirteen. On
the 12th of January, 1468, the Estates appointed an
embassy to treat, each Estate making a free gift of
£1,000 for its expenses. Its heads were the Bishop
of Glasgow, the Bishop of Orkney, Lord Avondale,
who was Chancellor, and Arran, the brother-in-law
of the King and Boyd's son and heir. It is worthy
of remark that it was the Estates, not Boyd or the
King, who gave them *full power to mary and bring hame
a quene*, to which is added a light-hearted clause that
if Scandinavia should not after all consent, they might
make a circular tour of certain courts in order to seek
for a suitable royal lady : those specified are England,
France, Burgundy, Brittany (whose heiress was the
King's cousin), and rather surprisingly, Savoy.

The envoys did not have to make their tour of
inspection. Christian was trying at the time to
strengthen himself against his neighbour the Emperor :
the alliance with Scotland was worth having, both in
itself and as a link with France. Recent troubles in
Sweden had left him short of funds, and there was
difficulty over the dowry, but terms were agreed on at
last, and in September Arran returned with them.
The bride was to bring 60,000 Rhenish florins, of
which 10,000 were to accompany her, the important
strategic point of the Orkneys being pledged for the

balance. In fact, she brought with her only 2,000
florins, and the Shetlands were therefore added to the
pledge.

Arran returned in the spring, to fetch the bride. Her
portrait shows her scarcely beautiful, but with a gentle,
serious charm of bearing, borne out by the little that
is known of her : within a year of her death there were
proposals for her canonisation. She landed in July of
1469, and was married, with great pomp, at Holyrood,
on the 13th, a date whose ill-omen was to be fulfilled.

HERE
ENDS
CHAPTER
IX

R

CHAPTER X

JAMES III : 1469–88

' . . . Bellique causas et vitia et modos
Ludumque Fortûnae, gravesque
Principum amicitias, et arma
Nondum expiatis uncta cruoribus. . . . '
Horace, *Odes*, II, 1.

JAMES III was eighteen three days before his wedding, a spare, blackavised young man with a taste for the arts and for the more abstruse and fantastic side of learning : he was a student of mathematics and astrology, a lover of letters, and even more of music : the thing that led directly to his death was his provision for a choir of singers who should accompany him everywhere. A true Stewart in certain ways, he loved splendour and beauty, building much : one can trace a good deal of him in the list of his jewels, in the great serpent tongue set with precious stones, the ring with a toadstone and the unicorn's horn, and such glitter of the more splendid and less fantastic as the ouch of gold made like a rose of diamonds, the collar of rubies set with threes of pearl, or that other *of gold made like swannis, with rubeis and diamantis and viii quhite swannis set with double perle.*

There is something enigmatic about the man : it is difficult to arrive at the truth about him. On the one hand he is represented as turning from those who by

birth were his companions to waste his time with
mignons of base extraction, on the other as shutting
himself from uncultured boors in a tiny brittle paradise
of artists. Neither happens to be very accurate. The
circumstantial tales of his debauchery, of his neglect
of the Queen for his mistress ' the Daisy,' the darker
scandal of his relation with his sister Margaret, have
no evidence earlier than Buchanan, who was intensely
hostile to the Stewarts, and had a commodious power
of turning to slander events of his own time that he
knew at first hand : there are no records, either, of
any illegitimate children of his, any more than of his
father or his grandfather . . . while as for the opposite
picture, his favourites included a tailor and a fencing-
master, and though both occupations are highly
skilled, and both, in those days, were very necessary,
they hardly rank as branches of the fine arts. Looking
closer, one finds that Drummond was not far wrong
in declaring that he ' had too much of the *Stoical*
virtues, little of the *Heroical.*' He appears as a gentle,
sensitive young man, affectionate and avid of affection,
overshadowed by his brilliant younger brothers, not
unmindful of weighty responsibilities, but feeling them
burdensome on those quieter matters, of study and
arts and intimate friendship he cared for, conscious
of his own weakness to shoulder them, and shrinking
from men who made him feel that weakness to the
companionship of those whose position forced them
to depend on his will, on a will that called for no effort.
Yet there was some of the Stewart fire in him : the

growing lethargy of his later years—he was not quite thirty-seven when he was murdered—is due, one guesses, as much as anything to a strain of his great-grandfather's melancholy, well based on his betrayal by the brother whom he had loved and pertinaciously trusted . . . on the Stewart malady of a broken heart.

James, in spite of the weakness he was to show at times when his affections tangled with his will, was capable of energetic action : and as his father had done, he saw in his marriage the occasion to assert himself as King. Before his bride had come over the North Sea, he was already planning a *coup d'état*. He had submitted to Boyd's dominance when he was a child who could not help himself, but clearly it irked him, and he planned to win clear. He must have revealed some part of his intention, for before Arran, who brought the bride, had landed, his wife, Princess Mary, fled to him with a warning, and he turned his ship and went back with her to Denmark. The half-revelation may have given James pause, for he did not act at once : but in November, when the Queen was crowned, the Estates were convened to Edinburgh. The elder Boyds, suspecting what was coming, arrived with an armed force, but it melted away. Lord Boyd fled to England, where he died soon after, but the Regent, Alexander, was arrested, tried for the King's abduction three years before, and beheaded out of hand on the Castle Hill. Their great estates were annexed to the Principality of Scotland : one observes—it is the set-off to their genuine service—that they had got into their power the royal estates of the earldom of Carrick, the lordships of Bute and Renfrew, and the castle of Dundonald, all closely linked with the houses of Bruce and Stewart. Arran was out of reach, but was forfeited of his earldom. He went into the service of the late Queen's cousin, Charles of Burgundy, going as his ambassador to England : he died soon after, in 1473, and his widow, Princess Mary, returned to Scotland and was remarried, to Lord Hamilton, to whom her father had promised her as a child.[1]

The parliament which witnessed this violent reversal seems to show the young King setting affairs in order. Besides the chronic question of currency—the copper was already causing trouble, for foreign copper coins were barred as tender—there was vigorous administrative reform. A commission elected from all three Estates was to codify the laws, and provision was made for better control of the legal officers, with heavy penalties for *jugis ordinaris quhilk wil nocht execut thare office and minister Justice to the pure pepil.* Notaries and tabellions (the latter are ancestors of the Writers of the Signet) were to receive their qualification from the Crown, after due tests, and to take the place of the Imperial notaries, though those who held the Papal qualification were still allowed to practise. ' Purveying ' (forced levies of food, etc., by officials) was forbidden. Land tenures were overhauled, and the

---

[1] Their grandson was that Duc de Châtellerault who for a while was Queen Mary's heir-presumptive : and Lennox, Darnley's father, was their great-grandson by another line.

constitution of the legal courts. The privileges of sanctuary were discussed, with a view to the prevention of their abuses. There was an attempt to cope with the rowdiness of municipal elections, by the dubious method of letting the old Town Council elect the new one, while, rather significantly, no governor of a royal castle might hold municipal office at the same time : the burghs, as such, had become formidable, as indeed they proved with a vengeance in the next century, before the Religious Wars ruined Scottish trade. While the towns, like the trades, were developing into little oligarchies, there is evidence of the constant Stewart care for the mass of the people, the peasantry on the land, who were the bone and sinew of the country. *Pure men inhabitaris of the ground* were no longer to be distrained on for their landlord's debt, beyond the sum actually due to him as rent : if the debt amounts to more than the rents owing, distraint must be made on the landlord's other goods, and if he has none, the land itself may be sold, the tenants' rights being guarded by earlier statutes. In the last case, however, the debtor has a seven years' option of reclaiming the land by paying the purchase price. A small provision shows the same humanity : the poinding of bestial for arrears of rent must not be done at the actual terms of Martinmas and Whitsunday, but three days later, not to disturb the feast. And as ironic comment on the admirable intentions revealed above, the hospital commission has not yet acted, and there is a forlorn attempt to induce it to do so.

Through much of the 'seventies, and his own twenties, James bade fair to follow in the steps of his father and grandfather. There was a foreshadowing of later trouble in the increasing debasement of currency, but in the main there was growing stability and a strengthening of those allies the Crown and the Law. On 17th March of 1473, a prince was born who was to be James IV : and as the King had besides two brothers, both grown to manhood and the elder married, the dynasty seemed safer from encroachment than it had done for the last half-century.[1]

In 1472 there was another accession of territory. The instalments of the Queen's dower had never been paid, and the Orkneys and Shetlands were formally annexed as compensation, and attached to the Crown, the Earl of Caithness, who was (Norse) Earl of Orkney, being given Ravenscraig as compensation. Their organisation, as in land tenure, was retained, and still exists in a certain measure, and their Norse speech was to last until much later, and still strongly colours their local dialect. The reign, in fact, saw Scotland arrive at last at its present shape, with the final loss of Berwick, the recovery of Roxburgh, the final cession of the Western Isles, and the addition of the Northern ones.

[1] Two more sons—he had no daughters—were born to James, a second James, Marquis of Ormond, in 1476, and John, Earl of Mar, in 1479. The title of marquis, like that of viscount, which also appears for the first time in this reign, was borrowed from Continental usage, as in England a few years earlier: but in neither country had they any significance beyond indicating intermediate grades of nobility between those of duke and earl and earl and 'lord.'

The early 'seventies brought about an important innovation within the Church, in key with the growing tendency to define what may be called the margins of national life.   The Scottish Church was in the unusual position that its dioceses were on a parity, directly dependent on Rome, without an intervening Archbishop [1]—a position which had the practical disadvantage that it allowed the nearest archbishopric, which happened to be the English one of York, an excuse for making claims of superiority which more than once, when the countries were at war, had been exploited against the Scottish clergy, hot nationalists almost to a man.[2]   Now, Bishop Kennedy's half-brother and successor, Patrick Graham, resolved that it was time the Scottish practice conformed with the more general one of the Church.   His motives may have included personal ambition, but it seems fairly clear that whatever may have moved him, he was trying to forestall a recurrence of the claim of York, which, in view of the connection of the English reigning dynasty with its Archbishop, and their general attitude, was not improbable, and in fact was soon made : and Spottiswoode, his post-Reformation successor, is likely to be right in thinking that Graham desired to strengthen his hands

---

[1] *Archbishop* is not a sacerdotal order, but an administrative grade. The orders of the Catholic ministry are deacon, priest, and bishop, and no more, so that this absence does not imply any ecclesiastical incompleteness, but merely a local peculiarity in administration, which is retained at the present day by the Episcopal Church of Scotland.

[2] At least one previous English attempt on Scotland had been given something the colour of a *jihad*.

before undertaking a general reform of abuses, not only within but without his diocese.

The innovation began with a tragic failure. The see lay vacant some time after Kennedy's death, before Graham, then Bishop of Brechin, was appointed. What happened after that is far from clear. He had been involved in the Boyd *coup d'état* of 1466, but escaped the fall of their faction three years later : it may, however, have been because of his connection with them that King James refused him leave to go to Rome in order to receive his consecration. Graham waited awhile, but still could not get permission, and in 1471 he went without it. Just at this time Archbishop Neville of York chose to raise the old question of supremacy. Graham had the matter out with Sixtus IV, who trumped any further claim on the part of York by giving Graham the pallium and erecting his see into an Archbishopric, with the twelve Scots dioceses for its suffragans. At the same time he made him Legate for three years—Spottiswoode says ' for his more gracing ' in the reform of abuses, but Sixtus undoubtedly wanted a *quid pro quo*, in the shape of recruits for a sorely needed crusade : the Turks had swept now through the whole of Greece, and were actually threatening Italy.

Graham returned to Scotland late in 1473, and found himself at once in a hornet's nest, with the worst side of the national character rampant. The dioceses to the north of Forth had always admitted St Andrews to a certain rather vague seniority : but Glasgow, the old ecclesiastical capital of Strathclyde, had held aloof from the system established under David I. Candida Casa (Galloway) for long had really been suffragan to York, as the Isles had to Drontheim, while until the previous year Orkney had never had any Scots connection, and it still was under Drontheim. Moreover, if Graham really did share his elder brother's attitude towards reform, he would not be popular with the worldlier clergy. And the Estates had recently passed a statute, during Graham's absence—perhaps to his address— prohibiting any Scottish benefice from being procured henceforth at the Papal court.

The spear-head of the opposition was Schevez or Shivas, a priest and astrologer who had won James's favour. James wished Graham now to make him his Archdeacon, and Graham took exception to the astrology, as being too near art-magic, and refused. Shivas was a resourceful enemy. Graham was cited for contravening the statute referred to above, and inhibited from using the title of archbishop or exercising the regular legatine functions, while his power of defence was seriously crippled by inducing his Roman debtors to distrain, and by a further charge of heresy. Shivas also allied with the Rector of the University of St Andrews, who proceeded to excommunicate Graham, his own Chancellor. The Pope ordered an investigation, which was not concluded till 1476, and ended by declaring Graham mad. The madness, it is clear, was real enough, but whether it caused or was caused by the whole affair is impossible now to say :

one may guess the latter. He died a prisoner in Loch-leven Castle, and the King gave his vacant see to Shivas, who lost his objection to the archiepiscopal title. And the abuses that Graham had attacked continued to flourish, encouraged by the King's facile presentations, which caused the extrusion of prelates canonically elected, and a consequent re-laxation of authority at a time when discipline was badly needed.

Foreign relations, during most of this decade, went on improving, in appearances. In fact, new and very serious trouble was brewing, and partly perhaps owing to the apparent release from foreign pressure, the gentry had returned to their old pastime of private and vindictive war with each other. Edward IV had seemed secure on his throne after Hexham, and through the late 'sixties was inclined to an attack on France, where Louis XI had offered him an opening by quarrelling with Charles of Burgundy. Louis, in consequence, wanted nothing so much as a renewal of Anglo-Scottish war, while Charles desired a breach between France and Scotland. Edward realised that this last was improbable, so tried to keep Scotland still at peace with himself, and as far as he could from peace within herself. In 1469, however, he had to fight at home for his own existence : he quarrelled with Clarence, his brother and the son-in-law of Warwick, who had been the most powerful supporter of York.

The two fled to France, joined the exiled Margaret, and in October of 1470, landed. Edward's army deserted : he fled to Flanders in a fishing-boat . . . and returned the next March. The wheel swung. London, where Edward was popular, let him in : Warwick was beaten with ghastly slaughter at Barnet, and Margaret, who landed at Weymouth that same day, at Tewkesbury by the Severn on May Morning. Her son was murdered in cold blood after the battle, and Henry in his prison in the Tower, and the Wars of the Roses seemed to be ended at last.

Edward's apparent security made the Scots nervous : they recalled, no doubt, the truculence of his father, and the statutes of these years pay much attention to questions of armament and to the provision of artillery. At the same time, the Scottish government did not wish for a war if one could be avoided. In August of 1471 an Anglo-Scottish meeting took place at Alnwick, to deal with breaches of truce on both sides of the Border, and the next May brought a truce for fourteen months. France and Burgundy came to open war that year,[1] and in July of the next the Estates requested James to intervene. His position was difficult, for the previous March he had ratified treaties with England and Burgundy : his brother-in-law Arran was stirring up the latter against both France and Scotland, and Douglas, who had married Edward's

---

[1] Charles was aiming at an independent kingdom. Burgundy at this time, though one of the most powerful states in Europe, was nominally dependent, partly on France and partly on the Empire.

niece and been given the Garter, was doing precisely the same thing in England.

Louis nearly drew James to an awkward foreign commitment, that would almost certainly have meant an English war. He sent the Scot, Concressault, on a mission to induce James to conquer Brittany, promising to surrender his not very effective sovereign rights over the duchy to the Scottish Crown. James, whose niece was its Duchess, actually consented, and went so far as to try to raise men and money : the Estates, however, intervened, suggesting as a better objective Saintonge (to which James had an admitted right) and Gueldres, whose heir, James's cousin, had imprisoned his aged father and seized the duchy. The Estates wished James to induce his grandfather to cut out his son and make the King his heir : but the old man adopted his nephew Burgundy, and though the choice was fortunate for Scotland, Scoto-Burgundian tension was increased.

The clouds dispersed, however, for the time. Embassies were sent to all three of the bickering powers, and peaceable relations were maintained. Another Anglo-Scots conference at Alnwick made elaborate arrangements for Border peace, and the English agreed to pay compensation to the Scots Admiral for the wreck of Bishop Kennedy's *St Salvator* which had gone ashore on the English coast, and been looted.

Anglo-Scottish relations then seemed to improve for a while. Edward, still feeling his way towards war with France, decided to try for a definite Scots alliance, for the old Franco-Scottish bond had been weakened of late both by the death of the strongly pro-Scottish Charles VII and by the dynastic link with Burgundy. In June of 1474 negotiations were opened for a marriage between the young Prince of Scotland, aged fifteen months, and Edward's third daughter, Princess Cecily, who was four. On the 26th of October, a new truce of forty-five years was concluded, and the marriage treaty was signed at Edinburgh by Crawford and Scrope as proxy for the parties, and James looking on in cloth of gold lined with satin. The treaty declares that *this Nobill Ile callit Gret Britaine can nocht be kepit and maintenit bettir in Welth and Prosperite* than by an established peace between Scotland and England, and that the purpose of this alliance by kinship is that each King shall help the other against his rebels—a clause of which Edward's observance will soon be described.

The next year brought Edward's inglorious but profitable expedition to France, that ended in the Treaty of Pecquigny, while James used the new security to deal with Edward's old ally in the West. In November a parliament forfeited John of the Isles, and Crawford and Athol were sent with a fleet against him. John surrendered, and resigned the earldom of Ross, with Knapdale, Kintyre, and the hereditary sheriffdoms of Inverness and Nairn, whereon James showed his accustomed leniency by confirming him in the lordship of the Isles, and attempting to draw him within the ambit of central Scottish affairs by creating him a Lord of Parliament.

The first decade of the reign, comprising most of the fourteen-seventies, and of James's twenties, had been marked by success. Now the internal feuds grew more dangerous. The mid-fifteenth century, as a matter of fact, saw a bitter struggle over the whole of Europe between the new national centralising powers and the swarm of little half-independent princes who were the relics of the feudal system. Shrewd Louis XI was at grips with his nobles : so was the Emperor Sigismund with his. The Wars of the Roses were in essence no more than a sort of polarisation of such a struggle. Scotland's condition, though the violent energies of the national temper made it extreme, was far from peculiar. Spain, Scandinavia, Poland, the Low Countries, the Italian states, were all similarly affected, while the Renaissance quickened in Italy . . . and the Turk was pressing merrily north-westward, and pushing inward the Marches of Christendom.

From the later 'seventies onward the Highlands in special were in a continual state of violent disturbance. The forfeitures of 1476 had broken the dangerous united power of Ross and the Isles together, but had left most of the ancient inheritance of the MacDonalds. John of the Isles had accepted his defeat, and the King's leniency appears to have caused a real reconciliation : but the standard of revolt was raised again by John's natural son Angus, a ' stirring chiel,' who rebelled against both his father and the King. The

MacLeans, MacLeods, MacNeils, and MacKenzies supported John, but the last of these clans introduced a fresh complication, as MacKenzie of Kintail repudiated his MacDonald wife, with circumstances of sufficiently brutal ignominy, and replaced her by carrying off a daughter of Lovat. The natural result was a first-class feud, which affected Scots politics into the eighteenth century.

Young Angus's rising was dangerously successful. He defeated Athol and Kintail at Lagabread in Ross, then Crawford and Huntly, then Argyle and his own father John, and in the naval battle of Bloody Bay, off Ardnamurchan in 1481, was victor again. Within three years of John's forfeiture, indeed—at the beginning of 1479—the Estates were calling for some kind of government action to end no fewer than five private wars, from Sutherland to Annandale in the Marches, and a worse one was growing within the King's own household.

By that year, James was rising twenty-eight, and already his energy had begun to slacken, and the Sisyphus-load of government to bend him. He began to retire more and more from public life and to devote himself to his private amusements, which apart from dabbling in astrology would seem to have been harmless in themselves . . . like the locksmith work that so occupied Louis XVI. He found pleasure in the men who shared his tastes—Rogers, an English musician of great talent, whose pupils were well-reputed in the next reign ; Cochrane, a brilliant swashbuckler young architect, who caught his eye by prowess in a duel and built his great hall and chapel in Stirling Castle; Torphichen, a *maître d'armes*; and some humbler men. And meanwhile his two brothers had reached manhood, and made glittering figures in the popular eye, throwing their senior farther into shadow. Alexander, Duke of Albany, now in his twenties, was a strikingly handsome young man, with very fine eyes, a good judge of a horse, an expert in all athletic accomplishments, and open-handed. (James, to the cost of his popularity, was economical save in the arts.) John, Earl of Mar, who was newly out of his teens, had gracious and charming manners, the same good looks, and the same tastes : in fact, he ran a stud. He, for all that is really known to the contrary, may have been loyal to his brother and nephews. Alexander, most undoubtedly, was not, but as ugly a traitor as cursed even the fifteenth century . . . and he held the earldom of March and a Wardenship, and was Governor of Berwick, holding thus the keys of the eastern frontier.

Now, James was still bent on the new English alliance, and the forty-five year truce. In 1478, indeed, there was some talk of two further marriages, between James's sister Margaret[1] and his brother Albany on the Scottish side, and Edward's brother and sister on the English, Clarence and the now widowed

---

[1] She had just completed her education with the nuns of Haddington Priory, where Sister Alison Maitland was her governess.

s

Duchess of Burgundy.[1]   Clarence's murder immediately afterwards put a stop to the one match, and the other fell through.   Some complicated intrigues ensued thereafter.   Edward, quite possibly urged on by Douglas, seems already to have been working on Albany, and there was a not unnatural jealousy between the King's brothers and the favourites, of whom they and their followers loudly expressed contempt.   Albany embroiled himself in some March trouble with the Homes and Hepburns, who won the ear of James's favourite Cochrane, and induced him to set James against the princes.   Cochrane produced a convenient astrologer, who prophesied in a concatenation according.   A Lion would be devoured by his own whelps. The King would die at the hands of his near kindred. (And if the prophecies were perhaps *ad hoc*, they both came true enough, as it turned out.)   James took them seriously, but like most Stewarts he had strong family affection.   He loved his brilliant brother, and for a time, though he brooded, he would not act.

Then the two princes were suddenly arrested, Albany on a charge of treasonable intromissions with England, Mar on plotting against the King by means of witchcraft, and lodged one in Edinburgh and the other in Craigmillar.   How far the charges were justified, at

---

[1] Albany had already been married, to Lady Katharine Sinclair, a daughter of Caithness, and had children by her.   He got the marriage annulled about this time, and the children were declared illegitimate and barred from the succession.

this point, is not clear : Albany, certainly, was an unsatisfactory Warden, and his later treacheries have a shameless breadth that suggests something much less excusable than a man made bitter by false accusation : and Mar, like many gentlemen of his time, had undoubtedly dabbled to some extent in magic, though quite possibly it was only for amusement, as a prevalent and fashionable vice. Albany, strong, quickwitted, and resourceful, made a dramatic escape, and got away. His friends sent in to him two small casks of wine, containing a letter and a coil of rope. The Duke and one of his gentlemen, imprisoned with him, invited the governor of the castle to supper : he came, bringing with him three of his officers, and they were seated by an enormous fire, and made a wet and lively night of it. In time, between wine and the heat, they showed signs of wear, and the two desperate men set on them and stabbed them, flung the bodies, with ugly vindictiveness, on the fire, and made their escape by the rope. It was short : the equerry, going first, fell and broke his leg. Albany slipped back, took the sheets from his bed, lengthened the rope and got down, and carrying his companion on his shoulders contrived to reach the ship that was in waiting, and win to France. The picturesque escape completed the popular legend of his dashing and attractive personality, and set popular sympathy further against the King . . . and Mar's fate, a little later, enhanced the ill-feeling, for he died in highly suspicious circumstances, and current scandal accused James of his murder. What really

happened will never be clearly known. The popular
tale was that he had been stabbed in his bath. Another
version avers that his associates having been tried
for witchcraft, found guilty, and burnt, he was given
the chance of suicide, and took it. Drummond declares
that in the private papers of Bishop Elphinstone (who
was in a good position to know the truth) he found a
statement that Mar fell sick of a fever, was taken to a
house in the Canongate to be nursed, and there bled,
according to current medical practice, and put into a
hot bath, where he tore off the bandage in his delirium
and bled to death before his keepers noticed. This is
possible, for the baths of the time, as may be seen in
contemporary pictures, were often covered with a sort
of tent [1] : and it may be remarked that the insurgent
lords who brought several serious charges against
James, more than one of which was demonstrably
false, did not bring this, which would have been most
convenient. But the popular voice at the time found
the King guilty : and he very foolishly weighted the
scandal by giving at least the revenues of Mar's earldom, and perhaps the earldom itself, to his favourite
Cochrane. In his isolation, he turned more and more
to his little personal clique : Cochrane, in special, was
all-powerful at court, and feathered his nest handsomely with bribes. Between his influence, sheer
timidity, or avarice—the last, of course, was blamed—
James seems to have made an attempt at amassing

---

[1] The Treasurer's records have an entry of cloth to make such a
tent to cover Queen Margaret's.

money,[1] possibly as safeguard, for the treachery in his
household had shaken his nerve. He consented,
apparently through Cochrane's influence, to a fresh
and serious debasement of currency, the silver being
heavily adulterated. The base coin, called in derision
Cochrane-placks, caused rising prices and trade dis-
location, increasing general hatred of the King, and
alienating those stable elements, the burghs and
traders, who had supported his father and grandfather :
and Cochrane, confident in his hold on the King,
flaunted his power and jeered at all complaints.

Albany, meanwhile, in France, attempted to stir up
Louis XI. Louis treated him with courtesy, at least,
and allowed him to marry Anne de la Tour d'Auvergne
(a very great house) but refused to act against Scotland.
Instead, he sent an envoy to King James, a Scots
priest, one Dr Ireland, to mediate between the
brothers, and persuade the King, if he could, to an
English invasion. Ireland was a fine scholar, and
James showed him a good deal of personal favour : for
the rest, he went so far as to postpone his brother's
forfeiture, but would neither pardon him, nor break
the truce. Indeed, he made a fresh gesture towards
England, by suggesting a new marriage for his sister.
Clarence was dead and Richard of Gloucester married,
so the proposed bridegroom now was Edward's

---

[1] To judge from the inventory of his possessions after his death,
the attempt was not remarkably successful : but his savings may
have stuck to other men's fingers, and we know that some of his
baggage had gone missing.

brother-in-law Earl Rivers. Edward, however, was much annoyed just then with both Scotland and France, for Louis had been keeping him in play with a proposal for marriage between the Dauphin and Princess Elizabeth, which he had no intention of carrying out. Albany may have perhaps betrayed his intentions : Edward undoubtedly suspected them, and refused in consequence to trust his ally. Relations grew more strained, and in the spring (of 1480) James decided on war. Bishop Spens of Aberdeen, they say, protested, and being unheeded, died of a broken heart. Edward put his fleet and army on a war footing, with provision of ' bombards, cannons, culverins, fowlers, and serpents,' and gave his brother Gloucester the command. James sent him an envoy, to warn him that if he persisted in aiding Burgundy against France, he himself was bound to act on France's behalf. Edward dismissed the herald impolitely, and there were some actual hostilities. Angus raided the Border, and burnt Bamborough, and an English fleet attacked the south-east coast, and were smartly defeated by Sir Andrew Wood, who was given Largo for his services. Plague, famine, and the economic results of the base coinage worsened the situation.

James mobilised, and was going to march into England, when the Papal Nuncio intervened, much as the League of Nations might do now, and appealed to both sovereigns (backing the appeal with a threat of excommunication) to desist from inter-Christian hostilities in view of the Turkish menace to the south, which indeed was as serious as it well might be, for the Turks were now attacking Italy, and they had swept, in the last twenty years, through the Balkan peninsula right up to the Danube. James halted, but Edward would not : and public opinion, roused by a clash with the Auld Enemy, swung round, and violently, in the King's favour. The Estates of March 1482 were hotly for him, and very fierce against Edward, who by a regrettable adoption of English diplomatic manners was described throughout these proceedings as *the Revare Edward calland him King of Ingland*. They did not, however, decide definitely on a war, but offered a reward for the capture of James Douglas, set on foot arrangements for mobilisation, and decided to wait and see what Edward was doing.

What that was would have interested them greatly, and it was unlucky for James that they did not know. Albany had come over from France to England. It may be that he thought his brother had wronged him : he had certainly been an unsatisfactory Warden, but evidence of any actual treason, before his arrest, seems vague. Now he more than justified any such charges. To his own greed and to his hate of his brother he was ready to sacrifice Scotland itself, to say nothing of a trifle like his honour. At Fotheringay, on the 10th of June, he put his name, as *Alexander R.*, to a paper in which as Alexander King of Scots he binds himself to help and aid Edward against all earthly princes and persons. He will do fealty for ' my realm of Scotland.' He breaks the French alliance, and promises to make

no more without Edward's leave, and to hand over
Berwick. Then, having slept on that, he amplified it
with another paper next day. Edward now binds himself to help Albany to the realm and crown of Scotland
and all that is in the hands of ' James now holding the
Crown of Scotland,' and to defend him against the said
James. Liddesdale, Eskdale, Annandale, and Lochmaben—the West and Middle Marches—are added to
Berwick. The fealty clause now appears with embroidery, so as to admit that fealty was owed in the
past. As soon as Albany can ' clear himself from all
other women ' he is to marry Princess Cecily, his
nephew's betrothed : and if he fails to rid himself of
his Duchess, he must marry his heir to a royal English
bride.

He signed that. Then he marched with Gloucester
on Berwick. James assembled his army on the
Boroughmuir of Edinburgh, with Cochrane in command of the artillery, and marched to defend threatened
Berwick. He got to Lauder, and camped there.
Angus, Huntly, Lennox, Crawford, Buchan, and Gray
were with the army : and they chose this time to deal
with the favourites. They held an unofficial council in
Lauder Kirk, and fumed their indignation, whereon
Gray rose and drily told them the fable, of the mice
who decided the cat should wear a bell . . . and then
came on the problem, Who was to bell the cat ? The
huge Angus sprang to his feet, and cried that he would.
(He was Archibald Bell-the-Cat for the rest of his life.)
And then there was a knocking at the door, and into

what he thought was an officers' council swaggered the Master of the Artillery—Cochrane himself, superb in black velvet and gold. Angus faced him and laid hold of his golden collar, crying that a halter would become him better, and another Douglas, Sir Robert of Lochleven, snatched his bugle, saying he had hunted mischief enough. Cochrane had courage, and he took it boldly, demanding whether this were jest or earnest : and at that they broke loose and seized him and bound his hands. He offered them a silk rope from his own pavilion, but a hair tether was the best he got. Then they marched to the King's tent, and before his face seized the others, Rogers, Leonard, Torphichen, and Preston, sparing one more, young Ramsay of Balmain, who was only a boy, and hanged them with Cochrane over Lauder Bridge. It appears there was some competition to offer halters. Then, with the King a prisoner, the army marched, not towards Berwick, but to Edinburgh, where James was warded in the Castle, in charge of his uncles, Athol and ' Hearty James,' the Earl of Buchan.

Gloucester, unopposed, made an easy capture of Berwick, which thus was lost for good, and advanced through Lothian, Albany still with him, *Arcades ambo*. Angus wanted to give the King into their hands, for Edward and Albany had tampered with him, and the Red house now was on the road of the Black. With the English on Scottish soil, this was too much. His associates refused, and marched to Haddington, barring Gloucester's advance. Archbishop Shivas, the Bishop of Dunkeld, Lord Avondale the Chancellor, and Argyle intervened to mediate between the brothers, and with success. James knew nothing yet of the Fotheringay affair, and remembering Mar, may have felt that he had treated his brother harshly : what Albany's motives were is not very clear, but from his subsequent actions one may fear that control of James's person was the strongest. On the 2nd of August the four conciliators signed a band undertaking to go surety for Albany's safety if he would promise loyalty to his brother, and to procure the return of his lands and offices : whereon the Duke calmly went back again to the Scots, and Gloucester, who since he seems to have had some humour, was probably enjoying the situation, returned unmolested to reduce Berwick Castle. The burgesses of Edinburgh sent with him an offer to repay at their own costs the instalments of the Princess Cecily's dowry.

Then, with the aid of the said burgesses—they might hate the favourites, but the King was the King— Albany rescued his brother from the Castle. James was deceived, believing what he wished, that his brother was loyal and he no longer alone. He rode through cheering crowds to Holyrood, and gaily made Albany ride behind him *en croupe*, in visible token of reconciliation. To his good townsfolk he gave their Golden Charter, making the Provost henceforward their Sheriff, with the right to raise the citizens in arms under their famous banner the Blue Blanket. To his brother he gave his trust and his affection : the two of them lived, ate, even slept together, and a Parliament on the 2nd of December not only gave Albany Mar and the Garioch, but made him the King's Lieutenant of the Realm, to defend it ' with all his extreme power.' They were making ready for war, if it should come, but they did not want it. The final clause of their business is that *Pece be takin with Ingland, gif it can be had with honor but [without] inconvenient.* They are still willing that the Prince shall marry Princess Cecily, and protest that if there is war, it is not by the King's will. Then they proceed to make ready if it comes, by ordering the lieges to *purvay thame of hors, harnes, and vthir abilzement,* and of *victalis,* warn the Wardens to be vigilant . . . and go on to deal with adulterated wine, to encourage various imports by foreign traders, defend some Scots merchants who are in trouble in France, discuss Princess Margaret's marriage to Earl Rivers, and—a common habit of James III's parliaments—re-enact several statutes already passed.

A month to the day after James and the Estates had put the keeping of Scotland into his hands, Albany sent Angus, Gray, and Liddel of Halkerston to Edward, to renew the secret treaty of Fotheringay. Scrope and Northumberland met them, and on the 11th February 1483 they all signed a truce between Albany and Edward and ' their lovers and well-wishers.' Albany agrees now to marry an English bride without any dowry, to serve against France (where he had been very well treated) and to furnish a list of those lords on the Marches who are likely to be loyal to King James.

Angus and the rest promise allegiance to England and
hostility to James (how James Douglas, remembering
Arkinholm, must have grinned !) and Edward will
supply three thousand archers, and more if needed,
and restore the worthy James Douglas to his lands.

Their patron Albany, still at the Scottish court, was
enjoying the sunshine of his brother's favour.   It is
likely that he was planning a *coup d'état*, for he set
about rumours that James wanted him poisoned.   By
the middle of March, someone opened the King's eyes.
On the 19th he dealt with Albany, who had to confess
the poison tale was baseless, admit his dealings with
Edward and renounce them, and undertake to forward
peace with England.   He was deprived of the Lieutenancy, and he, Angus, with Athol, Buchan, and their
brother the Bishop of Moray, forbidden to come within
six miles of the court.   That was all his punishment.
He was allowed to keep his lands and titles, and
astoundingly, his Wardenship of the March.   James
may have tried to shame him by trusting him : but
even yet he did not know his brother.   Albany promptly
fortified Dunbar, and sent Halkerston, with whom he
had sworn to break, to renew his band with Edward.
An English force marched to Dunbar, and was admitted : and then, on the 9th of April, Edward died.

The fresh treason was soon known.   On the 27th
June, the Estates at last found Albany guilty of treason,
and forfeited him of life, lands, and goods.   He had
fallen between two stools, and heavily, for Gloucester,
who had usurped his nephew's throne a few months

after his elder brother's death, did not wish for war. William Elphinstone, the great Bishop of Aberdeen, who in character was Kennedy's successor, was sent with Crawford to renew the truce, and the French alliance was ratified again, on the accession of Louis XI's son, Charles VIII, whose ambassador was the great Franco-Scottish soldier, Bernard Stuart d'Aubigny.

The Estates, it appears, were not sure of King Richard's mind, for in February 1484 they enacted that all men liable to serve should stand by for mobilisation at eight days' notice. The sentence on Albany's associates was repeated : it is clear that they were weary of disorder, and of over-leniency of the King. Absentees from Parliament were censured, a day of accord was appointed for all feuds, and there was a statute, very significant, to the effect that for a year to come the King

has closit his handis fra gevin of Remissionis and Respettis for tresoun, slauchtir, or forthocht felony, common thift, and manifest Refe.

In late July, Albany made his last throw. Richard refused him help, and in the congenial company of Douglas, with men of his own, he made a thrust for Lochmaben. It was the annual fair, and the town was crowded. The people thought they were an English raid, and set about them : the garrison turned out and took a hand. Douglas was captured at last, but instead of being headed was returned to his original profession, and forced to become a monk of Lindores Abbey, where he died in peace some four years afterwards, the last of all the Douglases of the Black. Albany got away across the Border, and since nothing more was to be had from Richard, went to France, and was killed in a tournament the next year.

A few weeks after this raid both James and Richard were appointing envoys to discuss a truce, and a new marriage for the Prince. Edward's daughters had been bastardised by Parliament, and Richard had none, so the lady now was his niece, Anne de la Pole, Suffolk's daughter. In September a truce for three years was agreed to, *tam per Terras quam per Mare et aquas dulces*, provision being made for a sort of by-truce for six months at Dunbar (where Albany's legacy of English troops were still sitting still and probably thinking hard) after which James might retake it if he could without the general truce being considered broken.

The parliament of next May wore a peaceful aspect, save for a hopeful statute recommending the trial and execution of all notorious offenders, and the perpetual worry over the coinage, which was now worth only a third of that of England. The act against purchase of benefices at Rome was re-enacted, but as a counter-gesture of politeness Archbishop Shivas was sent to the Papal court to ask the new Pope to confirm the alliance between Scotland, France, and the Scandinavian kingdoms.

August brought violent changes in English affairs. The last male left of the House of Lancaster was the son of Margaret, Countess of Richmond, a Beaufort, by Edmund Tudor, son of a handsome Welshman who had caught the eye of the widow of Henry V, in whose service he was. He was therefore half-nephew of the dead Henry VI, whose name he bore, and for some time had found it healthier to live a nomadic life on the Continent. It made him cool, shrewd, humorous, and close-fisted, and rid him of any inconvenient scruples. Richard's dealing with his nephews had shocked even fifteenth century consciences, and Henry saw his opportunity. The long-headed young French Regent, Madame Anne, who was a singularly able woman, perceived the advantage of a friendly England, and backed the gambler's throw with five thousand men, of whom a thousand were Scots in the French service.[1] They landed, and on the 22nd of August defeated Richard and killed him on Bosworth Field. The affair was to turn out of importance to Scotland : in the long run it brought the Scots Kings a second throne.

Now, Henry had not the least use for superfluous war. Moreover (though few men were less moved by emotion) he had grounds of personal gratitude towards Scotland. Scots sympathy had been with Lancaster. He had been brought up as a boy at the Breton court, where the Scots Duchess Isobel had been kind to him, and Major says that as a starving exile he had been befriended by one Patrick King, a Scots merchant of Rouen, who had housed and fed him and set him

[1] Drummond says Bernard Stuart was in command, but Major, a Haddington man, makes it ' John of Haddington,' who may be John de Conyngham (Cunningham), Captain of the Scots Guard about that time.

up in funds. The Scots too had fought well for him at Bosworth. And he was very uncertain on his throne, since besides the Parliament's ban on a Beaufort succession, there were no fewer than sixteen people living who had a better claim by descent than he had. He improved his position by marrying the senior of them, Edward IV's eldest daughter Elizabeth, recognised now as legitimate for the occasion, and sent Northumberland to negotiate. King James agreed to a new three years' truce, and to another proposal for a marriage—this time of the Marquis of Ormond, his second son, to Henry's sister-in-law, Princess Katharine; and again Anglo-Scottish affairs seemed settling down, for the sensible Henry's major policy was to restore the wreckage of civil war, and England seemed to approve of his intentions.

James by this time appears to have withdrawn as much as possible from public life, and his temporary return to popular liking had not endured. Queen Margaret's death in July 1486 increased his solitude. Disaffection was again lifting its head. The Prince, an eager, sensitive, brilliant boy, was in his teens : his mother's death and his father's late retirement made it easy to poison his mind against the King.

The parliament of October 1487 seems to show some sense of the growing internal danger. The nobles demanded a general amnesty, and the Church and the Commons joined to counter them by praying the King to give none for seven years, while at the same time they made acknowledgment of James's good relations with the Estates. The lords and freeholders were made to promise that they would not maintain traitors, thieves and robbers—a provision nullified by the saving clause that they would not be prevented from taking part, *in sober wys,* with their kinsmen and friends in defence of honest actions. Those who did not attend parliament would incur the King's displeasure, and be fined. A statute which shows the growing importance of the merchant class established a Convention of Burghs to meet yearly at Inverkeithing, in order to discuss municipal affairs and *the welefare of merchandis.* And there is one little inconspicuous statute, on a trivial point, that led to tragic results : no one might hinder Coldingham Priory from being united with Stirling Chapel Royal.

Six weeks later, Carlisle Herald came as envoy, and Snowdon Herald received him at Edinburgh. They discussed the terms of a formal alliance with England. The current truce was extended to 1489, Ormond's marriage to Princess Katharine was re-settled, and there was a further suggestion that James should marry the widow of Edward IV and the Prince one of her daughters : his original betrothed, Princess Cecily, had been married off by now to an English peer. James intervened, and made a condition, the return of Berwick. The envoy was not competent to answer, but a commission to discuss the matter was arranged for May, and a meeting of the two Kings for July.

T

James never saw that July. The trifling affair of Coldingham was his end. He had given his new chapel in Stirling Castle a double choir of singing men and boys, one half of them to be in residence and the other to go always with his person : to support its expenses he had annexed to Stirling the Priory of Coldingham in the Merse. Now, the local magnates, who were the Homes and Hepburns, no peaceful set, had in a manner that was grown too common come to consider that the Priory, or at least its Priorship, was their perquisite. They made a band with other disaffected lords, the chief of them being Angus and Argyle. Matters hung so, for a little. At the parliament of January 1488, the question of Coldingham was raised once more, but the King and the Estates do not seem to have grasped that anything lay behind the opposition. They were busied in sending an embassy to England to agree formally to the marriages, on condition that either Berwick should be returned, or its castle should be razed.

By the time that James had become aware of the band, the greater part of the South was arming against him. He tried to detach Angus, and merely precipitated an outbreak. Thereon, having deposed Argyle from the Chancellorship and given it to Bishop Elphinstone, he garrisoned Stirling, gave its governor, Shaw of Fintry, whom he trusted, the custody of the Prince, placed his treasure in Edinburgh, and fled across Forth in a ship of Sir Andrew Wood's—barely in time, for his baggage was seized at Leith.

Both sides sent envoys to England for support, and the rebel lords proceeded to march on Stirling. Shaw surrendered the Prince, and they proclaimed him King, announcing that his father was deposed ... on a charge of having sold the Marches to England. The North, however, was loyal. James raised Fife. (They say that he saw Douglas at Lindores Abbey, and asked him to fight—with that record !—but the old man told him that he and the King's 'black box'—*i.e.*, the treasure-chest of the popular legend—had been under lock and key too long to be useful.) Then he went on through Strathearn and Angus, to Aberdeen, and thence to Perth, being joined by Athol and the magnates of the North-east—Huntly, Crawford, Ruthven, and Lindsay of the Byres.

The rebels had carried the young Prince to Linlithgow, under the royal banner of the Lion. James marched on them and met them at Blackness, and Huntly and Errol tried to mediate. There was some fighting, but the prestige of the Crown had survived even James's ineffectual reign, and the insurgent forces were falling away. If he had struck he might have won through even then. With his fatal leniency, he compromised. The lords were to make formal submission to him, and have security for life, lands and gear. Feuds were to be arbitrated. The King and Prince were to be reconciled. The King, if his person might be guaranteed in honourable security and freedom, gave his consent to the forming of a council of prelates, lords, and others of wisdom for the guiding of the realm.   And the insurgent lords were left still armed, with the young Prince in their keeping.

The pacification had barely been arranged when James found its hollowness.   He took the field once more, making his second son Ormond Duke of Ross, as if he meant him to take his brother's place, and Crawford at the same time Duke of Montrose.   He sent envoys to France, Rome, and England for support in what looked like becoming a Scots War of the Roses. Then he marched on Stirling and sought to take refuge there.   Shaw closed the gates in his face, and refused to admit him.

On the 11th of June, the two forces met.   It was near the day, and the place, of Bannockburn, two miles from Stirling, but farther to the west than that great battle. James wore Bruce's sword, and Lord Lindsay had brought him a gift of a grey horse, a mettlesome brute that Albany might have managed, but James could scarcely keep in his control.   The Lion Banner faced the Lion Banner, for the rebels had brought with them the young Prince.   The battle was a queer half-hearted business, as if neither side were confident in its cause :   there were few casualties, but one of moment.

James, with his son against him, was not the man to be in any sort of a fighting mood :   and his uncertain mind unsettled his mount, as a rider's does with any sensitive beast.   Whether he chose to fly or the grey horse bolted, or both, the beast galloped him through the summer evening away from the field, down the valley of the Bannock.   A mill they call Beaton's—the blind walls are there yet—stands a little to the west of Bannockburn village, and a woman came out to go to the burn for water. She saw an armed man riding down on her, and fled back to the house, letting her pitcher fall, and the beast shied at it and threw his rider. They were kindly folk, and seeing him lie there stunned, they carried him into the mill and tended him. How far he may have been hurt was never known, but ill with grief and the shock of the heavy fall, he begged for a priest. The goodwife asked his name, and the broken man cried ' I was your King this morning.' The poor woman—she was kind, and probably loyal— ran to the door and called to one of her neighbours to hurry and bring a priest to shrive the King . . . and a strange man (who he was was never known) had come up and dismounted. It may have been Lord Gray, the son of the Gray who had struck down the Black Douglas, or Stirling of Keir, or one Borthwick, who was a priest : all three had been seen to ride in pursuit of the King. At her cry he came forward and said that he was a priest, and she took him innocently to the King. He knelt, and asked James if he were mortally hurt. James said no, but he craved the comfort of absolution. ' This shall shrive thee,' said the stranger, and struck with his dagger.

CHAPTER XI

JAMES IV : 1488-1513

' ' Fortune is so variaunt and the whele so meuable there nys noone constant abydyng.'

Sir Thomas Malory, *La Morte Darthur*, xix, 17.

THE new King was fifteen, a brilliant attractive boy who was to become the ideal Renaissance prince. The dreadful catastrophe that ended his reign has caused him to be severely judged by historians : but it is possible that some at least have used it to ' rationalise,' as our cant word has it, a temperamental aversion, less justly based. There is a revealing passage in Hume Brown. He quotes Ayala's praise of James's scholarship and gift for languages, and puts side by side with it Buchanan's verdict, that he was *ab literis incultus*. Now, Ayala knew James personally and well : he was a responsible diplomat, writing a secret and confidential report : Buchanan lived nearly a century later, and was writing propaganda against James's grand-daughter and her house in general : but Dr Hume Brown, having quoted the two verdicts, declares that Buchanan's ' is probably nearer the truth.'

In fact, there is very little occasion for guess-work. We know a great deal about James the Fourth. We are fortunate in possessing not only Holbein's portrait which, like most of that painter's work, is almost a biography in itself, but a detailed and confidential description of him by a shrewd if certainly friendly observer, Ayala, the Spanish ambassador, who knew men. Writing when the King was twenty-five, he mentions his remarkable good looks : James was fairer than most of the princes of his house, but he had their auburn colouring, and the strong vitality that goes with it. He passes on then to praise him as a scholar : the young King was a good Latinist, and spoke, besides his country's two vernaculars, French, German, Italian, Flemish, and Spanish. He was a student of history in special—the art of kings—and we know from other sources, of science also, with an interest in its practical, humanitarian side, not least in medicine, in which he had some skill. The Spaniard notes also that he had a real reverence for religion, was truthful ' even in jest,' a rare virtue in the princes of the day, and generous. Also, he was brave to rashness. Ayala, on occasion, tried to hold him back, and condemns him as too hasty for a soldier : ' he begins to fight before he has given his orders.' He quotes also James's own defence on the point. ' He told me his subjects serve him with person and goods, in just and unjust quarrels, as he chooses, and therefore he thinks that it would be unjust to embark on any warlike undertaking without himself being the first man in danger. Nor do his actions fall behind his words.'

The point of view is entirely characteristic. Under the eagerness of his grasp on life (Ayala knew him in his happiest years) was a passionate responsibility as

King—as King of all Scots, not of a class or faction. Like James I and James II—like all the best of the Stewarts—he saw, and tried to rule, Scotland as a whole : but by no means in terms of doctrinaire abstractions. A man was a man, not a unit of an equation. Below the dry detail of his Treasurer's records, one can see not only his thoughtful consideration for even the most humble of his servants, but his open-handedness and accessibility to any poor man who found himself in trouble. Yet neither was he only the poor man's King : it was he who broke down, by sheer personality, the long opposition between the Crown and the nobles. Twelve earls and fourteen lords gave their lives beside him in the red sacramental unity of Flodden. It was he who won the Highlands for his house, made them for good the stronghold of devotion to the Stewarts. He made Scotland again the one united nation she had not been since the death of Robert Bruce.

Nor did he see Scotland merely as a whole. He saw her as a part of something greater. It is under him that she attains the climax of that fifteenth century process of growth which made her a power to reckon with in Europe : she was, in spite of the disaster of Flodden, to hold that place for another hundred years, but her position in the sixteenth century was partly due to adventitious circumstances, partly a living on the capital of a tradition established in the fifteenth. And his reign, to a large extent through his influence, is one of the two peaks of our intellectual history. From

his son's time onward there is a progressive decline to
the intellectual blank of 1700, not remedied until the
too brief brilliance of the later eighteenth and early
nineteenth centuries.

In many ways, James resembled his great-grandfather. He had his accomplishments, his intelligence,
his personal charm, and his warm humanity. There
was steel in him, but—it is both a quality and a defect—
there was not the same vein of hardness in his nature,
and he had less of that deep stability that underlay the
fire of the earlier man. One has of course to remember
that James I came to the throne at twenty-nine : James
IV had fourteen years—some three-fifths of his reign
—before that age, and it makes a difference. James I
had watched the statecraft of Henry IV, the disasters
of France, through ten years of intelligent young
manhood, without being involved himself in responsible action : and his son had the wise Kennedy
to guide him. Still, there is temperament concerned
in the difference. Comparing the Stewart kings with
Robert Bruce, it has been well said that they ' were
amateurs to his magnificent combination of all that is
best in both professional and amateur.' They had
not, in fact, his heroic weight and strength, his *robur
et aes triplex* : they fought in their shirts. But they
fought gallantly, and James IV not least, pressed with
a real steadiness to their goal, the good of Scotland,
not unwisely conceived, if at times their attempt to put
the conception in practice was marked by unwisdom
in the practical details, as in Charles I, or in James III

and Robert III failed for lack of strength to bear a crushing burden.

James's impulsiveness has been over-emphasised by unfriendly historians : he carried out a consistent policy, and only the pressure of most part of Europe drove him to leave it, ruinously, at last. Yet he had something of his father's moodiness, enhanced perhaps by his Scandinavian blood. It comes out in certain sides of his religion. Some part of his liking for religious forms may be that which goes with a natural courtesy, a sense, as they say in France, of *les façons* : even when it goes no deeper than the forms it need not be either hypocrisy or pose. Under the forms, one can see other things. The religion of the day, when it was real, had a dark strain in it, as of desperation, that is not in the heights and depths of the age of faith. His century is the time of the *danse macabre*, the lust of the flesh and the eye and the pride of life, but a sense of the skull behind the laughing beauty . . . the time of Dunbar's procession of the dead poets, of Villon's ladies vanished like the snow and the pride of dead lords gone down the wind like dust. Sauchieburn, at an impressionable age, may have marked the boy—the death of a King, his father, struck treacherously from life in a roadside cottage, and himself at the head of the men who were to blame. It is worth observing, too, that we do not know how far these sudden flights to retreat and penance, perhaps the result of weakness, resulted in strength. There is much to be said for making one's soul in silence.

It is common form, in referring to James's religion, to set by it, with a sneer more or less polite, some reference to his profligacy also.   In fact, his amours cross queerly with his devotions.   But certain points are worth remembering, not merely as a mitigation of judgment (and a king has a right to fairness like other men) but as throwing a good deal of light upon the man, and therefore on the king who is our concern.   It was an immoral age (if any is not, except in its theories) and James was in the high-road of temptation, deliberate as well as incidental : he came to the throne too old to be stolen or bullied, young enough to influence easily through the affections, hot-blooded, loving all beauty, with the loneliness of youth called too early, and with bitter circumstance, to bear the load of an enormous task, and a ready gratitude towards easing kindness. He shows no sign of the callous or merely impulsive profligate, the *homme à bonnes fortunes*.   What his legend comes down to is four mistresses : he was generous and responsible to them, and to their children : he seems really to have loved Margaret Drummond at least : and he did not give his power into their hands. It appears too that as a husband, *il se rangea* : he was kind and considerate to the child he married, won so much affection as she was able to feel, though neither by her age nor her character could she give him the rest and security that he needed.

In the long run, he bears a strange aura, like a man fated.   It shows in the pity of the Holbein portrait, done when his heart was broken to end a war.   Under all the gaiety and the eager brilliance, there is a sort of endurance of dark knowledge. The Iron Belt of his penance may be legend, but the hunger of the eyes and the set of the mouth reveal that the legend has an ultimate truth.

When his reign began, the boy was still half a prisoner. The dead King's body was found, after some search, and buried at Cambuskenneth by his Queen. On the 26th of June the new King was crowned at Scone, with his gentlemen round him in black velvet mourning—the last King of Scots to be crowned there save Charles II. At once, as had happened in past minorities, a number of new men came into power. Indeed, the very day after the battle, the Homes and Hepburns acquired a grant of lands, and the rise of the Kers and Argyle dates from this time. Argyle became once more the Chancellor, the Master of Home replaced Crawford as Chamberlain, Lyle was Justiciar of the South, Glamis of the North, and Lord Home and Hepburn were Wardens of the Marches, the latter becoming High Admiral as well, while Angus assumed a sort of Regency. The faction were not vindictive to their opponents. Crawford was ' pardoned,' and so, in spite of his seaman's frankness, was Andrew Wood.

An embassy of announcement was sent to England. Henry received it politely, and made a three-year truce . . . but strengthened Berwick. Scandinavia sent over the young King's uncle, the Count of Oldenburg, who was a good deal at court till the end of the year. In

July a Spanish embassy came to Linlithgow : they had negotiated the marriage of the Infanta Katharine to Arthur Prince of Wales, and now came north, to try to lure Scotland from the French alliance with some hazy suggestion of a Spanish match. Spain, under Ferdinand and Isabella, was on the verge of clearing herself of the Moors (Granada fell in 1491) and already embarked on that opposition to France that determined so much of the next two centuries in the history of Europe. By a queer freit like a rhyme they brought the boy King the gift of a sword and dagger, that were taken from his corpse, twenty-five years later, after the mortal battle that was to be bred from that very Hispano-French antagonism : they are now preserved in the English College of Heralds.

The new court was a lively and a splendid one, bright with masques and pageants, tournaments, dancing, hunting. There was steel under the velvet, all the same. The intransigents of the losing side were hunted down. Buchan, Forbes, and Ramsay of Bothwell (the lad who had escaped the rope at Lauder) were charged with treason, and sent for trial at the next parliament, and the King went on circuit with his new Justiciars, a progress perhaps impressive and certainly gay, for he took his huntsmen and minstrels and English fool.

His first parliament met on the 6th of October, with a full and possibly apprehensive house, and the winning side in the recent civil war proceeded to apply the needed whitewash.

There wes proponit the debaite and cause of the feild of

Steruelen (Stirling, *i.e.*, Sauchieburn) in the quhilk vmqhile James king of Scotland quham god assolze faider to our souerane lord happinit to be slane.

The leaders of the losing side were charged (in agreeable irony, by the mouth of Angus) with attempting to subject Scotland to England. Lord Glamis showed the Blackness Capitulations, under James III's Great Seal, and declared them broken. The winners pronounced themselves whitely innocent, and sent a declaration to that effect to the Kings of France, Spain, and Scandinavia, and to the Pope. One observes that they omitted Henry VII, who knew a good deal about the late *coup d'état*. Buchan confessed his sins, and was absolved, but the rest were forfeited. Bothwell's earldom was given to the Admiral, Hepburn of Hailes, a gift to be avenged on the young King's house. He and Home had the charge of Edinburgh Castle, and of the Duke of Ross, the heir-presumptive. And, the affair of the late King's death disposed of, the Estates debated on fishing with foul tackle.

Even though it may have been from selfish motives, the men who were now at the head of Scots affairs worked intelligently for stable government. They enriched themselves at the expense of their more prominent opponents, but were conciliatory to the rest. In an early parliament it is enacted that the heirs of those killed at Sauchieburn, on both sides, are to succeed, and the poorer men not to suffer. *All the gudis movabill belanging to the pure unlandit folk* that were looted before the battle must be returned, a statute which caused a certain amount of ill-feeling among the followers of the successful party. Various other, more general, provisions were made in these years, in the tradition of Stewart legislation. The parliament of 1490 demands arbitration of all disputes, and *scharp Justice* for *the partiis quhilkis ar obstinat*. The act against the obtaining of benefices from Rome was re-enacted, and in forcible terms. The second of these early parliaments, soon after the first Christmas of the reign, made an important ecclesiastical innovation, proposing a second Archbishopric, of the West, in the university city of Glasgow. The proposal was tentative : the privileges of the new province were to be debated by its Bishop and the advisers of the King. St Andrews did not relish the idea, and it was not until three years after that (9th January 1492) that Innocent VIII gave the necessary Bull.

There was various commercial legislation, such as the enactment of a standard salmon-barrel and of an assay of goldsmiths' and silversmiths' work, and some more attempts at the chronic currency problem. Merchants were now to import four ounces of *brynt siluer* for every *schirplar* of wool, last of salmon, or four-hundredth of cloth, to be sold at a fixed price to the Royal Mint.

It is clear that an influential part of the nation did not want the dog-fights of past minorities. One observes that both the Church and the Third Estate concurred in trying to emancipate the King : they had grown accustomed by now to trust the Stewarts. The first step to the assumption of personal rule by his father and grandfather had been their marriage : and at their first meeting the new King's Estates brought forward a proposal to hasten his, with *a nobill princeis borne and discendit of ane worschipfull house of auld honour and dignite*. An embassy was to be sent to the courts of France, Spain, and Brittany,[1] the Estates providing £5,000 for their expenses, £2,000 apiece from the First and Second, and £1,000 from the Third, canny provision being made that the nobles' share should really fall on them, *nocht on the comoun pepill*.

The summer of the year after James's accession brought a renewal of the civil war. Lennox and Lord Lyle were up in the West, and Lord Forbes in the North, with the bloodstained shirt of James III for a banner. A contest threatened on the lines of the old Livingstone-Crichton wars. The insurgents declared that the young King was misguided by men who were using the power for their own profit : and although as has been said the government would seem to have been well handled, there was some excuse, for Hailes in a year had progressed from minor baron to Earl of Both-well, High Admiral, Keeper of Edinburgh, Thrieve, and Lochmaben, Warden also of the West and Middle Marches, and guardian of the King's heir, the Duke of Ross.

The rebels seized Dumbarton. Argyle was sent to

[1] The future Duchess Anne (she succeeded to the Duchy a few weeks later) was daughter of the first cousin of James's father, and one of the greatest heiresses in Europe : by her marriage to two successive Kings of France she brought her great semi-independent dominion under the French crown.

reduce it, and with the King at their head the ruling faction took Duchal and Crowliston, which had been garrisoned against them. Lennox attempted to cross the Forth at Stirling, was repulsed, and went up river to Talla Muir : and Lord Drummond with the King and the royal troops fell on his force in the October night. They broke it, and the revolt. Lennox and Lyle with their associates, the Earl of Huntly, Lord Forbes, and the Earl Marischal, were tried at Edinburgh early the next year, and having been tried were pardoned, and received to favour. It was the last Lowland threat of civil war in this reign, at any rate against the royal power.

Friction with England was not long in beginning. The English privateers were a curse to the coast. Early in 1489 a squadron of five of them appeared in the Clyde, and chased a royal ship, which had to slip her cable and run for safety. James sent out Andrew Wood with the *Flower* and the *Yellow Carvel* : he met the whole five, and brought them home as prizes. James and his captain were within their rights and Henry could do nothing—officially. Unofficially, he was very far from pleased. He dropped a discreet hint to a London merchant, one Stephen Bull, who made preparations for a handsome vengeance. He fitted out three ships, with picked crews and a large complement of crossbowmen, and learning that Wood was on his way home from Flanders, anchored behind the May and waited for him. Wood sighted them in the early dawn of summer, and managed to get both the weather-gauge and the light. The well-gunned English ships opened heavy fire, but much of their shot passed over the smaller Scots ones, and Wood ran up under their guns, grappled, and boarded. The fight raged all day, and at night they cut loose and drifted alongside each other, patching their wounds, till dawn. Then—they were in the Firth of Tay by now—Wood grappled again, and held on till all three were taken. He handed over Stephen Bull to his master, who scolded him amicably and sent him back to Henry free of ransom, but with a warning he would not do so again.

The episode increased Wood's favour at court, and it may have impressed the King's mind with the importance of sea-power, which in these years of discovery [1] was growing. It may also have made Henry aware of possibilities in his young neighbour. In the April of 1491, at least, just when James was sending the Archbishop of St Andrews to arrange a commission to see to Border peace, Henry, at Greenwich, was drawing up an indenture with three émigrés, Ramsay, ex-Lord Bothwell, Sir Thomas Todd of Sereshaw, and Buchan, the King's great-uncle, son of Queen Joan, by which the latter agree that they shall

Take, Brynge, and Delyver into the said King of England's Handes the King of Scottis now Reynyng and his brother the Duke of Ross or at the leste the said King of Scotland.

The economical Henry kindly lent them the sum of £266 13s. 4d. for expenses, which they promised to

[1] The Equator was crossed in 1471, Diaz reached the Cape in 1487, and Columbus the Bahamas in 1492.

repay by Michaelmas, Todd's son and heir being left to Henry as pledge.

It is to be hoped he got his money back, for the King of Scots and his heir remained safe in Scotland. He balanced the attempt by tampering with the other faction as well. Angus went on a visit into England. Only part remains of the document which ensued (Henry always preferred to stick to the forms of sound business) but it shows an agreement to hand over Hermitage, the key of the West March. Apparently something of the affair transpired, for on his return Angus was met by the Lion Herald, and sent to ward in his own house of Tantallon. James, however, had much of his father's longanimity. Angus received no other punishment than the transference of Liddesdale to the more reliable keeping of Lord Bothwell.

These conspiracies, no doubt, might have led to very sinister results, but compared with the violent events that had marked the opening of the two previous reigns—with the Douglas Wars, even the Boyd *coup d'état* and what followed on it—they are mere ghosts of disturbance. By the early 'nineties, the Lowlands at any rate were settled down, and in spite of the events that began his reign the young King had already won the affection of the best of his father's men, notably the great seaman, Sir Andrew Wood, and a greater man, William Elphinstone, Bishop of Aberdeen, a churchman and statesman in the tradition of Kennedy, who had already been the Chancellor, and in 1492 received the Privy Seal, which he held till he died, heart-broken, after Flodden.

The busy domestic legislation was continued, and side by side with it one observes a stabilising of foreign relations and the growing importance, and influence, of the merchants, who had thriven steadily under the fostering care of the last three reigns.[1] An embassy was sent to renew commercial relations with Scandinavia, and Bothwell and the Bishop of Glasgow were despatched to France to renew with the now major Charles VIII the *aliauncez . . . maid before of auld and of new*, to seek for a Queen of Scots, and ensure reciprocity of commercial privileges. French relations, in fact, continued intimate, though without the binding of a royal marriage, for there was no French princess of suitable age. The embassy tried for Maximilian's daughter Mary, but she had been betrothed to the Infante of Spain, so they returned very early in 1492, and received a polite vote of thanks from the Estates.

This parliament of 1492 shows the last repercussion of the civil war. An investigation was demanded, of the fate of the late King's treasure and of himself,

for the eschewing and cessing of the hevy murmar and voce of the peple of the ded, and slauchtir of vmquhile our souerane Lordis faider and progenitor quham god assolze king James the thrid.

A reward was offered for the murderer, but the action

[1] James carried on his predecessors' policy. His correspondence with foreign courts shows clearly his continual deep interest in the ventures of Scots merchants, and his readiness to give them all possible help.

seems to 'have been no more than a gesture : at all events the man was never found.

The parliament of the next May, 1493, shows much, and very assorted, legislation, including a grant of over £1,000 *for the honorabill hamebringing of a Quene* —premature, for it was ten years yet to James's wedding. There is a lowering of prices, and two important groups of legislation. The first is a naval-commercial one, characteristic of the reign, a Shipping Act : it laments the decay of the fisheries, and the *grit innumerable rychis that is tint in fault of shippis and buschis* (busses) and enacts that all coastal burghs are to build vessels of twenty tons, equipped for fishing, and press crews from their able-bodied unemployed— *stark idill men.* The other group is ecclesiastical, a fresh expression of the ' Gallican ' attitude of the Scots Church. It reaffirms the King's right to present to benefices, on the diplomatic ground not of principle but of the distance from the Court of Rome. Detailed regulations are drawn up to govern the relation of the Scots Church and the Curia—among others that no non-Scottish Legate will be received, unless he has the rank of Cardinal. The Scottish ambassadors in Italy are to exhort those of their nationals who have litigation in progress at the Papal courts to withdraw their pleas and have them heard at home. And as a rider to these general enactments, the two Scots Arch-bishops, Glasgow, who was supporting his new dignity, and James III's old favourite, Shivas of St Andrews, who strongly objected to a rival pallium, are adjured with vigour to cease their *contentione and pley* (plea) and submit their quarrel to the arbitration, not of Alexander VI, but of the King.

A few weeks later, there was a new move in Anglo-Scots relations, which though only partly effective at the time, was to lead to others of much greater importance. At the end of the month (May, 1493) Henry sent proposals for a *vera firma perpetua et realis Pax,* or alternatively for a truce to last for the life-time of both Kings, or for such other period, less or more, as might be decided, and offering as guarantee, since his daughter Margaret was only four, the hand of his kinswoman Katharine, daughter of the Countess of Wiltshire, and grand-daughter of Edmund Beaufort, Duke of Somerset. The Scots declined the marriage, and refused also to commit themselves to a perpetual peace, but a truce of six years was signed at Edinburgh on the 22nd of June. The allies of both parties are to be included if they so wish, and give notice to that effect within six months, and the appended lists are of interest as showing the balance of international politics. Those of Scotland are France, the Scandinavian kingdoms, Spain, Naples, the King of the Romans (Maximilian), Austria, Burgundy, and Milan. The English ones are the Emperor, the King of the Romans, Spain, Portugal, Naples, Austria, Burgundy, Ferrara, Savoy, and the merchants of the Hansa. The Italian commitments are worth noting, as within the next twenty years Italian affairs were violently to affect both Scotland and England.

The young King was now twenty, and without any
sort of sudden *coup d'état* had been gradually attaining
active rule. The five years of a reign so inauspiciously
begun had seen much progress towards stability.
There was a decent prospect of foreign peace. The
Lowlands had settled down from their recent disturbance, and young as he was James had shown his uncommon power of winning the liking of different types
of men. Since the Stewart dynasty had reached the
throne, there had never been so little hostility to the
Crown on the part of factious and ambitious nobles.
But since Bruce's day the kingdom that the Kings
between Kenneth I and Alexander III had forged
together had been tending again to divide into two by
no means friendly nations : and the steady spread of
English as the Lowland vernacular had made the
separation definite.[1] The Highlands, in fact, or at
least the still semi-independent principate of the Isles,
had ever since the reign of David II presented a
recurring and urgent problem to a centralising and
unifying government. James set to work to solve it,
and he did, very largely by sheer power of personality.
He allowed himself to be maladvised into one bad and
almost disastrous blunder, but overcame even the
results of that, and founded the traditional and well-
grounded trust of the Highlands in the House of

---

[1] As late as 1553, however, the pupils of the Grammar School of
Aberdeen, then approaching its tercentenary, were bidden to con-
verse in Latin, Greek, Hebrew, French, or Gaelic, English, or rather
by that date, Scots, being barred.

Stewart, which made them the last support of that dynasty, thrice over, when it fell on evil times.

When the reign began, Angus of the Isles was still in active and successful rebellion. In 1490 he was murdered by his own harper, but the disturbance he had created continued, and in the next year the old feud between the Isles and the Crown blazed up once more under new leadership. John was old now, and seems to have taken no active part, but apparently he felt that his past reconciliation had been with King James III, not with the Crown. Apparently with his concurrence, at least, the titles of Lord of the Isles and Earl of Ross were assumed by his nephew, Alexander of Lochalsh. The latter's onslaught was a dangerous one. Assisted by Clan Chattan, he ravaged the Mainland as far as Inverness, where he took the royal castle : then, joined by Clan Cameron and the Clanranald Macdonalds, he attacked the Mackenzie lands in Easter Ross, burning Conon Kirk above its congregation. That clan defeated him bloodily at the battle of Park, famed in Highland history for the generalship of Kenneth of Kintail and the exploits of Big Duncan of the Axe, and took him prisoner. His uncle appealed to England, without success : Henry VII was anxious then for peace with James.

John was old, Angus was dead, Alexander of Lochalsh a prisoner, and Angus's young son, Donald Dubh, a prisoner of his uncle the Earl of Argyle, who was a King's man. In 1493 the Estates decided that there must be an end : they forfeited the actual Lordship itself, which passed to the Crown, and is held now by the heir to the Scottish throne. Old John submitted, retired to Paisley Abbey, and five years later *excellentissimus princeps Johannes Dominus de Insulis* gave up the ghost in a common inn at Dundee, in debt to his landlady for board and lodging.

The action of the Estates might have been ineffective, had it not been for the King's personality, and his gift of attaching to him men of all kinds. He set himself to win over the Isles, by force if he must, by liking if he could. In 1493 he went to Dunstaffnage and to Mingary, where he received the homage of the chiefs. Next year he went thrice, in force, but peaceably, investigating fisheries, encouraging shipbuilding, and above all making himself known and liked. (His knowledge of Gaelic would of course help immensely.) His vigour and charm, his natural sympathy with Highland ideals, and his readiness to take the Gael on his own terms, had a strong effect. The expeditions were gay, but exceedingly useful. The King hunted merrily, yachted, entertained . . . and worked hard, repairing Bruce's castle of Tarbet, building a dockyard there, and garrisoning the same King's old refuge of Dunaverty, while the chiefs who had supported John were pardoned, and received their lands again under Crown charters. There was still a certain amount of opposition. John Macdonald of Islay swooped on Dunaverty as the King left it, and hanged its captain in sight of the royal fleet : the place, however, was recovered shortly by the MacIan MacDonalds of

Ardnamurchan, and the recalcitrant John and his four sons sent to Edinburgh and shortened by the head.

In May 1495 the King returned to the Highlands, and was welcomed. The Highlanders had resisted, and were prepared to go on resisting, the feudal conception of the state, but the personal rule of a king who would stand to them in the patriarchal relation involved in chiefship, was another story, and a pleasanter one. When a little later the freed Alexander of Lochalsh fell foul of Kintail, the Island clans would not rise in his support, and the MacKenzies and Munros together put him down easily.

The years of the pacification of the Highlands saw the founding of a peaceful institution, initiated by Bishop Elphinstone, but supported and highly favoured by the King, whose purpose was to give the Far North an easier access to scholarship and the various arts of peace. This was the third Scots university, founded by Elphinstone in 1494, within a few hundred yards of his Cathedral. Its bull of foundation is of the 10th February 1494 (*i.e.*, 1495 by our reckoning). The Bishop, who had taught at Orleans and Paris, was a great administrator, and no mean scholar. His new university, modelled on that of Paris, the Mother of the North, was most carefully organised from the beginning.[1] It shows the new interest in science,

---

[1] Aberdeen is said to be the only university in Europe that retains the full mediaeval form of the election of a Rector by the *procuratores* of the Nations : the procuratorship, now found nowhere else, is the oldest of all academic offices.

shared by the King, that its original Chairs included the first university foundation in Great Britain for the teaching of medicine.[1] The initial mistake of Elphinstone's Alma Mater, Bishop Turnbull's university of Glasgow, was avoided, and the new institution was adequately endowed, and provided from the start with both a salaried staff and suitable buildings, whose tower, in token of King James's favour, carried, as it still does, the royal crown. The magnificent woodwork of the original chapel, saved by main force from a Reforming mob, is still extant, the finest of its kind in Scotland, but Elphinstone's library, his organ, his cloth of gold hangings and jewelled altar plate, have vanished like so much else : and in spite of his pair of tombs, so has his body, laid to rest after Flodden before the Chapel altar, and removed in secret to save it from profanation by the Reformers.

Two other important educational provisions of the reign may also be mentioned at this point. 1505 saw the foundation at Edinburgh of the College of Surgeons, which received its royal charter the next year. Earlier than this, in 1496, and with the warm approval of King James, the Estates had passed the famous Education Act, compelling all barons and freeholders, under a penalty of £20, to send at least their eldest sons, at the age of eight or nine, to the grammar schools, to remain there

quhill thay be competentlie foundit and have perfyte latyne. And thereftir to remane thre zeris at the sculis of art and jure.

[1] Cambridge acquired one in 1540, Oxford five years later.

Few historians trouble to quote the reason annexed, characteristic of Stewart policy.   It was to supply an intelligent ' officer class,' and especially one acquainted with the law, so that in acting as Sheriffs, or as lords of regalities and baronies (who had their own courts) they might

haue knawlege to do Justice that the pure pepill suld haue na neid to seik our souerane lordis principale auditoris for ilk small Iniure.

In 1495 the twenty-two-year old King embarked upon a curious English adventure, that came near precipitating an English war, and possibly a larger conflagration.   Henry VII had then been ten years on the English throne, and although his own claim was, to put it mildly, doubtful, his marriage to Elizabeth of York made his son at any rate the lawful heir . . . so long as her brothers, the little Edward V and Richard of York, should be content to lie quietly in their grave. The Yorkist *émigrés*, whose head was the Queen's aunt, the Duchess Dowager of Burgundy, disliked the situation very much.   In 1487 a young man of the name of Lambert Simnel proclaimed himself the son of the murdered Clarence, and his claim was backed by the son of Clarence's sister, John de la Pole, Earl of Lincoln.   The affair was effectually put down, Lincoln killed in action, and Simnel given a job in the royal pantry, whence he later graduated to the mews.   Five years after, there was another, and very much more plausible, attempt.   This time the candidate was a

young Fleming, Piers or Perkin Warbeck, who claimed
to be the murdered Duke of York, Queen Elizabeth's
brother. He was a personable young man, of uncommon charm, and when Duchess Margaret took
him up with enthusiasm, and declared that he was
certainly her nephew, many Yorkists sincerely believed that he was the Duke : indeed, it would seem he
came near to believe it himself. Charles VIII accepted
him when he visited France, and appointed him a
prince's guard of honour, with the Scoto-Frenchman
Concressault in command.

Now, ever since the beginning of the reign, the
Yorkists had tried to get Scotland to act against Henry.
Even within a few months of Sauchieburn, Duchess
Margaret was already sending envoys, and in the next
years there was much coming and going between Burgundy, Scotland, and Ireland, in which country there
was still a strong Yorkist feeling. Warbeck betook
himself to Ireland, and James was informed. In
November of 1494 Duchess Margaret herself sent to
tell the King that ' the Prince of England ' wished to
visit him. James gave permission, and preparations for
the guest were made at Stirling, but the visit was postponed by an abortive Yorkist *coup d'état*, betrayed by
Clifford, which cost their party some heads. In the
next year, the Duchess tried once more to enlist King
James, sending to him the O'Donnell of Tyrconnel.
James, apparently, showed signs of being won over.
He had no hostility towards England itself, but he had
no cause for affection towards Henry, who had not only

tried to kidnap him, but intrigued with Angus, virtually
the Regent, to hand over secretly the key of the Border
... not to mention his intromissions with the Isles.
The young ' Duke of York,' if he really was Duke of
York—as his aunt and other people who should know
were informing Europe in general that he was—was the
lawful King of England, extruded by force and
treachery from his throne.   To a young man of James's
chivalrous disposition, this itself would have been some
motive for support.   In fact, there were other, more
politic, reasons as well.   Henry, efficient but grasping
and without charm, was not much loved by the country
that he ruled : if Scottish arms should help the
restoration of a young, attractive, and legitimate King,
there was every reason to anticipate that the venture
would make for Anglo-Scottish friendship.   We know,
of course, that the reasoning was wrong, because
Perkin Warbeck was *not* the lawful heir : but to dismiss
it as mere chivalrous folly—still more as a piece of
folly pure and simple—is considerably less than just to
James, who must act on what he knew in 1495.

Henry took fright, and sent up an embassy, offering
James now the hand of his daughter Margaret, who was
six.   James refused the match.   In November, Warbeck
arrived, and was royally entertained in Stirling Castle,
where the enigmatic ghost of another putative Richard
Plantagenet, Albany's luckless ' mammet,' may have
watched him.   James treated him with his usual
open-handed generosity, allowing him £1,200 a year,
and many rich gifts.   It is not clear how far, in the

beginning, he meant more than kindness to an unfortunate prince and courtesy to a possible future
neighbour. He did not commit himself at once to
action : but after a month Spain precipitated matters
by endeavouring to break the threatened alliance with
the Yorkists, and reconcile James with her ally Henry.
An embassy arrived with the suggestion that since
James had refused an English bride he might accept
a Spanish one instead. The offer was no more than a
desperate and short-sighted playing for time : that it
should be made was a wild expedient that shows the
quality of Henry's alarm, for the three Spanish princesses were all disposed of, to England and Portugal
and the Emperor's heir. James, as might have been
expected, soon found this out. He would not quarrel,
but tactfully shifted the matter to the Greek kalends,
by agreeing to send the Archbishop of Glasgow on the
long road to Spain, and promising that *if* the marriage
were made he would certainly consent to peace with
Henry. Then, in the next month, as a quiet counter-
gesture, he proceeded to arrange another marriage,
of the ' Duke of York ' to Lady Katharine Gordon,
Huntly's daughter, and grand-daughter of his own
great-aunt, Princess Annabel.

Affairs hung there for a while. Warbeck and his
beautiful wife took their share in all the functions of a
gay court. Henry sent fresh proposals for an English
marriage, and Ferdinand and Isabella for a Spanish
one, sending up a fresh envoy, Don Pedro de Ayala,
who in spite of his task was a wise and able man who

won James's friendship and gave him back his own, and has left us vivid portraits of king and country. France took a hand as well, and for once did not want an Anglo-Scottish war, especially if it were going to en-throne a King of England thirled to Burgundy. Charles, by the recent Treaty of Etaples, had made peace with Henry, and wanted no English enmity in his rear to hamper him during the war in Italy he had opened in September 1494. He sent over Concressault with a suggestion that he should mediate between James and Henry, and according to the report of an English spy, to offer 10,000 crowns for the person of York.

The proposal that he should stoop to sell his guest, if it were made, would certainly not please James. The flagrant dupery of the Spanish offer, and well-grounded doubts of Henry's sincerity, were clearly hardening the King's resolution, and apart from personal feeling in the matter, the Yorkists had promised a liberal *quid pro quo*. One of Henry's spies, in the autumn of 1496, reports that Warbeck had undertaken not only to restore the town of Berwick but to hand over certain lands in the Marches as well.

At length, when ' York ' had been nearly a year in Scotland, James decided on active support of the Yorkist rising. Henry, of course, was working by underground means, in the normal Tudor manner, as well as by open ones. He sent up Ramsay, the ex-Earl of Bothwell, who won over Buchan, his old associate in Henry's plot against James in 1491, and along with him Buchan's brother the Bishop of Moray, and more important, the young Duke of Ross, who was still the King's heir. He induced them to oppose the war, which in fact does not seem to have been popular, as Warbeck's arrogance and extravagance were alienating those who had been friendly. Ross even went so far as to offer to put himself under Henry's protection if James should invade . . . a step which may perhaps have been well-intended, but suspiciously recalls his uncle's conduct : and a plot was formed to seize Warbeck in his tent and hand him over.

James, now pledged to the attempt, was as good as his word, though one gathers that he himself was by now growing weary of his guest. He called up all men of military age, including those of the Isles, to a muster at Lauder, and gathered together the artillery : Mons Meg was taken from Edinburgh Castle, with minstrels going before her *doun the gait*, in spite of which she ungratefully broke her carriage. It was a costly venture, and Warbeck had already proved expensive : James had to coin his ' great chain ' to raise ready money : it was 13½ lbs. weight, and worth £1,500 simply as bullion. Certain English Yorkists arrived, and the Duchess of Burgundy sent over two shiploads of military stores, with a small contingent of men-at-arms.

In September James met his troops, and war was declared. Warbeck was proclaimed in England as Richard IV, and issued a manifesto accusing Henry of usurpation, murder, and extortion, offering £1,000 reward for his person, and pledging himself to lower

x

taxes and maintain the rights of Church, nobles, and merchants. (The significant omission would not please James.) The affair fell flat. His English partisans, like those of Charles Edward, refused to rise for a King over the Water unless he brought substantial foreign help, and were scandalised out of loyalty when he did. Warbeck announced that he would not shed the blood of his own subjects, and fell back on Coldstream ; in fact, it is possible that a man who had sufficient imagination to live his romance in such a convincing fashion might find it a considerable shock to find it plunging him in authentic bloodshed. James, more secure—he at least was convinced of his cause— raided Northumberland : but it was growing late, and food was scarce. He withdrew, and ordered another muster for spring. Henry and the Spaniards negotiated again, but though James had been further chilled by Warbeck's slackness, he would not give up his guest. In early June Lord Dacre invaded Scotland, and was defeated by the Master of Home. James met his troops at Melrose a little later : but by now he was most reluctant for a war. Before he could move, Henry sent up the Bishop of Durham, Foxe, with instructions to make peace on any terms so long as they included Warbeck's surrender. Before he reached Scotland, Warbeck himself had cut the situation. On the 6th of July, he sailed from Ayr on a ship of Robert Barton's : James, although thankful by now to be rid of him, treated him well to the last, fitting the ship commodiously for his comfort, and equipping his wife with appropriate travelling gear, including a sea-gown of *rowane cannee*. He tried the other end of England this time, landing in Cornwall with no more success : in fact he bolted and left his men to Henry. He was taken and hanged, and it is to Henry's credit (as shifty as he was, he was never vindictive) that his widow, the unlucky ' White Rose of Scotland,' was kindly treated. She ended her odd adventures by marrying, one hopes happily, a Welsh knight, and became the ancestress of the Earls of Pembroke.

With Warbeck out of the way, Henry was only too thankful for peace with Scotland, and James had no longer any motive for war : and he never desired to make it for war's sake. Ayala arrived once more with proposals for a truce, and one was made at Aytoun in September, for seven years. It was nearly upset at once by the Governor of Norham, who caused an ' incident ' on the East March by a piece of heavy-handed officiousness : but by December the hard-working Ayala induced the two Kings to extend it for their joint lives, and accept Spanish arbitration of any breach. The allies are included as before. France and Venice have been added to the English, Milan, Gueldres, Cleves, Holstadt, and the Mark of Brandenburg (*i.e.*, incipient Prussia) to the Scots.

James ratified the amended truce in February of 1498, and set out for the Isles. At Campbeltown he received the homage of Alexander MacLeod of Dunvegan and Torquil MacLeod of the Lews, and attempted to settle a feud betweeen two branches of the MacDonalds. Then, probably through the influence of Argyle, he made one of the big mistakes of his career. He suddenly reversed his Highland policy, which until now had been uniformly successful, and turned from a patriarchal to a feudal relation, revoking all charters, and making Argyle Lieutenant of the South Isles and Huntly of the North, with commissions to feu the lands again to new tenants. The natural result was hot indignation : it is the least defensible action of James's career. Even then, his earlier policy had made so profound and far-reaching an impression that there was no immediate revolt. In 1501, however, the rising discontent found a spearhead in young Donald Dubh, the son of Angus, who escaped from his uncle Argyle and took refuge in the Lews. Even so, it was not until 1503 that the West really rose. Then it did so formidably : Badenoch was laid waste, Inverness burnt. In the next spring the general legal organisation was extended to include the Isles, where new sheriffdoms were created : but it needed two years of hard fighting to quiet them down. Indeed, it was not until 1506 that Huntly stormed Stornoway Castle, and forced MacLeod of the Lews to surrender. Donald Dubh escaped to Ireland, where he died. King James, who had by this time seen his error, went back to a policy of conciliation, and in spite of the mistrust he had created, carried it out again with so much success that the clans were pacified, and returned to a friendly relation with the Crown, that endured until the conclusion of the reign.

While these affairs were in progress in the North-west, there were others of much moment farther south, that led first to the second peace of the Three Hundred Years' War [1] and later, though not for another century, to so complete a reversal of that war's initial purpose as the placing of a Scots king on the throne of England. In the autumn of 1499, Henry renewed his proposal for an Anglo-Scots marriage. James, now twenty-six, was reluctant still, perhaps for personal reasons. His earlier connection with Marion Boyd, the mother of his beloved son Alexander, was probably over by now, but he was certainly entangled at this time with Janet Kennedy, the ex-mistress of Angus, and a lady with considerable talent for ex-tracting substantial gifts of land from her lovers ; and besides this there was a more serious affair, with Margaret, the daughter of Lord Drummond, whose *portrait parlé*, the poem *Tayis Bank*, has a suggestion of silver-point grace and charm below the phrases of its courtly convention. James was deeply in love : it was thought he might marry her, and rumoured that he had done so secretly. Whether that would have been wholly a misfortune is questionable : the match had no political advantage, and would have caused very dangerous jealousies : and there might of

---

[1] The first ' perpetual peace ' of 1328 had lasted for five years : this one endured a little more than eleven.

course have been no Union of Crowns, which would probably have meant more futile wars. But there is another side. A marriage that satisfied his personal needs might have given James that stability of being, that assurance of strength that is in his great-grand-father, and have saved him in the deadly stresses of his last years. One cannot tell : we do not know enough of Margaret Drummond . . . only that James, until the end of his life, had masses said for the repose of her soul. And we do know much—too much—of Margaret Tudor.

The insistent King Henry continued his proposals, and even applied for a provisional dispensation. (James's great-grandmother, Queen Joan, was sister of Margaret's great-grandfather Somerset, so they were just within the forbidden degrees.) It was granted in July of 1500. Still James held back. And then, a few months later, Margaret Drummond and her two sisters, seated at breakfast, were suddenly taken violently ill, and died.

In October of 1501, James gave in at last, and deter-mined to accept the politic marriage : the fact that his bride was only a child of twelve may conceivably have made him less reluctant. He announced his intention in Letters Patent from Stirling, bearing that

quo Matrimonio et ipsius sacro Foedere Hostilitates, Inimi-citiae, et alia Enormia quamplurima inter Reges et Regna multotiens sedantur, atque ex animis pelluntur Principum : Amor, Dilectio, Comitas, Pax, Tranquillitas, atque Caritas radicantur, multaeque aliae Felicitates et Bona innumerabilia consequuntur firmantur et stabiliuntur.

Bothwell, with the Archbishop of Glasgow, and For-
man, the Proto-notary Apostolic, were despatched as
envoys to discuss the terms, and at Richmond on the
24th of January 1502, Henry signed the double treaty,
of marriage and of perpetual peace and friendship. On
the 22nd of February, in Glasgow Cathedral, near the
right horn of the altar, James ratified it.[1] There was
to be a

bona, realis, sincera, vera, integra, et firma Pax, Amicitia,
Liga, et Confoederatio, per Terram, Mare, et Aquas dulces ac
ubique Locorum . . . semper perpetuis futuris Temporibus
duratura.

Each King promised not to shelter the other's rebels,
and the usual passport and extradition arrangements,
common to many previous truces, were made. The
town of Berwick was specially included, to be un-
disturbed, which amounted to virtual cession. James
clearly was in no mood to argue his terms, nor dared
his advisors try to induce him to do so. The so-long-
refused bride was only to bring £10,000 . . . and if
she died without issue the unpaid instalments of that
were to be remitted.

Even in the details of his long-cherished plan,
Henry avoided extravagance with some care. A letter
of that summer throws an amusing side-light on his
habits, as well as one that is somewhat less amusing,

[1] The documents of the ceremony are extant, and very decorative.
The marriage treaty, the work of one Thomas Galbraith of the Chapel
Royal of Stirling, is specially rich, with a splendid border of roses,
thistles, and daisies, the royal arms, and the monograms of the
spouses.

if one looks under the surface, on the attitude of his son-in-law to the match.   It is a reply from James to his *Derrest Fader*, who wants him to

> supersede or cesse the Confirmatione of the AULD LYIG and BAND had and observit of lang tyme betuix Ws and the Maist Cristyn Prince the King of Fraunce our Predecessouris Realmes and Subdittis.

James consents to postpone the ratification until he can see Henry and discuss the matter . . . and goes on to the pay of the Queen's twenty-five English followers.   Henry has asked what he is going to pay them :   James replies quietly that he is not bound to pay anything at all, but if his *Derrest Fader* prefers him to stand their salaries, he will.

The settlements were agreed on by the lawyers, the Queen's jointure of £2,000 a year, her dower lands of Ettrick, Newark, the Earldom of March, Linlithgow, Stirling, Menteith, Methven, and Doune :   and on the 17th of December 1502, they were all confirmed over again at Edinburgh, with a significant little incident. James signed the indentures, and then when he had signed, discovered that since the document had been drawn up in England, Henry's name appeared on it as *King of France*.[1]   James may possibly have suspected that he was being trapped :   he certainly would not insult his oldest ally by assenting to this preposterous claim of a new one, and at once had drawn up a notarial instrument bearing that he had signed the

[1] All the French soil that had been in English possession for fifty years now was the town of Calais :   but till 1801 this title, and the quartering of the lilies, were still a regular part of English usage.

thing inadvertently, and ordered another copy to be made, from which the offending title was omitted.

During the preparations for his marriage, James intervened with success in a foreign war. The great Scandinavian disturbances of the early century that were to end, though not until 1523, in the separation of Sweden under Gustavus Vasa, broke out in this time, and the Swedes captured and imprisoned Queen Christina, the wife of James's uncle King John : he sent a squadron, the *Eagle, Toward, Douglas,* and *Christopher,* with two thousand men under his father's cousin Hamilton, now made Earl of Arran : and they released the Queen.

Enormous preparations were made for the marriage. James may have been something of a reluctant bride-groom, but he went about the matter with an air. He did not quite touch the splendour of his son's gown of cloth of gold with forty-nine thousand five hundred fine orient pearls, but his wardrobe had its points, undoubtedly. The Treasurer's records glitter with cloth of gold and gold-flowered damask, velvet of cramoisie and Rissillis black. The new palace that he never lived to finish was building at Holyrood, where one tower is left yet (Cromwell's men wrecked the rest) and the Queen's Chamber was hung with a hundred and forty-seven ells of velvet, red and *purpure blew,* with seventy-seven of cloth of gold for her bed. All the Royal Household went braw in the King's gifts, from Hamilton's sixteen ells of gold-flowered damask to the porters strutting in French tan cloth and satin. All the Southern ladies were bidden to the Border to greet the bride, and a garden of colours they must have made at Newbattle. The great winged lawn towers of the last reign were out now before the little close French hood, but they shimmered in cloth of gold, crimson velvet and black, satin and ' tinsel ' and many-coloured damask.

The bride set out in the summer of 1503, in charge of Surrey, whom James was to meet again in ten years' time. Northumberland and the Archbishop of York, the greatest men of the North of England, came with her. They reached Newbattle on the 3rd of August. James arrived, and there was a stately supper, whereafter he returned to Edinburgh, coming back next day to find his bride at cards among her ladies. As a substitute for talk, he played to her on the clavichord and the lute, she danced for him, and was duly complimented : then he sprang to his horse without setting foot in the stirrup, and was off at the gallop. Four days after that he met her outside Edinburgh, and she rode pillion behind him through the city, on a magnificent bay horse trapped with gold, past pageants of saints and angels and goddesses, streets hung with tapestry, fountains running wine. They were married at Holyrood on the next day . . . and the morning after, James, to please his bride, allowed Lady Surrey to cut off his beard, and gave her fifteen ells of cloth of gold as a barber's fee.[1] There were masques and pageants and plays and tournaments, and it may have been then

[1] It cost £180—perhaps the largest hairdresser's tip on record.

that James founded the Order of the Thistle : it had been the national emblem for some little time. And according to a letter of Margaret's own, Surrey was in great favour with the King : she seems, poor child, to have been a little jealous.

The next few years, with James in his early thirties, saw a good deal of active and successful work. The pacification of the Highlands, accomplished during that time, has already been mentioned. Now he attempted the same thing for the Borders, where disturbance, though on a smaller scale, was endemic. In the year after his marriage he went on a round of police-work, and took with him Lord Dacre, the English Warden : there is a touch of gay picnic about the proceedings, but there was a very practical side as well : among the Treasurer's entries for huntsmen and minstrels are such others as that of a certain eightpenny rope, *for the thevis at the Hallinbus* ; and the Border clans were quieter for a while.

The parliaments of these years show a good deal of detailed domestic legislation. All the country, including the Isles, now came under one law, and the administration of that was in several points reformed. Stiff qualifications were laid down for notaries. The expense of legislation was reduced. No ' remissions ' were to contain a general clause that should cover any unspecified offences. A daily court was to sit in Edinburgh, which more or less confirmed that town's place as the capital, which it had held in practice through the last reign. It was sought to make Parliament more representative by compelling the attendance of all freeholders of over 100 merks, while those under that sum could choose between appearing in person or sending procurators. An important act gave security of tenure : the King or any man else could feu his whole lands, and the feu should stand for the feuar's heirs as well, thus definitely commuting military service for rent. All sasines had to be duly registered. One notices the amount of legislation that has special reference to the merchant class. The burgh privileges were secured. Merchants abroad could only litigate among themselves in the Conservator's (a kind of Consul's) court, while to secure fair dealing when they did so, he was to be supported by a council of six from among the most able merchants, and keep himself in touch with home affairs by a return to Scotland every year. And there is a significant attempt, now the long exhausting war seemed over for good, to repair its desolations. Timber is to be conserved, and more to be planted : the lairds are bidden to improve their lands with plantations and orchards, parks and warrens and hedges. There is some evidence that these peaceful labours were not without result. Soon after his marriage James made the personal experiment of riding quite alone from Stirling to Elgin : he did it, unmolested, in a day, slept for some hours in his clothes on top of a table, and went on to his favourite shrine of St Duthac's at Tain, where having heard a mass and made thanksgiving for the quiet of the

country, he returned to the South again in a splendid
' progress.'

Foreign affairs seemed as prosperous as domestic,
though the quarrel of France and Spain in 1503, over
the kingdom of Naples, made Louis XII eager for a
Scots breach with England, who was Spain's chief
ally. James succeeded, however, in keeping on good
terms with all three countries. He had ended, perhaps
at a bitter personal cost, the long English war of two
centuries and a quarter : for the rest of his reign, till
the very last weeks of it, he strove passionately for the
peace of Europe, for unity in face of the dangerous
East. Love of peace, indeed, was a Stewart characteristic. Almost all of that house had plenty of
personal courage, and most, indeed, showed a hearty
zest in fighting when that had once become unavoid-
able. Nearly all, too, had a large fund of *moral* courage,
of a willingness to undertake great risks to support the
values of the code they followed. But their passion
as rulers, the passion especially of those of them who
were born and nourished fighters, was for peace, and
for the wholeness of the nation. That last desire had
a side that was dangerous. In those who were narrow
mentally, like Charles I, it could be disastrous, since
it ran easily into an attempt at not only unity but unwise
uniformity, which is unity imposed from the outside.
None the less, when we look at the whole dynasty, it
is their glory that they were Kings of Peace . . . and
to be that, a ruler must face long struggle, and the
chance of something like martyrdom in the end.

Through this first decade of the century we find James constantly acting as mediator between quarrelling powers. He took a hand again in his uncle's affairs, and succeeded in reconciling Scandinavia with Lubeck and the cities of the Hansa. One small ally gave his *corps diplomatique* a good deal of work. In 1505, James was adjuring Gueldres to be civil to his father-in-law King Henry, and get rid of Suffolk, the last hope of the Yorkists, who was sheltering there. The Duke acted on his advice, and as reward, demanded assistance against the Emperor; and James, enlisting the help of Louis XII, achieved a settlement of the dispute. In the next year and the next again, his protégé was again in trouble, first with Flanders, Holland, and Brabant, and then with the Emperor once more. James intervened again, and again with success, though the last intervention had strange, far-reaching, and unhappy results, for the reconciliation of Maximilian and Gueldres was to lead directly to the League of Cambrai. All these affairs were matters of peaceful diplomatic procedure, though to be sure that had the sanction behind it of an efficient and enlarging fleet and a country whose high military reputation had not been lowered by the successful issue of two centuries and a quarter of war against odds. The only armed intervention was with Portugal, which had seized John Barton's *Lion*, and would not disgorge. James gave letters of marque and reprisal to Barton's sons, that cost the Portuguese Indian and African fleets a good deal more than the value of the *Lion*.

In February of 1507, a Prince of Scotland was born, and James was delighted, giving the lady who was first with the news a hundred gold pieces and a silver cup. Indeed, there was general rejoicing, and with good reason, since a hard-riding King without a son had cost Scotland very dearly in the past, and the King's younger brother, John Earl of Mar, had died unmarried a few months before James's wedding, while the Duke of Ross, the titular Archbishop of St Andrews, had followed him within a year of it, so that the next heir was the Duke of Albany, half French, brought up in France and a traitor's son, and after him Arran, a reckless, light-headed fool.

The opening decade of the sixteenth century is one of those eras of our history that show the fairest promise for the future. All through the first twenty years of James's reign one sees the old dangers— England, the wars between the Crown and the nobles, between Highland and Lowland—lift their heads, and couch. ' The clouds of pride and madness and mysterious sorrow '[1] that darken so much of the fifteenth century and make stormy night of so much of the fourteenth, seemed clearing before a sane and steady daylight, and after sunrise. The shattered country had forged now into a union that she had not known since the last years of Robert Bruce. Churchmen and nobles, burgesses, country people, felt a

[1] G. K. Chesterton on the Scottish nobility, in *The Innocence of Father Brown*.

common and personal loyalty to the King, more deep and widespread than for two hundred years. Scotland, indeed, had recovered, and increased, the prosperity of the thirteenth century, of the peaceful and thriving years of the last Alexanders. She was not, of course, wealthy, as Flanders or Venice knew wealth. Her natural resources forbade that, for one thing : our country is richer than most in the matter of beauty, but not in much else : and Ayala, with a dry chuckle, gives other reasons. ' The people,' he says, ' are not industrious : they prefer to spend their time in making war, or if there is no war, to fight with one another.' He liked them, for all that : his picture is a friend's. The men are handsome, well-dressed, hospitable, courageous, strong, quick of mind and body, their vice being jealousy. He admired the women, whom he found courteous, chaste, but friendly and frank of bearing, independent, mistresses of their own property, and incidentally, of their husbands also. They are, he says, very pleasant to look upon, and dress better than their neighbours across the Border.[1]

It is clear, however, and not only from Ayala's description, that if Scotland was poor beside Flanders or even England, her poverty was only comparative : there is grim testimony to that effect in comments on the physique of Scottish corpses after more than one

---

[1] He specially admires, but unluckily does not describe, their head-dress. Perhaps French influences, not to speak of the climate, put them early into the graceful black velvet hood : the change from the lawn wings would come about the time when he was writing.

battle : the common people were sturdy and well-
nourished. What is left to us of the building of the
time (there is a good deal) is further evidence : indeed,
the fifteenth century opens one of the three great times
of our architecture, not only religious, like its predecessor, but secular as well : the delicate richness and
restraint of Melrose are mated by many castles, built for
splendour and even comfort—a later desire—as well
as for strength, in a beautiful arrogant mode inspired
by France but fully naturalised, the characteristic stark
and masculine shaft with its crown of arrogant orna-
ment at the summit. Many are left, though most of
the more important have been incorporated in later
buildings : the ' magnificent abbeys ' of which Ayala
speaks are known to us only as rickles of shattered
stone, and the bien houses of the solid burghers, the
town ' lodgings ' of the nobles, are gone completely.
Ayala says of the houses in the towns that they are
' good, all built of stone, and provided with excellent
doors, glass windows, and a great number of chimneys.
All the furniture that is used in Italy, France, and
Spain is to be found in them. It has not, either, been
bought recently, but inherited from the past.' There
were gardens also, like that in which the spoilt beauties
of Dunbar exchanged those very unbeautiful con-
fidences : we can trace the ghost of the great formal one
under Stirling Rock, where the King's white peacock
sauntered in silvery pride.

    Of the other arts, we have only such scanty traces as
the splendid screen at King's College, Aberdeen,

Y

fragments of plate, the wall-paintings at the Kirk of Foulis Easter.[1] Not a scrap of the coloured glass the age so loved survives of all its saints and armorials. A great part even of its literature has been swept into nothing—half of Dunbar's procession of dead poets are *nominum umbrae* : but there was much of it, flamboyant coloured stuff, highly formalised but almost brutally living, the most vital in Northern Europe at the time. The contrast between fifteenth century Scotland and England, with regard to creative work in literature, is no less marked than the Victorian one : only then the balance was the other way. The music is lost now, but there was much : there are references to it everywhere, and phantasmal recurrent traces of growing drama : what there is left of the next generation's, the first from which any whole play has survived, shows it more advanced than in England at the time.

We have seen already the growing provision for national education, and that scientific as well as humanistic : besides those foundations that have been already mentioned, the end of the reign saw another of importance, the College of St Leonard at St Andrews, founded by Prior Hepburn and the young Archbishop, Alexander Stewart, for the training of poor students in logic and theology. Nor was education confined to the home schools and universities. Latin was still a spoken tongue throughout Europe, and the wandering Scot still took his free-

[1] In the mid fifteenth century two Scots sculptors were in the service of the Duke of Burgundy.

dom of it, from the north of the Empire to South Italy.[1] The close link with France had of course its special effect : Ayala remarks how commonly French was spoken. In 1507 the new tool of learning—it was not yet that of ignorance—the press, was brought to Scotland by Bishop Elphinstone. *Prentit bukis* had been on sale by 1501, for the King bought several in that year from a Frenchman, Quintilian and Vergil and some books of devotion. In September of 1507, however, the first actual Scottish press was set up in Edinburgh by Walter Chepman and Andrew Myllar, who were given the royal licence to print

the bukis of our lawis, actis of parliament, croniclis, mess bukis and portuus efter the use of our realme [2] . . . and al utheris bukis that sal be sene necessare, and to sel the sammyn for competent pricis.

Abroad, Scotland was to be reckoned with throughout Europe. She was small, but a nursery of hard-fighting soldiers, that made her valuable as an ally. To quote the Spanish diplomat once more, ' Scotland has succoured most of her neighbours. With regard to France and Flanders this is notorious.' Her position in a day where sea-power had suddenly become of such vast importance was greatly enhanced by James's important fleet, to which he himself devoted much

[1] In the fourteen-nineties the Prior of Kelso is mentioned as a friend of Politian : it is not quite clear if it is he himself or a brother monk who is the Dom James of Kelso who somewhat earlier was writing Greek hymns for Lorenzo de' Medici.

[2] Elphinstone's *Aberdeen Breviary*, incorporating the ' propers ' of the Scottish saints, was among the first, and is mentioned in the licence, which bans the *Sarum Breviary* hitherto used.

labour, inspecting his dockyards, going on trial trips, bringing shipwrights trained in the latest modern methods from France and Italy and the Low Countries, and showing favour to such brilliant sailors as Sir Andrew Wood, the family of the Bartons, Sir Alexander Matheson, and William Merrimouth, called the King of the Sea.

There is a darker side to the brilliance, of course. Scotland did not escape the spiritual decadence that is the note of the age all over Europe, the hard brutality underneath its splendour. The Church, that should have provided the medicine for it, was corrupt and worldly, the Orders in decay, poisoned by their own wealth. The corruption can be, and has been, exaggerated. There were still churchmen like Bishop Elphinstone, a man of blameless life, a sweet strength of spirit,[1] fine scholarship, and a wise passion for reform ; or Bishop Brown of Dunkeld, who was at pains to send Gaelic-speaking friars, carefully chosen, on missionary journeys through the Highlands : and these were not the only men who worked for a spiritual and intellectual reformation. One instrument for that, or meant for that, was the collegiate churches that are a characteristic of this age : thirty were founded under the first four Jameses. These were small communities of secular priests, St Giles's, Edinburgh, which was the most important (it was not a Cathedral till the seventeenth century), had a provost and curate,

---

[1] Boece, who as Principal of his university, knew him well, describes him in age : *senectus ei iucunda et veneranda, non morosa, non anxia, non difficilis, non tristis.*

sixteen prebendaries, four choristers, a sacristan, and a beadle, while many also had schools attached to them. But although it is unjust to ignore the active measures of reform from within, or to take too literally the writings of a satirist (and a disappointed courtier-priest) like Dunbar, there is no doubt but that reform was needed. One fount of corruption was the evil custom, far from peculiar to Scotland, but rampant there, of regarding the higher offices of the Church as convenient endowments for younger or illegitimate sons of great houses, who accepted them as mere means to livelihood. Again it is possible to exaggerate. Bishop Elphinstone, the virtual though not the nominal head of the Scots Church through great part of this reign, was a poor man's son,[1] and though James gave the Primacy first to his brother and then to his natural son, at an age too early even for the priesthood, the choice in the latter case at all events would certainly seem to have been well justified, for Alexander Stewart has been described as ' the Marcellus of the Scottish Church.' The threnody for him of his tutor Erasmus suggests not only a distinguished young scholar but a lad of nature as fine as his person was handsome. He died, aged twenty, beside his father at Flodden.

Allowing most amply for its darker side, the time has the vigour, the cheerfulness, the promise, the sense of eagerness and of morning daylight that one finds two

---

[1] His father is said to have been a parish priest : this does not necessarily mean that he was illegitimate, as many widowers have taken orders.

generations later in England, at the opening of the great age called Elizabethan. James, and the men he had chosen to group round him, had built on the battered but substantial foundations of his great-grandfather and his grandfather, had recovered what was ruined after 1290, and more, for though the Scotland of the last Alexanders was very decidedly a part of Europe, she was not the power she had grown to be under the Jameses. Small as she was, no country, in 1505, seemed more ready to share the new life of the Renaissance. But the sunlight was eclipsed before that noon.

HERE
ENDS
CHAPTER
XI

CHAPTER XII

FLODDEN

' Still from the sire the son shall hear
Of the stern strife, and carnage drear,
Of Flodden's fatal field,
Where shiver'd was fair Scotland's spear,
And broken was her shield : '
Sir Walter Scott, *Marmion.*

SCOTLAND has been ill-served by her own historians, but there are not many episodes of our past, at any rate of our mediaeval past, that have been so much distorted by omissions as the catastrophe that closed this reign. The common account is that James, for amusement or glory, invaded wantonly a friendly neighbour : heroic conduct when, as with Henry V, the invasion chances to end in a success, but otherwise deserving of all reprobation. A few historians, somewhat more thorough, remark that the invasion was in French interests, and point out what a shocking thing it was to prefer an old friend to a very new one. The irony is all the more rich in flavour in that James worked harder, perhaps, than any man to avoid the general European war in which this fatal campaign was an incident. He feared in it the undoing of Christendom : it brought, indeed, the ruin of his work, and by mercy, his death before he had time to know that. No brave man has gone to war with more reluctance : he struggled for years, speaking sense to the insane greed of his fellow-monarchs, before their united stress grew too strong for him, and he was forced to the *ultima ratio regum*, and went down at last with an arrow in his throat, within a lance's length of the English commander, that Surrey who had brought him home his bride.

The causes of Flodden tangle like a tree's roots, in the strange and complicated course of events that when Scotland, France, Spain, and England were growing to nations, left Italy a chaos of small states. The jealous conflict of Milan and Venice, in the mid-fifteenth century, was quieted for a little after Lodi : but in the fourteen-eighties, in James's childhood, Venice found herself fighting again, not only Milan, but Naples and the Pope : and she was beaten. Then the blaze spread outwards, in a manner with which the present generation is more familiar than that of its fathers. Venice sought for revenge, or, as her statesmen conceived it, for a balance of power in the Peninsula : and she looked for an ally against her enemies. Now, France had some claims on both Milan and Naples. Louis of Orleans, the brother-in-law and heir-presumptive of Charles VIII, had a right to the former through his grandmother, against the Sforze who were its actual holders, by their descent from her illegitimate niece. Charles himself had some claim, less clear, but not unplausible, to Naples : the reigning monarch of that little kingdom, Ferrante, was of illegitimate birth, but by blood a cousin of Ferdinand of Spain. The young Charles was tempted into attacking Ferrante's kingdom.

In 1494 he crossed the Alps, and the history of modern Europe begins.

He took Naples, and easily. Spain, which held Sicily, was alarmed and indignant, suspecting in Charles a design of reuniting the severed parts of the old kingdom of the Two Sicilies. Maximilian of Hapsburg, not yet formally Emperor, suspected that Charles might seek the Imperial Crown, still nominally given by election. Venice realised that Charles had been too successful, that in inducing him to march on Naples she had brought a foreign power into Italy : and the Pope looked on France's entry with no more liking. There was a rapid political setting to partners. Spain, Maximilian, and all of the Italian states save Florence joined against France to form the League of Venice : and she was driven out.

Charles was killed by accident in 1498, and succeeded by his very distant cousin, Louis d'Orléans, now Louis XII. He married Charles's widow, Anne of Brittany, and carried on his predecessor's policy, adding now to the claim to Naples his own personal, and valid, one to Milan. The League of Venice had broken up as soon as it had won its victory, and its members were quarrelling among themselves. In 1499 Louis attacked again, with the aid of Venice, and easily took Milan. Being thus in control of Northern Italy, he pushed on towards Naples. Ferdinand, not then wishing for war with France, was content for the time to divide what spoils were going. By 1501 the lion's skin had been flayed, and the huntsmen fell out over the division. In 1502, the year in which James made perpetual peace with England, France and Spain were at war with each other in Italy, and the conflagration was threatening to spread much farther.

It did. England saw in a Franco-Spanish war an excellent opportunity against France. France looked to Scotland, as always, for help against England ; and, Spain, England's ally, did what she could for a Franco-Scottish breach, while Louis worked against the Anglo-Scots marriage. James, for the moment, was holding the balance of power in Northern Europe : and he used his position to keep peace not only for Scotland but abroad. So long as he, with his united country, its fighting reputation and strong fleet, should lie neutral on the flank of Spain's ally England, the cautious Henry would certainly think three times before committing his country to a French war ; and France would not care to provoke an English attack unless Scotland were active in her enemy's rear. James continued friendly relations with all three countries, exasperated them all by doing so, but made time in which international politics might conceivably have settled down in peace.

Then, however, in the year after James's marriage— that is, in 1504—a new factor appeared, ' the turbulent, unquiet, but magnificent Prelate,' as Drummond calls him, the soldier-pope Julius II.[1] He looked with dis-

---

[1] When Michael Angelo carved him holding a book, he is said to have grumbled, ' What do you mean by this book ? Give me a sword ! '

like on the narrowing temporal power of the Papacy, and attempted to recover the Romagna from Cesare Borgia and the Republic of Venice. It sounds domestic enough to Italy : it made a permanent mark upon Scots affairs. Venice, afraid, looked round her to find help, and the situation farther north was changing, as new international jealousies appeared. Certain deaths in the royal houses of Spain and Portugal had left the Infanta Juaña heiress to Spain : she was married to the heir of Maximilian, the Archduke Philip ; and their son, who was later to shadow Europe as Charles V, was betrothed to Claude of France, King Louis's daughter . . . and Louis had no son, or near heir-male. Philip died in 1506, Juaña went mad, and Charles was left heir to Spain : and still Louis had no son. The French Estates-general (the representative assembly) implored their King to break Madame Claude's betrothal : and in 1507, Maximilian, who was still only Emperor Elect, accused Louis of aiming at the Imperial Crown, and marched south to receive it and forestall him.

Pope Julius took the Emperor's side against France, and endeavoured to upset the Northern balance by breaking its keystone, the Franco-Scots alliance. He named James ' Protector of the Christian religion,' and sent to him the jewelled hat and sword which were by custom blessed by the Pope each year for presentation to some favoured prince. (The sword is still in Edinburgh Castle.) James received the gift with all due courtesy, and sent Julius in reply a civil announcement that he had word from his uncle of Scandinavia that the Czar, the latter's ally, meant to turn Catholic : but to all the Pope's political suggestions, of abandoning France, he presented a bland refusal. Instead, he made clear what line he would take if there should be a general war, by offering an army to King Louis.

Maximilian's invasion was unsuccessful, and Louis did not need active Scots assistance. Now, however, at the end of the year 1507, a piece of sharp practice by Henry VII caused friction with England. Henry disliked his son-in-law's refusal to permit France to be wholly overshadowed by a *bloc* of Pope and Emperor, Spain and England. His irritation made him act with less than his usual circumspection. Arran and his brother had been to France on a diplomatic mission, and returned through England. Henry, regardless of the peace, detained them, and refused to let them go, until they had sworn an oath of perpetual peace. They refused, and James protested. In the next March, that is of 1508, Henry, still holding to his *détenus*, sent up one Dr West to the Scots court, to propose a personal interview of the two Kings, and to detach James from the French alliance. Public opinion in Scotland was solid for France : it would seem, indeed, that the Queen and the Bishop of Moray were the only people who favoured Henry's proposal. James was in a very difficult position. His infant son had died in the previous month, and Arran, for practical purposes, was his heir. (Albany was senior in line, but at that time might not have been accepted.) He compromised : he would not act against France, but so long as Henry would stay ' his loving father,' he would postpone a formal renewal of the alliance. Louis disliked this ambiguous attitude, which—probably with design—was cramping his bellicose schemes in Italy. In May he sent a counter-embassy, headed by Sellat, President of the Parlement de Paris, and the great soldier, Bernard Stuart d'Aubigny, *le chevalier sans reproche*, ' the Father of War.' [1] Their purpose was first, to ask the advice of James on the marriage of King Louis's young daughter—to the Archduke Charles or the next male heir to France, François de Valois, Comte d'Angoulême—and secondly, to procure the adhesion of Scotland to a league against Venice, whose component parts were Louis and his old foes, the Pope and the Emperor. James advised the native marriage rather than the foreign, and his advice was taken : but while he would not share a war on France, no more would he share an aggressive war by France. He stayed courteously and obstinately neutral.

Explosives were piling up all over Europe, and Henry persisted in holding on to Arran . . . while the Queen's second child, a girl, born in July, died almost at once, leaving the King still childless. In December the Pope, the Emperor, and Louis made a definite league, known as the League of Cambrai, drew

---

[1] Grandson of the Connétable de Buchan's captain Sir John Stewart of Darnley. He died soon after his arrival in Scotland, and Dunbar lamented him in stately verse.

into it Ferdinand, the ally of England, and made further attempts at persuading James to join them. Still he held out, though Henry's attitude over the Arran affair was making England far from popular. And then, on the 22nd of April, that is of 1509, King Henry died, and the curtain rose on the last act of James's tragedy, with the entry of a new *dramatis persona*, his brother-in-law the new young King of England, whose first act was to marry his brother's Spanish widow.

Scottish relations with the young Henry VIII opened civilly enough. James sent the usual formal embassy of congratulations upon his accession. At the end of June Henry ratified the Peace of 1502, and James re-confirmed it before the end of the year, while Arran was released. Indeed, there was a delusive gleam of sunlight. The young Henry was charming, spirited, and accomplished—at first sight, in spite of his hasty Spanish marriage, a much more congenial neighbour than his father. A second Prince of Scotland, born in October, was politely christened Arthur, for the dead brother of Henry and Margaret. Very soon, however, there was friction again, both personal and international. Henry had not his father's economy—far from it : but he had his father's greed. Henry VII had left Queen Margaret rich jewels : her brother now refused to let her have them. She was indignant, and James, punctilious always to the wife he did not love, was annoyed in turn at this cavalier behaviour.

While both personal and national ill-feeling were

increasing between the neighbouring insular powers, the Continental disturbances grew and spread. Venice countered the League of Cambrai by submission to one member of it, the Pope. In February of 1510, Julius made peace with her, turned on his allies, and set to work with Venice and the Swiss, who had quarrelled with Louis, to drive the French across the Alps again. James tried hard to reconcile Louis with both Pope and Emperor, sending Albany and the Bishop of Moray to Julius, but without success, and by the latter part of the next year a fresh political combination had crystallised, in the shape of what called itself the Holy League, between Julius, Spain, and Venice, against France. Maximilian joined the three a little later : and Henry, bribed by the Pope with the French king's title of ' most Christian King,' was eager to take the old unlucky road into Guyenne, and joined them also.

France was thus isolated, save for Scotland : and before the Holy League was fully concluded, she had been working for active Scottish support : the preliminaries of a renewed alliance were signed at Edinburgh early in March. James wanted nothing so little as a war, which would check all his thriving plans for Scottish welfare. Yet he knew not only that an integral France was essential to the stability of Europe, but that if France were dismembered by her foes, the rest of Scotland's allies would be small help if it came to a return of English aggression : and by this time he knew his brother-in-law. Not only loyalty but the interest alike of his kingdom and of Europe at large held him to the *Auld Lyig*. He played for time, in which the Holy League might begin to quarrel : but meanwhile tension with England was increasing. Queen Margaret was clamouring for her jewels. French ships were plundered by English off the Scots coast, and there were a couple of troublesome ' incidents ' that bred more ill-feeling. Andrew Barton, pursuing the naval harrying of Portugal, already referred to, searched an English ship suspected of carrying Portuguese goods. Surrey fitted out two ships, and under his son Edward Howard, later Admiral of England, they caught Barton in the Downs with the *Lion* and a small pinnace, the *Jenny Pirwin*, and fell upon him. In a desperate fight Barton was killed by an arrow, and the *Lion* was taken prize into the Thames. Henry set free so much as was left of the crew, but kept the ship, and was anything but civil to James's protest. Then there was a disturbance on the Marches. Ker, Warden of the Middle March, and a disciplinarian, had been murdered by three Englishmen. It was before the death of Henry VII, and he had acted correctly, handing over two of the men concerned to Scots justice. The third had got away. Now this man went openly about his affairs, and Ker's sons, taking the law into their own hands (they were not the most peaceful family on the Marches) raided his house, and sent his head to Edinburgh.

Between these threatening small affairs at home, and the bristling complications overseas, James's position was desperately anxious : and he had further cause for anxiety, for since Prince Arthur had died in the previous year, it began to be doubtful whether the Queen could in fact give him an heir. He was forced to make ready for what looked now like inevitable war, though while he strengthened his fleet [1] and his army at home, he continued still to labour with all his might, for the whole of 1511 and 1512, to prevent a general European conflict, and unite the hostile powers on a single front against their common and imminent enemy. This King who is accused of fighting the Flodden campaign more or less ' for fun,' was in fact the only potentate in Europe who was capable of seeing political problems in terms of something larger than national greeds, and attempting to form a League of Christendom against the growing menace from the East, where the Turks were already on the Danube, had won a foothold in Italy itself, and in 1529 all but broke past Vienna. The sneers of insular historians at James's ' fantastic ' proposal of a Crusade show them ignorant of the history of Europe, and vilely unjust to a man whose political vision had re-covered a great lost mediaeval concept, to carry him far in advance of the minds of his time.

1512, the last full year of James's life, went by in

---

[1] The strengthening of the fleet included the building of the *Great Michael*, the largest and most powerful ship of her day. She was 240 feet from stem to stern, of a thickness of hull designed to be proof against shot, and carried 35 great guns and 300 small, with a ship's company of 300 seamen and officers, 120 gunners, and 1,000 soldiers.

z

desperate diplomacy. France in Italy had begun with unexpected success, but the arrival of a Swiss army turned the tide. James had to cope with envoys from Julius, Henry, Ferdinand, and Louis. He sent Albany to the Emperor, to induce him to mediate between the Pope and France, while the Bishop of Moray went to Rome to engage the Cardinals. To Spain he gave a refusal to join the League, to England a refusal to break with France, while to France he consented at last to a definite treaty, whose terms were drawn up in May. The two countries were to promise mutual help against England. If one of them were involved in an English war, the other should be bound to declare war also. The subjects of neither might enter English service, and neither of them should harbour the other's rebels. No truce with England should be made without mutual consent, and none by either country separately, while if either King died without an immediate heir, the other was not to interfere in the resulting problem of succession.[1] James agreed to the terms, save that of the separate truce, added a clause that neither party was to accept a Papal absolution from his oath, and on the 16th July signed the treaty at Edinburgh. Henry's response was to

---

[1] Such a problem was possible then to either country. A third son, who lived to see an unhappy reign, was in fact born to James a few weeks before this, but his three elder children had all died infants, and if the little Prince James should follow them, there might be strife between Arran and Albany, the latter of whom had great interests in France. Louis had only daughters, who were barred from succession by the Salic Law, and his next male heir was a very distant cousin.

mobilise the North, and order Surrey to call up *Arriatos, Triatos et Armatos, tam Homines ad arma ac Homines armatos et Sagittarios et alios Homines Equites et Pedites Defensibiles.*

Meanwhile, France's position had been growing desperate, and then, for a while, improving. The English had landed at Bayonne, and Ferdinand claimed a passage through Navarre, the small independent kingdom, France's ally, astride the Pyrenees. Its Queen had refused, and in July he had made himself master of the cis-Pyrenean part, Spanish Navarre. Content with this, his energies somewhat slackened, and he failed to co-operate with the English force ; and they, between disappointment, the weather, and too much *vin du pays*, were obliged to withdraw. For a while the cloud of war seemed to hang suspended. There were desultory Anglo-Scots hostilities, mainly at sea, and with the advantage to Scotland. A squadron under La Motte, the French ambassador, sank three English ships and brought seven into Leith, and a little later Robert Barton arrived at the same port with no fewer than thirteen English prizes.

Both countries, however, were still marking time. Henry was set on a fresh invasion of France, and did not want Scotland active in his rear : James still hoped that the threat of it might hold him back, and therefore, probably, Ferdinand as well, at all events until France had time to recover from the weakening of the Italian wars. All through this winter, that before his fortieth birthday, the last of his life, he still strove to deserve his title of *Rex Pacificator*. A letter to his uncle of Scandinavia, just after the New Year of 1513, says, and with truth, that he has been labouring for the last two years to keep France, Spain, and England from a war. Now France has authorised him to treat with England ... and Henry refuses safe-conducts for the ambassadors. He has, notwithstanding, offered to forgo any claim for reparations, and to renew the Peace of 1502 if Henry will consent to a general peace. The English parliament, however, have decided to attack both France and Scotland (they had got over the Wars of the Roses by that time, and were in a very chauvinist frame of mind) and are threatening to seize the Scottish coast, while Spain refuses to make a separate peace. Pope Julius, about the same time, was trying to induce him to put pressure upon Louis : and James's reply, written in February, describes again his unavailing attempts, and begs the Pope to fulfil his sacred function as Father of Christendom, and win Christian princes to unite in its defence against the Turk.

James's offer of free remission for all injuries if Henry would abandon the French war may have made the latter believe that the Scottish king was possibly becoming more compliant. He sent Dr West again to James in March. West's very detailed report is in existence, and reveals, incidentally, the trials of diplomats before the telegraph, for he is considerably exercised as to whether the Pope is really dead or not. (He was, on the 22nd February.) His shrewd commonplace mind found James bewildering and exasperating.

One can see through his letter James desperately worried, and jesting wildly in the bitter exaltation of over-worn nerves : he scandalised West's solemn literal mind with a threat to appeal from the Pope to Prester John. Nerves or not, West could not shake his resolution : he would not consent to action against France. West tried bullying the Queen into using pressure (the poor soul was with child again, and near her time) threatening that she should never see her jewels, and that her brother would take from her husband ' the best townes they hade.' (James came up at this point, and West had to mend his manners.) Henry had misinterpreted his brother-in-law's conciliatory attitude, to the point of asking, of all things, for the loan of his fleet. That, of course, was refused, and West could get nothing else from James for a long time but a reiteration of his major position, that he would hold back so long as Henry would. He frankly admitted to *wanting* peace with England, and West tried to get him to put that on paper. James refused, and was frank also about his reasons. If he were to put his name to such a paper, it would be used at once to embroil him with Louis. West's smug iterations were straining his over-wrought nerves, and he must have been irritated almost past control by the fact that it was impossible to argue, since the values that were determining his conduct were invisible to a mind of the type of West's, and the only words he could use would carry no meaning. He could only talk at that *plat* incomprehension—talk, possibly, to stave off

West from talking (West, in fact, found it difficult to
get audiences) and repeat and repeat the one compre-
hensible point, that he would not abandon his ally
France.   The only concession West could win from
him was a promise that he would not make war on
Henry without a formal declaration first : but the only
possible means to peace with Scotland was to refrain
from aggression upon France.   From that, nothing
would move him.

West went back with that, and an angry letter from
Margaret, whose fifth child, a daughter, was born then,
and died at once.[1]   The new young Pope, Leo X, a
Medici, had a splendid opportunity to make peace : he
refused, took the same line as his predecessor, and
proceeded to excommunicate King James.   The latter
asked for help from his Scandinavian kinsman, but he
just then had his hands full with the Swedes.   La
Motte, however, returned again from France, with
four ships of munitions, 14,000 *écus du soleil*, and a
letter and a turquoise ring from Queen Anne, who
begged James, in the manner of the romances, to march
three steps on English ground as her knight.   No
romantic trappings could gild the situation, but he
would not be ungallant to a lady.   He wore the ring :
it was taken from his body.

The diplomats worked on.   On the 5th of April, at
Mechlin, a new league of partition was signed against

---

[1] Margaret had most of the Tudor faults without their qualities,
but it is pleasant to be able to note that in spite of her natural and
most justifiable dislike of the quarrel, she was firmly loyal to her
husband, saying in this letter he ' is ever the longer the better to us.'

France, on behalf of the Pope, Maximilian, Henry, and Ferdinand, the latter, however, hedging, and making a secret treaty with Louis also. Three weeks later, French-English hostilities began. Prégent with four galleys drove back an English fleet, and was able to attack the coast of Sussex. Just after that, James made one final effort. On the 24th May he sent Lord Drummond to Henry with a letter, inviting him to be party, with himself, to the truce of a year that Ferdinand had just concluded with Louis. The letter is courteous and conciliatory, appealing to Henry to share his efforts for a general peace, and the union of Christendom against the Turk. But the Turk was a long way from the English Channel, or even from the wealthy towns of France : the Defender of the Faith sent a final refusal.

The ring closed on France, and on the 6th of June the French and Venetians were heavily defeated at Novara by the Swiss, who used Bruce's old tactic of Bannockburn, that James, to his loss, was to try some three months later. On the 30th, Henry, having subsidised the impecunious Emperor, who flattered the young man to the top of his bent, sailed for Picardy, and was joined by Maximilian : and France was in danger from north and south at once.

James knew that he was finally committed. On the 26th of July, he declared war, formally, as he had promised, sending Lyon King of Arms with an ultimatum ; on the same day the Scots fleet sailed for France, and now James made a most disastrous blunder, the Stewart one, of trusting the wrong man. Arran was in command. The fleet should have been a formidable weapon : there were thirteen three-masters and twelve lesser ships, besides the *Great Michael*, in a class by herself, and a large English ship, recently captured. And Arran wasted the long eager labour that had gone to the making of that force. He took on himself the completely pointless exploit of landing and sacking the town of Carrickfergus, a brutal business, and then . . . sailed back to Ayr again with the loot. James, with good reason, was furious : he sent old Sir Andrew Wood to supersede him, but the sane appointment had been made too late. Arran up-anchored before Wood could reach Ayr, and sailed. The Scots fleet disappears in mist. The only Continental battle of the war— Guinegate on the 16th August—was over before the Scots troops could reach France : and we simply do not know what became of the fleet that was one of James IV's major works as King. Part of it, possibly, was sold to the French King after his death, in his widow's regency : the *Great Michael* was. The ships that in the manner of the time belonged to private owners, as several would, and were only commissioned by the Crown, no doubt went back to private hands again. It was the end of Scotland as a sea-power.

Henry gave siege to the town of Térouenne, and there, on the 11th of August, the Scottish herald brought James's ultimatum, and even at this point made an attempt for peace. Lyon pointed out, before delivering his letter, that Henry had been for weeks before Térouenne, which was still untaken, while on the other hand he had achieved the avowed purpose of the war, in causing the French to withdraw from Italy : further hostilities would be merely wasteful. The argument failed, as it was bound to do, for Henry's purpose was a good deal larger than these fairly justifiable aims : he wanted the dismemberment and humiliation of France. Lyon accordingly presented his letter. The whole scene is vividly given by Holinshed, whose omissions, however, are not without some interest : they can be checked by the documents whose substance he professes to give. He does not include, for instance, James's reminder that Henry had refused safe-conducts to his ambassadors sent to treat for peace, and that he is only doing for his ally what Henry had bound himself to do for his own. The letter itself makes no further effort now : it merely gives James's reasons for making war, and sums up his position, as much, one is inclined to think in reading, for his own benefit as for that of Europe : he certainly could not have hoped now to influence Henry. He enumerated Henry's breaches of international courtesy, and his ill-conduct towards Scotland and France, and then recalled his own bond to the latter,

" wherefore he required him to desist from further invasion and destruction of the French dominions, which to do if he refused, he plainlie declared . . . that he would do what he could to cause him to desist from further pursute in that his enterprise."

Henry let fly in a violent verbal outburst, reported by the same historian. (Holinshed wrote a generation

later, but he seems to have had an eye-witness's
account, and the speech he gives Henry is highly
characteristic.) It is a wild blast of accusations and
threats. Henry claimed that *I am the verie owner of
Scotland, and that (James) holdeth it of me by homage.*
(He was used, of course, to call himself King of France,
so the mental process is not without precedent.) He
threatened to expel the Scots king from his realm, and
ordered him to cease the war at once. Holinshed says
that Lyon was ' sore abashed,' but even in Holinshed's
account he does not sound so, for he replied with firm
courtesy that as James's subject he had to deliver his
message, but he would not take his master what
amounted to another man's orders. He would, however, since that was his duty, carry back a letter. Henry
accordingly wrote one the next day. It assumes the
highest possible moral tone, charging James with

> surmised Injuries and contrived occasions . . . by you cause-
> less sought and imagined . . . in the ancyent and accustomable
> manner of your Progenitors, which never kept Faith and
> Promise longer than pleased them.

He refers to James's *sensuall opinions*, calls him a
schismatic for opposing the Pope, reminds him of the
position of Navarre, and has much to say of *the loue
and dread of God*, of *our Patron St George*, and the
favour of the Deity for himself. Lyon returned with
it, but he was held up by foul winds on the coast, and
the letter never reached his master's hands. Louis
countered by the gesture of announcing that all the
privileges of French nationality were open thence-
forward to all natives of Scotland.

The war continued. On the day before Lyon King had delivered his message, Primoguet with a small squadron of Breton and Norman ships met Henry's fleet off the coast of Brittany : he had the weather-gauge, and instead of retreating, bore down on them and sank several English ships. His squadron, how-ever, was too small for effective action, and his own ship, Queen Anne's *Belle Cordelière*, was fired : he dismissed her crew to the boats, and with a little party of volunteers ran her alongside the English flagship and grappled, and took her down with him as the flames reached his powder. Within a week, the one conti-nental land battle of the war was fought, or barely fought, at Guinegate : the French army, in spite of the efforts of Bayard, panicked and broke, and the dis-graceful flight goes down in French history as the Day of Spurs. And meanwhile the Swiss were marching through Burgundy.

Anglo-Scots fighting opened on the Border a day or two after the ultimatum to Henry. It began ill. The long spell of peace had loosened discipline and made men careless. Lord Home, the Chamberlain, by his own slackness in the matter of scouts, was ambushed by Bulmer at Brownrigg, and his force mown down by archers among the whins.

James had ordered a muster on the Boroughmuir. Scotland seems to have been reluctant for the war, but with a steady loyalty to the King : every man, says Pitscottie, loved his prince so well they would not dis-obey him. No more representative or united force had mustered in Scotland through her history, nor was to do until the time of those whose names lie in steel on the Rock of Edinburgh. But the King, who had seen his bitter effort fail, was worn out, a fey man with the knowledge of doom, and there were dark omens. The tales may be legend, or, it has been suggested, a desperate device of Queen Margaret, to check the strife of her husband and her brother. They tell of the strange figure clothed in blue who rose at mass in St Michael's Kirk of Linlithgow, warned the King not to go forward with the war, and passed from sight, no man preventing him : and Pitscottie has another and wilder story :

Thair was ane cry heard at the mercatt croce of Edinburgh about midnight, proclamand as it had beine ane summondis, quhilkis was called by the proclaimer thairof the summondis of Plotcock,[1] desiring all earles, lordis, barrones, gentlemen, and sundrie burgess within the toun to compeir befoir his maister within fourtie days. . . . But on indweller in the toun, called Mr Richard Lawson . . . ganging in his gallerie . . . fornent the croce, hearing this voyce thocht marvell quhat it should be, so he cryed for his servand to bring him his purs, and tuk ane croun and kest it over the stair, saying, I for my pairt appeallis from your summondis and judgment, and takis me to the mercie of God.

. . . Eftir the feild thair was not ane man that was called at that tyme that escaped, except that on man, that appailled from thair judgmentis.

In late August, with these omens for a dismissal, and the King himself at its head, the army marched, and an English one moved to meet it under Surrey. At Twiselhaugh on the 22nd, James crossed the Tweed : he was only to live for another eighteen days.

[1] Plotcock, Pluto.

The next lower crossing was commanded by Norham, and he did not dare to leave it in his rear. He gave siege to it : it was thought impregnable, but yielded to five days of fierce assault. The deep and treacherous Till bound the army into a corner of Northumberland, and since the weather was violently wet and stormy, it would be in spate. James set to work systematically to clear his road. He divided his force, and sent part of it over Till by the bridge at Twisel, to take Wark, which commanded not only a ford of Tweed but the gate of ' the Dry March ' between Tweed and Cheviot, and access to the middle Tweed valley and to Kelso. He himself with the rest marched on Etal and Ford, which commanded the bridges of the lower Till. All three were taken easily by the 3rd, and James halted then for a few days at Ford, until Surrey's movements should become clear. There is, incidentally, no evidence that Lady Heron had anything to do with this delay. The story does not appear until Pitscottie, a generation later, and his circumstantial account is full of contradictions of known fact. All that we do know for certain of the lady is that she was trying to get James not to raze Ford, and using as lever not her personal charm but a couple of Scottish prisoners begged from Surrey.

That general was advancing from the south, with an army of about 26,000.[1] He reached Durham on the

---

[1] Colonel Elliot's estimate in his *The Battle of Flodden*. There is, however, very little reliable evidence as to number. The sixteenth century figures make the Scots army anything from 200,000 (Hall) to under 26,000 (Holinshed and Buchanan) and the English from 50,000 (Pitscottie) to 26,000 (Hall). Modern estimates vary nearly

29th (the day Norham fell) and got into touch with Dacre's Borderers. On the 3rd he was at Alnwick, where he met the overseas reinforcements brought from Flanders by his son, the Admiral, Thomas Howard. He then lay on the narrow southern end of the quadrilateral of low ground bounded by the Tweed, Till, Alne, and North Sea, while James was at Ford on a bridge over the Till, commanding both the Dry March and the fords of Coldstream and Twisel, and able to move and block the crossing at Berwick. Strategically, they were thus blocking each other, and more completely than they would have done a generation before, for their artillery would be helpless to move on ground that hobelers alone could have crossed well enough : and the ground in that weather would be very bad.

The morning after he arrived at Alnwick, Surrey did a thing that shows that the Middle Ages were not yet over : he sent Rouge Croix Pursuivant to James, with a formal challenge to a pitched engagement, Thomas Howard adding a personal one of his own, with a taunting reference to Andrew Barton. On the 6th, Islay Herald reached Alnwick with James's acceptance. He would wait Surrey's coming till Friday the 9th, at noon.

as widely, and more acrimoniously. Colonel Elliot's is given tentatively, but has certain bases for at least a guess : there is not even that, however, for the Scots army, but it would seem to have been rather larger. We cannot, however, deduce as much as some gentlemen have done from the fact that one was drawn from all Scotland, and the other from only the northern half of England. England in Bruce's day had at least five times the population of Scotland, and now has eight.

He prepared then to do so. His position at Ford was unsatisfactory, depending on the bridge, but across the Till he might strike south by Wooler, and had open lines of communication by Coldstream and Kelso. He crossed, accordingly, at Ford itself, and being joined by the rest of his army from Wark, took up his position on the hill of Flodden, thus cutting off Surrey from an advance on Scotland except by crossing the Tweed below the Till. On Flodden he put in practice a new device, borrowed from the Continental wars, and unlike all Scottish traditional strategy,[1] which was based, at its best and most successful, on a fluid offensive by small, independent, and highly mobile divisions. This was a fortified camp, protected by entrenchments, with his guns in emplacements across the scarp of the hill, below his front. The Till guarded his left flank, a marshy valley his right, and his rear was probably on wood (there is one there to-day at any rate) and certainly with a long steep slope behind it.

On the 6th, the day on which he received James's reply, Surrey marched the fourteen miles to Wooler, which brought him within about six of the Scots army. Next morning he reconnoitred, and disliked what he saw, to the point of sending Rouge Croix again to James, to upbraid him with breaking his word by changing ground to a place ' like a fortress,' and inform

---

[1] There is a Scottish precedent, none the less, in Douglas's and Randolph's campaign in Weardale in 1327, where it was very successful. See *Robert Bruce, King of Scots*, pp. 332 *et seq.*

him that the gentlemanly thing would be to come down on the open plain by Milfield, where if James would let him know by nine next morning, he would be pleased to wait from twelve to three. James answered that he would choose his ground at his liking, and stayed where he was. Unfortunately, Surrey was a better general than this interchange of courtesies suggests. Having failed to bully James out of a strong position, he set, and with intelligence, to work at what was the next best thing, to make it useless. He could not afford to play a waiting game, for besides the vile weather, his provisions were failing, and as all the contemporary English accounts lament in toncs of the deepest commiseration, his army for three whole days had been short of beer.

On the next day, therefore, the 8th, he accordingly marched, not on the Scots, but past their front, out of effective gunshot (though shots were exchanged) moved north, crossing the Till by the bridge near Weetwood, and advancing to Woodend, north of the line Etal-Lowick, where he camped for the night. This movement rendered the Flodden position useless : Surrey was north of the Scots, within easy touch of Berwick as a base, and might strike into Scotland by Berwick, Norham, or Twisel. They descended therefore from their position on Flodden, made a short march, and camped for the night on the lower ground by the Till, somewhere south of the triangle Ford-Etal-Crookham. They were still on Surrey's flank if he marched on Scotland, and as the crossing by Cold-

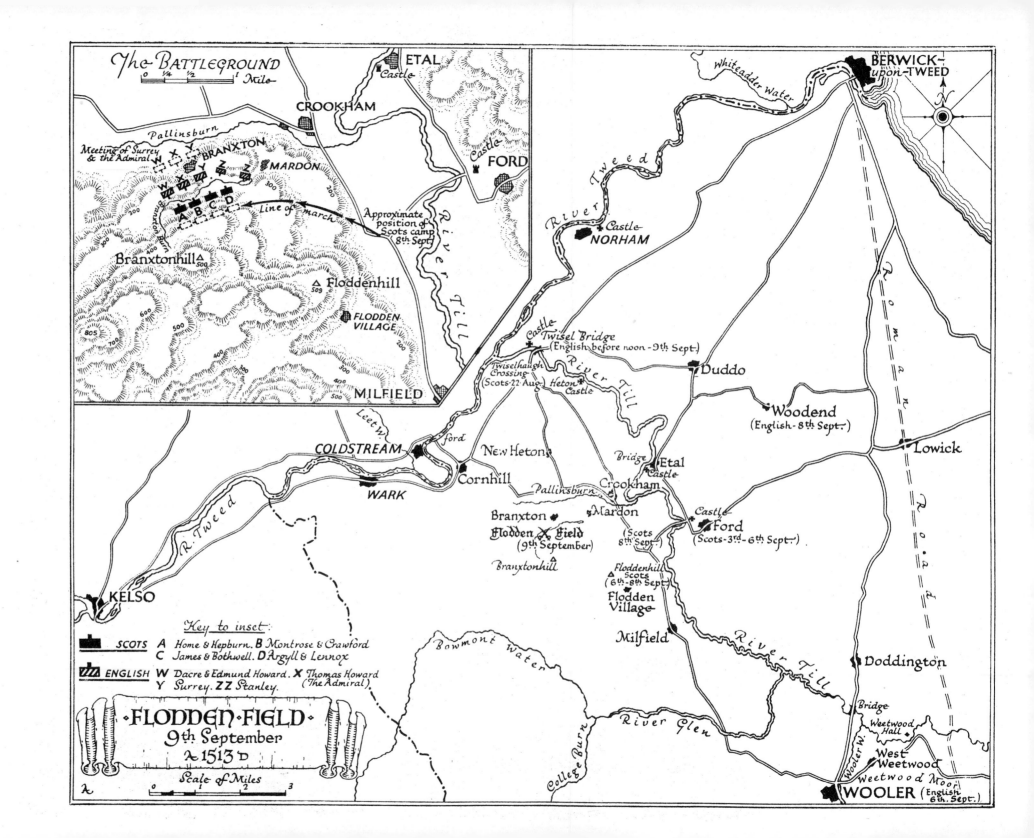

The BATTLEGROUND

0 ¼ ½ 1 Mile

ETAL
Castle

CROOKHAM

Pallinsburn

Meeting of Surrey
& the Admiral
BRANXTON
MARDON

FORD
Castle

300

200

Approximate
position of
Scots camp
8th Sept.

Line of march

River Till

Branxtonhill △ 500

△ Floddenhill 509

600

FLODDEN
VILLAGE

805 700 500

400

300

500

300

200

MILFIELD

BERWICK-
upon-TWEED

Whiteadder Water

River Tweed

Castle
NORHAM

Castle Twisel Bridge
(English before noon–9th Sept.)

Duddo

Twiselhaugh
Crossing
(Scots–22 Aug.)
Heton
Castle

Woodend
(English–8th Sept.)

Leet W.
ford

COLDSTREAM

New Heton

River Till

Lowick

Cornhill
Pallinsburn

WARK

Bridge
Crookham
Etal
Castle
Mardon

Castle
Ford
(Scots–3rd–6th Sept.)

Branxton
Flodden ✕ Field
(9th September)

(Scots
8th Sept.)

Floddenhill △
Scots
(6th–8th Sept.)

R. Tweed

Branxtonhill

River Till

KELSO

Flodden
Village

Milfield

Doddington

Key to inset

SCOTS   A Home & Hepburn. B Montrose & Crawford
        C James & Bothwell. D Argyll & Lennox

ENGLISH W Dacre & Edmund Howard. X Thomas Howard
        Y Surrey. ZZ Stanley   (The Admiral)

Bowmont Water

River Glen

Bridge
Weetwood
Hall

·FLODDEN·FIELD·
9th September
A.1513.D

College Burn

West
Weetwood

Weetwood Moor

Scale of Miles

0   1   2   3

Wooler W.

WOOLER (English
6th Sept.)

stream lay open to them, they had the inner line. One has, by the way, to remember at this point what is easy for the modern to forget, the engagement to meet Surrey. His challenge could not have been refused without disastrous results to the morale of the army—especially a Scottish army—and to break it, once it had been made, would have meant a mutiny on the breaking side. Surrey's march into space must have looked as if he were intending to break it : it gave him the initiative, even from a purely modern point of view : and the Scots waited to see what he was at. Probably —one must remember the age again—they could not believe that he would break his word in the face of two armies, after himself having issued such a challenge. As it happened, they were right : but he succeeded in making them doubt if they were, and halting their movements by the uncertainty.

The major evidence for the next day's movements—the 9th of September, the day of the actual battle—is the English official Gazette, written so soon after the action that it names some of the missing as still not accounted for, and signed by Thomas Howard, who was the English second in command. In the morning Surrey marched, and again north, or rather west by north, away from the Scots, leaving Stanley with the rear-guard to hold the bridges of Etal and Ford, and prevent the Scots from crossing in his rear.

The Scots and English were out of sight of each other, and there was no such thing as a field telegraph. Before James's scouts (who presumably knew the

2A

ground less well than Dacre's Borderers, who were Surrey's guides) could get back across the Till with definite news, Surrey had made the five miles to Twisel Bridge. James apparently decided that after all Surrey did not intend to keep that formal engagement and was marching on Scotland, though it was still possible that he might cross Till and return. The other alternative, however, must have seemed the more likely by then. James broke camp therefore, and marched west, along, and fairly well up, the long high wave of ground called Branxton Edge.[1] This commanded the country towards the Coldstream crossing, towards which he was marching. He could thus, if Surrey really was crossing Tweed, advance parallel with him and into Scotland, while if he should after all be crossing Till, he could swing right and meet him, in plenty of time to avoid being caught in column. The light troops, the Border men under Home and Hepburn, led the advance : there may have been some Highlanders under Huntly, whose rapid marching would keep up with the hobelers. Crawford and Montrose had the leading division of the main body : then came the King himself, with the centre, and Bothwell after : and finally, under Lennox and Argyle, the Highland rear-guard, who fired the camp, as was their common custom : the smoke, on the south-westerly wind of that time and weather (and thick from the damp of its fuel) blew like

[1] The English called the battle that of Branxton, and the name in fact is much more accurate. The actual field is over a mile from Flodden Edge, and farther, and out of sight, from Flodden village.

a fog between the Scots and Stanley, now advancing to get in touch with his commander : for Surrey, in fact, was not very far away.

What he had really done, on reaching Twisel, was to cross, not the Tweed by the ford, but the Till by the bridge. Then he divided his force. The Admiral (Howard) with something like a half of the men, and the guns, crossed the bridge about eleven in the morning, and marched up Tweed to Cornhill, opposite Coldstream, his purpose being clearly to hold the Scots from crossing. Surrey took the rest by a more easterly and less easy route, towards Pallinsburn, intending apparently to catch the Scots in flank if they did the natural thing and made for Coldstream. Finally, Stanley, when the Scots had moved, appears to have crossed the Till, by the bridges at Ford and Etal, to the left bank, and was following discreetly in their rear. The Scots apparently saw him prepare to cross, and James's master-gunner wished to stop and shell him,[1] but James, who by now knew that precious time had been lost, and that Stanley was not in force to tackle the army, forbade him : his strained nerves made him lose his temper, and historians have scolded him ever since. In fact, as it was to turn out, to have checked Stanley would have saved a largish number of Scottish

[1] This seems the likeliest place to fit in the incident as Pitscottie tells it. The crossing referred to is usually taken to be that at Twisel, where indeed to shell the English would have been useful. Unfortunately for both James and his objectors, it was also perfectly impossible, as Twisel was four miles off and out of sight. Pitscottie as it happens, does not say Twisel, but merely calls it the Bridge of Till : and there were four bridges in the relevant area.

lives : but in the circumstances of the moment, James's decision was perfectly justified.

The Admiral reached Cornhill, and found it empty : and the Scots had not passed through, either. In fact, the Scots were doing what he had counted on their doing, but Surrey's apparent flouting of his engagement had puzzled them into delaying over it. He had to discover what they were about, and accordingly swung east and marched towards Crookham (*i.e.*, by the road that led him across the line of his father's advance and towards the Scots) with the double purpose of getting in touch with his father and learning the whereabouts of the Scots army. Just past the first milestone out of Cornhill village, where the road passes over high ground (cut now) and bends, he would find out. He could see two important things. Ahead, to his right, he could see along the slope of Branxton Edge, and the advancing vanguard of the Scots, marching towards him roughly parallel with the ridge—that is, on their most natural route to Coldstream. Parallel with both the ridge and their line of march, and on his own side of the Branxton Burn, was another wave of ground, over which he would see the smoke of Branxton Village : this wave was much smaller, swelling gently up from a burn on either side, but high enough to mask his force, if he waited behind it, from the Scots artillery. He marched, and with speed, into this second valley, of the Pallinsburn, and as he marched sent off an urgent message to his father, with the Agnus Dei from his breast as token, to bid him come up as quickly as he could. Surrey did so, and they joined in this Pallins-burn hollow—the *petite vallée* mentioned in the Gazette—and forming line there, on a front parallel with the ridge, advanced *tout en vng front*, though one gathers that the *tout* does not include Stanley, in touch, but not in line, with their left flank, and some little distance off. He probably came up the branch valley at Mardon.

James, from Branxton Edge, was aware of this concentration. With Napoleon's guns, say, he could have blown Howard to pieces before he could have got into the Pallinsburn dip : with his own, though he could see him, he could not. Now, to have the English army close on his flank while he was in column of march was inviting disaster. In face of Branxton Village, accordingly—that is, in face of the yet invisible English —he halted and changed front to his own right, so that his force was in line, facing that of Surrey, who was keeping the settled engagement after all.

It was now about four of a stormy September day. The two forces, as the English appeared on the crest of the northern ' wave,' were facing each other across an open valley, the ground gently falling in front of *each* of them, towards the Branxton Burn that lay between.[1] It was slippery with wet : the Scots took off their shoes for a firmer grip.

[1] The map has misled Dr. Mackay Mackenzie, whose sense of terrain is unhappily inferior to his gifts as a researcher into texts, into saying that the ground *rises* from Branxton Village to Branxton Edge. In fact, it *falls*, with a steady gentle slope, for rather more than a quarter of a mile. *Both* forces were advancing downhill, and if there

There was a brief, ineffective, artillery duel, such effect as it had being in favour of the English, for the Scots guns, though Howard later speaks of them like a lover,[1] were firing from a line too high on their slope, and could not be depressed sufficiently to prevent their shot from going over the advancing, and descending, English, while the English ones got on to James's batteries and killed some of the crews and his Master-gunner. Their shot fell also among the advancing ranks, though since these were also descending below the range, to little purpose. Lang draws a dramatic picture of the English guns ' mowing down the charging spears,' but in fact the comments of the English them-selves make it clear that they did little execution. Home and Hepburn, with their mounted Borderers, charged Dacre and Edmund Howard, the English extreme right, broke their opponents, and drove them back. The Cheshire and Lancashire men, in this division, were routed and fled, the Yorkshiremen following them. Dacre's Borderers apparently made a stand, but not till they had been driven back a good distance, out of sight of the main action, going probably down the channel between the site of Branxton village

were any advantage in the ground, it was slightly—but very slightly —with the English : indeed the two ends of a football field could hardly have provided less difference. The wind, presumably, was with the Scots. The light, in that sort of weather, would be alike. So is the surface, at the present day, and it probably was then for all one can see.

[1] " Les plus cleres les plus neetes et les myeulx fassonees (façonnées) . . . et les plus belles de leur grandeur et longueur que jai viz (vues) oncques."

and the hillock of the battle memorial, the tall stone cross raised ' To the brave of both nations.' Unfortunately, their retirement had brought them on to their baggage train. The Scottish Borderers halted then to secure their prisoners and loot the tempting English baggage-waggons of what was to be costly booty for their country. Neither Home nor Dacre could get his men reformed in time to take further part in the actual battle : and Home, though he was useful in the retreat, became the most execrated man in Scotland.

The main bodies advanced on each other, in steady formation. The Scots were dismounted, officers and all, and came on close-ranked, in silence, *en la maniere que marchent les Allemans, sans parler ne faire aucun bruit.* That phrase, as Dr Mackay Mackenzie has pointed out, is the key to the whole mystery of the battle. In spite of the statements of historians, the two forces were on equal terms as to ground. But the Scots apparently were in greater numbers, and the weather was certainly in their favour : there was no panic, no quarrelling of commanders : they were well armoured, their enemies bear witness that they fought with the utmost gallantry till the end. Yet they lost, the severest defeat in all our history, and it was no Falkirk nor Poitiers, no archers' battle, but a fight of men foot to foot and body to body, where no archery could distinguish friend from foe.

What betrayed them was the arms in which they trusted. *The Almayn manner,* or some equivalent phrase, is a technical term, used technically by Howard,

who was a professional fighting man. It meant not
that they fought silently, as Howard's prose style
would incline one on casual reading to believe, but
that they used the arms, and the tactics, associated
in all the military science of the time with the lanz-
knechts, the famous Swiss and German infantry, that
Spain, France, and Italy had all adopted. Dr Mackenzie thinks that the Scots may have taken its use
from certain French officers sent over by Louis : but
that is unnecessary. The Scots had used at least the
germ of it more than a generation before Sempach, in
Bruce's charging schiltroms at Bannockburn, then a
piece of brilliant originality which had met spectacular
and resounding success : and its characteristic weapon
(as indeed he remarks himself) the eighteen-foot spear,
was a new thing in Swiss hands as late as the fourteen-
nineties, but appears in Scots Arming Acts twenty
years before. It is in essence the tactic of the phalanx,
a charging body of foot in close formation, with (this
is the Bishop of Durham, just after the battle) *long
speres . . . wherin was their truste*—the close hedge of
eighteen-foot *pointed* spears. Courtrai had first shown
its effect on the defensive :[1] the genius of Bruce had
proved it a formation that *so long as it was unbroken,*
could attack, could send footmen through cavalry like
a plough through soil.

But as always happens, war was developing : an

[1] Wallace had used it earlier, at Falkirk, but though it sorely dis-
concerted Edward's best cavalry, its effect was countered by that
novelty, his Welsh long-bowmen.

" irresistible " weapon begets its counter. Bishop Ruthal has the key-word here, the bill.

> Our billes qwite them veray welle, and did more goode that day thenne bowes, for they shortely disappointed the Scotes of their long speres wherein was their greatest truste.

There is other evidence to the same effect. Now, the bill was an eight-foot shaft with a spear-point *and axe-head*—a Lochaber axe or partisan, in fact. Any fencer will realise what this would mean : it gave, in effect, a rather greater advantage than a breech-loading rifle against a muzzle-loader. The Scots *phalanges* may conceivably have broken formation on the slippery ground : but even this would hardly be necessary, and indeed they seem to have been notably steady, even when the battle turned into massacre. The bill-man could swing his axe on the pike shaft, reducing it to a mere wooden pole . . . and a quarter-staff, even in hands trained to use it, has small chance against a sharp axe with an eight-foot sweep. The Scots secondary weapon was the sword : we know these were used, from Bishop Ruthal again :

> Whenne they came to hande stroke though the Scotes faght sore and valiauntly with their swerdes, yet they coude not resiste the bills that lighted so thicke and sore upon theym.

Indeed, they had little chance of doing so. The idea of the sword as a defensive weapon did not dawn until later in that century, and in any case the Scots sword of the time was a cutting weapon, not a thrusting one. The bill, with its long arc of sweep, would be slow enough for a lunge beneath its shaft *with the point* to get home, or at least have a very good chance of it : the cut, however, was no faster than the bill-stroke, and hopelessly outreached by the long ironed axe-shaft the sword had not sufficient weight to cut.

The lines crashed on each other in the broad shallow valley. The Scots left apparently made contact first, the shock running fairly quickly from left to right. Montrose and Crawford met the Admiral : both earls were killed, and their force suffered heavily, exposing the flank of the King, who joined by Bothwell was next on their right and facing Surrey's division. It seems there was time, before the centres met, for the English archers to do some execution. The extreme right, the Highlanders, suffered most. They were presumably more lightly armed, and they were certainly the last to make contact, leaving the longer time for the English archers : and they were unlucky in their moment of impact. They were opposed to Stanley, who seems, as has been said, to have come up the burn from Mardon steading, not on their front but on their flank. They tried to form front to their right in order to meet him, and he caught them before the movement was completed. He shattered them, drove through, and turning on the high ground, seems to have found himself above the locked centres, the King engaging Surrey. Re-forming, he charged in on James from either flank or rear.[1]

---

[1] Buchanan is always a doubtful authority, but General Carruthers, who has been so good as to read this chapter, considers he is probably right in making Stanley's division attack in *two* sections, one, by the

Once the full lines had met, it was plain hand to hand fighting. Save for Stanley's return swing, there is no manoeuvre : men simply fought where they stood, till the darkness fell, after some two hours and a half of bitter conflict. The length of what, after the first quarter-hour, was clearly a lost battle, needs explanation. The Scots had no officers left to bring them off : these had led, with pikes, on foot in the front rank, and met the first furious onslaught of the bills. James himself went down a lance's length from Surrey, and the hotly English Hall pays him generous tribute :

O what a noble and triumphant courage was this, for a Kynge to fyghte in a battayl as a meane souldier !

With no officers left to give the word to retreat, the rank and file resisted where they stood till they went down. Their magnificent physique and their heavy armour—there is testimony to both—prolonged the struggle : but the armour, after a time, would hinder, not help, a swordsman so circumstanced, and the weighted axe-heads shatter it in the end.

The darkness came down on the rain and the bloody field, where the stream was choked in its course with trodden corpses. The King lay dead there, and the young Archbishop, the Bishop of Caithness, the Bishop of the Isles, twelve earls and fourteen lords : four men were left of the whole body of the Scottish peerage, that would not so have followed a king since

Etal bridge, taking the Highlanders in front and drawing their attack, while the other crossed by Ford to the position the Highlanders had abandoned, thus taking them in flank and rear.

Bruce. No family of note in the whole of Scotland but had lost a man, and very few of the humbler. The number of the dead will never be known, but there may have been as many as ten thousand 'gaping against the moon' when she rose over Till. It was the direst defeat in our history . . . and yet no battle in European story is more honourable to both sides engaged. It was valiantly won, valiantly lost, alike.

There were few prisoners taken. One deserves remembrance, Skirving of Plewlandhill, who bore the banner of the dead Earl Marischal : when the day was lost he tore it from its staff and wound it about his body beneath his doublet, where he carried it through two years' imprisonment, bringing it home to Scotland in the end.[1]

With the fall of the early dark, the fighting slackened, and what was left of the Scots army retreated, on Coldstream Ford. It was a retreat, even yet, and not a rout : Home covered it, and they drew off in such good order that the English stood to their arms all through the night, uncertain even then of their victory. 'The Teviotdale men '—so says Hall—attacked their camp : these would be a part at least of Home's division. In the morning there was an attempt to save the guns, but the Scots who tried it were only a small body, and were driven off after a fierce little action. The whole of the artillery was captured.

[1] When the Scottish Women's Hospital in Serbia was captured in the war of 1914-18, Dr. Alice Hutchison saved its Union Jack in precisely this fashion.

The news swept across Europe. There were bonfires in Venice. It reached home sooner. They say on the night of the battle that the young Archbishop's ghost was seen to say mass before the high altar of his own cathedral, for the dead army lying around their King. Edinburgh had the news on the day after, that the loved King was gone and all his leaders, and men from every kindred over Scotland, the Border unguarded to the enemy. There was cause for panic, but there was no panic. The Town Council's proclamation is still extant.

The x day of September, we do you to witt, for as mekill as thair is ane greit rumber now laitlie rysin within the town, tueching our Soverane Lord and his army, of the quhilk we understand thair is cumin na veritie as yet, quhairfore we charge straitlie and commandis, in our Soverane Lord the Kingis name, and the Presidents, for the Provost and Baillies within this Burgh, that all manner of personis, nyhbours, within the samen, have reddy thair fensabill geir and wapponis for weir, and compeir thairwith to the said Presidents at jowing of the comoun bell, for the keeping and defens of the toun against thame that wald invade the samyn.

And also chairgis that all women and specialie vagabounds that thai pass to thair labouris and be not sen upon the gait clamourand and cryand, under the pane of banesing of thair persons but favors : and that the other, women of gude, pass to the kirk and pray, quhane time requiris, for our Soverane Lord and his army, and nyebouris being thairat, and hald thame at thair privie labors off the gait, within thair houses, as affeirs.

For all the magnitude of the disaster, the military sequel was but slight. England, certainly, was safe from immediate invasion, but Surrey, though records give him low casualties, was unable to follow up his victory in the manner his superiors desired. He foundered, like so many English commanders, on the question of supply. The provisions of the Scots, and their excellent beer, had been joyfully acquired as loot of the battle : but even so he had to disband his troops. (The English side of the Border, it must be remembered, was and is much poorer country than the Scottish.) Indeed, at the beginning of October, Home and Dacre, the opposite Wardens of the East March, met once more, but more peaceably, to discuss a truce : and the Scots were by no means pliable over terms. Dacre, in fact, got into serious trouble with his own government for doing nothing : they were not in the country, or weather, and he was ; and probably with good reason he blames ' the waters,' though on the 23rd of October he could announce a raid ' to keep Tividale waking.' Flodden was fought not much more than four miles from the March, but it was not until five weeks afterwards that any English troops crossed into Scotland. The Borders were still organised for defence, and the Border division had suffered least in the battle : and though in November a strong English raid was launched on Jedburgh, it had no success, and one can read under Dacre's discreet dispatch that in fact it was fairly heavily defeated : he even expresses fear of a counter-invasion, and by the next year he was in trouble again, over successful Scottish raids on England.

The general war dragged on for six months after

Flodden. France was saved, not by herself or by her ally, but by the jealousy of her assailants. Neither Ferdinand nor Leo, in the long run, dared allow their companions too great a victory. The Pope was therefore reconciled with Louis, safeguarding the interest of his house, the Medici, by balancing Spain with France in Italian affairs. Ferdinand, fearing to see Maximilian's power increased by a broken France and an allied England, contrived a breach between him and King Henry. France slipped from between them. Young Henry, disappointed of his war, held out until the August after Flodden, and then was bought off by an annuity and the marriage of his sixteen-year-old sister to Louis, whom she danced into his grave by New Year's Day. In April of 1515 the new King, Louis's son-in-law, Francis I, made a fresh treaty with England, and invited the Scots to be a party to it. Their reply to the offer is willing, but not eager. It speaks of success since their late heavy misfortune, but agrees to a truce for the sake of King James's desire, the union of Christendom against the Turk : and for seven years an armed and menacing truce stood against a Scotland that glittered with civil war. Then it broke, with Surrey's son ravaging the Marches . . . and the Turks well up the coast of the Adriatic, and pressing cheerfully on Buda Pesth.

James, who had given Scotland unity, died on Branxton Hill with an arrow in his throat. His people would not believe that he was dead : he had gone to Jerusalem, and would come again. But Dacre found his body on the field, took it to Berwick, and gave it over to Surrey. They had it embalmed, and sent it to King Henry, who refused James burial, on religious grounds, for being in contumacy towards the Pope. Leo himself, more merciful or at least more politic, sent him a dispensation in November, permitting burial in St Paul's Cathedral. But the corpse lay above ground at Sheen, wrapped in lead, among lumber. Many years after, idle inquisitive workmen were allowed to cut off the head : one took it home for the sweet smell of the spices, kept it awhile, and then, seized perhaps with compunction, induced the sexton of St Michael's, Wood Street, to bury it in the common charnel-house. What became of the headless body is not known. James, who had loved both splendour and human kindness, was to lack not only the pomp of a prince's tomb, but even the common decency of a beggar's . . . and that a nation not ungenerous should so treat the corpse of a brave enemy displays in a single hideous revelation the things that are engendered in men's minds by a long and unsuccessful war for ' glory.'

That war had come to an end, for the time being, with Scotland beaten and maimed, but unconquered yet, even almost uninvaded. Yet the legend of popular tradition is right that gives Flodden the colour of sunset, and in storm-cloud. The brilliant King was gone, and the men with him who should have been the leaders of that generation, passed the torch of its achievement to their sons : and the splendid promise of the late fifteenth century sinks gradually to a bloody twilight.

The inveterate civil wars blazed up once more, with no man capable of quenching them, for the government was in weak and foreign hands, Queen Margaret's first, then the Duke of Albany's. James V, king from babyhood, when he came to rule, had his father's work to begin all over again. For two generations also the English war still sapped the country's strength : one of its fiercest and most vindictive onslaughts, if not the most dangerous, comes thirty-one years later, when King Henry's personal orders were to spare neither women nor children ' if there should be resistance.' And before the Three Hundred Years War came to an end—within a matter of fifteen years from Flodden—there was beginning the long and bitter struggle, a religious war, or rather, deeper than that, a strife between two sides of Scots civilisation, which sent that civilisation, by 1700, into something like the eclipse, in the things of the mind, of the black middle fourteenth century. That last struggle seemed to close on Culloden Muir, two hundred and thirty-three years after Flodden : it was more than a kirk and a dynasty that went under. Yet it revived again, in terms not of arms. Life sprang up once more to a brief and brilliant flowering : but its roots were in a soil that had grown thin, and again it seemed to go down into the dust before the Genius of the Victorian Age, the darkest side of whose shadow

2B

fell upon Scotland. Whether that victory in turn was
final has grown more doubtful in the last ten years.
King James, perhaps, may ride home from Jerusalem
yet.

BIBLIOGRAPHY

MOST of what survives of the primary material—*i.e.*, the actual state papers, etc., of the time—is collected in the following: Rymer's *Fœdera*, vols. iv-xiii, *The Acts of the Parliament of Scotland*, vols. i and ii, Macpherson's *Rotuli Scotiae*, Maitland Thomson and Balfour Paul's *Registrum Magni Sigilli*, Stuart and Burnett's *Exchequer Rolls*, Dickson's *Accounts of the Lord High Treasurer*, the facsimile *National MSS. of Scotland* (Record Series), Ruddiman's *Epistolae Regum Scotorum*, the eighteenth-century *Epistolae Jacobi IV et Jacobi V*, and Stevenson's *Letters and Papers illustrative of the War of the English in France*. Palgrave's *Documents illustrative of the History of Scotland* deals with an earlier period, but includes Hardyng's forgeries in an appendix. Abstracts of many documents are to be found in Bain's *Calendar of Documents relating to Scotland*, Brewer and Gairdner's *Calendar of Letters and Papers ... of Henry VIII*, Bergenroth and Gayangos's *Calendar of Letters ... relating to ... England and Spain*, Rawdon Brown's *Calendar of State Papers ...* (English) *... in the Archives of Venice*, and Teulet's *Inventaire chronologique des documents rélatifs à l'histoire d'Écosse*. Gregory Smith's *The Days of James IV* is a useful teacher's book, giving extracts in modern English from contemporary documents.

Early historians include Wyntoun's *Orygynale Cronykil*, Fordun and Bower's *Scotichronicon* and its supplement, and the anonymous *Liber Pluscardensis*, by a servant of the Dauphine Margaret. John Major in his *Historia Majoris Britanniae* is the father of modern philosophical history, as Boece in his *Historia* is of modern popular *histoire romancée*. There is more historical value than in Boece in Lindsay of Pitscottie's *Chronicles*, though he needs careful handling. Bishop Leslie's *Historia* is soberer, and like Boece has a racy Scottish version. Drummond of Hawthornden's *Five Jameses* is better literature than history, but his comments are often intelligent and interesting, and he has an excellent turn for vivid phrase. The Asloan MS. includes a short account of the reign of James II.

Of foreign writers one cannot omit Gray of the *Scalacronica* and Jean Froissart, who both knew Scotland at first hand, the *Chronicon de Lanercost*, Knighton, Hall, Holinshed, or Jean Chartier, or the brief but vivid account, by a contemporary Englishman, of James I.

Among modern histories, there is surprisingly little on this period in general. What there is is part of large general histories, and suffers severely, as a rule, from the strong anti-national and anti-Stewart bias of the dominant school of the nineteenth and early twentieth centuries, and their ignorance, or at any rate ignoring, of anything outside *this nobill Ile callit Gret Britaine*. In spite of its heavy prose and some errors of detail (though not as many as Andrew Lang tried to prove !) by far the best is still that in vols. i and ii of Fraser Tytler's *History of Scotland*. (Hill Burton, to whom one would have expected the time to appeal, is oddly perfunctory in dealing with it.) Aeneas Mackay's articles in the *Dictionary of National Biography* give compact and lucid summaries of events. There is a very short and much *romancée* life of James I by Prof. Jusserand, *Le Roman d'un roi d'Écosse*, and a *Life of James IV* written over twenty years ago by I. A. Tayler.

More useful are the discussions of various aspects of the time in the following : Sir J. B. Paul's *The Scots Peerage*, T. Innes's *Scots Heraldry*, Grub's *Ecclesiastical History of Scotland*, Bellesheim's *History of the Catholic Church in Scotland*, J. Mackinnon's *Constitutional History of Scotland*, J. Davidson and A. Gray's *The Scottish Staple at Veere*, Miss I. F. Grant's *Social and Economic Development of Scotland* and *Economic History of Scotland*, D. Gregory's *History of the West Highlands*, W. C. Mackenzie's *Short History of the Highlands*, Miss A. Cunningham's *The Loyal Clans*, W. Fitzwilliam Elliot's *The Battle of Flodden*, W. M. Mackenzie's *The Secret of Flodden*, J. Forbes Leith's *The Scots Men-at-Arms in France*, J. Hill Burton's *The Scot Abroad*, F. Michel's *Les Écossais en France*, H. Rashdall's *The Universities of the Middle Ages*, D. MacGibbon and T. Ross's *Castellated and Domestic Architecture of Scotland* and *Ecclesiastical Architecture of Scotland*, the Reports of the Royal Commission for Ancient Monuments, the present writer's *Historical*

Survey of Scottish Literature, Cosmo Innes's *Scotland in the Middle Ages*, E. S. Kerr's *Scotland under James IV*, L. A. Barbé's *Sidelights on the History of Scotland* and *In Byways of Scottish History*, and P. Hume Brown's *Early Travellers in Scotland*. Professor C. de Chavrebière's *Histoire des Stuarts* deals mainly with the generations from James V onward, but contains an account óf the French house of Stuart d'Aubigny.

The foreign background may be studied in the relevant volumes of the Cambridge *Mediaeval* and *Modern Histories*. The chapters on Scotland itself are affected by a strong pro-English bias, but have valuable bibliographies. A good short survey of Europe at the period is Sir R. Lodge's *Close of the Middle Ages*, which goes to 1494. The wars leading to Flodden are described in A. H. Johnson's *Europe in the Sixteenth Century*. Fuller surveys of the concurrent history of the two countries most closely linked with our own may be found in vols. iii, iv, and v of *A Political History of England* (ed. Professor Tout) and vols. iv and v of *L'Histoire de France* (ed. E. Lavisse).

INDEX